Defining Issues in English Language Teaching

Debrah
Jeager
(905) 935-1261

Defining Issues in English Language Teaching

H. G. Widdowson

OXFORD
UNIVERSITY PRESS

OXFORD
UNIVERSITY PRESS

Great Clarendon Street, Oxford OX2 6DP

Oxford University Press is a department of the University
of Oxford. It furthers the University's objective of excellence
in research, scholarship, and education by publishing
worldwide in

Oxford New York

Auckland Bangkok Buenos Aires Cape Town Chennai
Dar es Salaam Delhi Hong Kong Istanbul Karachi Kolkata
Kuala Lumpur Madrid Melbourne Mexico City Mumbai
Nairobi São Paulo Shanghai Taipei Tokyo Toronto

Oxford and *Oxford English* are registered trade marks of
Oxford University Press in the UK and in certain other countries

ISBN 0 19 437445 9

Printed in China

Contents

To my granddaughter Fernanda

Preface

This book is about the teaching of English as a foreign or other language. Its central concern is to investigate issues relevant to the definition of English as a subject, how its learning objectives might be realistically specified, and what language and language activities are appropriate to the purpose. The enquiry involves the consideration of a number of current and controversial issues, including the international role of the language, its use for specific purposes, competing claims for its ownership, norms of correctness, the promotion of real or authentic English, appropriate methodology, and the advocacy of task-based instruction.

Like its predecessor, *Aspects of Language Teaching* (Widdowson 1990), this book is substantially composed out of a number of papers I have presented and published in the preceding ten years, as some readers will recognize. It is, however, a composition and not a compilation and takes the form of a continuous, and I hope reasonably coherent, argument.

The argument follows a particular line and plots its course through various areas of enquiry, taking up issues which seem to me crucial in defining English as a foreign or other language (EFL or ESOL) as a subject that is taught in schools. There are two points about my purpose that I would like to stress so as to indicate to readers how I would hope the book will be read.

To begin with, the book makes no claim to comprehensive coverage. It does not pretend to map out a survey of the different areas of enquiry that, in one way or another, have claims to be relevant to English teaching, and if it is read as such, it will be found to be seriously wanting. It is rather more like the detailed directions for taking a particular route: the directional map of an argument through these areas, and I have taken note only of those features that help me on my way. Those who work their claims in the different areas I have passed through (second language acquisition research, language testing, for example) might well feel some justified resentment that I have trespassed too casually on their patch. Like all maps that trace a line of argument, the one I draw here gives a selective and necessarily incomplete description of the whole terrain that is traversed, and little indication of alternative possibilities of finding a way through it.

The book is then partial in that it gives only as much detail as is needed to follow a particular direction. It is also partial in a rather different sense, and this is the second point I would want to make about it. My concern, as I have said, is to enquire into the nature of EFL/ESOL as a *subject*: what factors we need to take into account in defining it as a pedagogic construct, which like other school subjects, has to be designed in the light of local curriculum specifications, timetabling constraints, and classroom conditions. The issues I have explored in this book all relate to this basic question of how this English subject is in principle to be defined. The process has involved me in the detailed consideration of a number of well entrenched assumptions, and I have been critical of a number of current positions in arguing for my own. This, then, is no impartial account, and although some readers will agree with the line I take, many, we can safely assume, will not. But it is not really agreement or disagreement that matters. Obviously I must believe in the validity of my own argument, or otherwise I would not have bothered to write this book in the first place. But I do not expect it to be accepted without question. On the contrary, my purpose is to prompt critical thinking into the issues I raise, and there are times when I have been deliberately provocative to that end. If my criticisms are unfounded, then how can they be countered? If my argument is awry, then how can it be set straight; if entirely misconceived, then what alternative is to be proposed?

So this book is designed both to exemplify and to stimulate a process of critical enquiry into issues that I identify as relevant to the definition of the English subject. This is not the first time I have undertaken such an enquiry with this purpose in mind. How far the purpose has been achieved in the past, or will be achieved this time round, is open to doubt. And the doubt has to do with the effectiveness of the kind of applied linguistic enquiry that I am undertaking here, and that I have spent my professional life in trying to promote. A word about this seems to be in order.

As time goes by, ideas about English teaching come and go, articles make an ephemeral appearance in journals and then become part of a forgotten archive, books go out of print and out of mind. What is dated is assumed to be outdated. But although publications have a limited shelf-life, and one suspects are, like other consumer products, sometimes deliberately designed for rapid obsolescence, the issues they deal with, and the ideas they express, continually reappear and are given the guise of novelty. Whether this is true of other areas of enquiry as well I do not know, but in the field of EFL/TESOL, there is, it seems to me, a striking absence of cumulative development or intellectual continuity. In 1886, the German scholar Wilhelm Viëtor published a celebrated pamphlet, *Der Sprachunterricht muss umkehren!*, which is generally rendered in English as *Language teaching must start afresh!* (See Howatt 1984), and as such it has been used in our field often enough since then as a rallying cry for change. Fresh starts, or better perhaps fresh fits and starts, have been much in evidence. But 'to start afresh' is not really a very satisfactory translation of *umkehren*. A closer rendering would be 'to turn around' or 'to retrace one's steps'. This suggests going back in the direction you came from, but looking out for where you went astray. This kind of considered pathfinding is rather different from the idea of starting afresh by just returning to square one. But changes in English language teaching over the past half century are better characterized as fresh starts rather than as a retracing of steps. Ideas and proposals have generally been heralded as entirely new departures, new approaches, new directions, new ways, without going back to see how they might link up with paths that have already been taken. Retracing one's steps seems so retrograde.

I find myself reacting in two quite different, and indeed contradictory, ways to this lack of developmental consolidation. On the one hand, it is irksome to find old ideas appearing in new packaging without knowledge, or acknowledgement, of their origins, and the discussion of issues in ignorance, or disregard, of how they have been dealt with in the past.

But on reflection, this process of rediscovery seems entirely natural and desirable. Like any other human activity, English teaching needs continual novelty to sustain its dynamism, even if the novelty is in some sense an illusion. The very fact that ideas and issues, no matter how old their provenance, are taken up again makes them new, gives them a recharged vitality; and every new generation needs to think afresh for itself, appropriate the past and make it demonstrably their own. Rather than complain about the repossession of ideas, one should welcome it, and it does not matter where they come from but what is made of them now. Change in English teaching is often dismissively described (I have done it myself) as mere shifts in fashion. But there is really no call to be dismissive. Fashion shifts so as to accommodate to changing perceptions, different social circumstances, and when the designs of the past make a reappearance now, they are renewed and made relevant to the present.

And so, I conclude wisely, it is the continuing process of enquiry that really matters, not its cumulative development, and in this process, ideas and issues are taken up anew, language teaching does indeed start afresh. I would argue myself that a knowledge of how they figured in the past can provide insights that can be drawn upon in their new-found reformulation in the present. But this does not depend on explicit acknowledgement. It is the appropriation that counts. Indeed the influence of the past is likely to be effective to the extent that it is absorbed into the present without trace.

The purpose of this book is to activate critical thinking about the subject, English, and so to make a contribution to this continuing process of enquiry. By my own wise reasoning, this purpose can be most effectively achieved without my being aware of it. This is, of course, a particularly comfortable thought to keep me company in retirement. And it is one that I need to bear in mind whenever I look at future publications in the field, and am tempted, unwisely, to look first to see whether my name figures in the list of references.

HGW, Vienna, July 2002

Acknowledgements

As I state in the Preface, this book has its origins in a number of papers which I have written over recent years. None of these papers appear here in their original form but the way they have been incorporated into chapters is indicated by the following list:

Chapter 1
'Coming to terms with reality. Applied linguistics in perspective' in *Selected papers from AILA '99*. Tokyo: Waseda University Press. 2000.
'On the limitations of linguistics applied'. *Applied Linguistics* 21/1. 2000.

Chapter 2
'Parameters in language teaching' in *Actes des Etats Generaux des Langues 1: Bilans et perspectives*. Paris: AEGL. 1989.

Chapter 3
'Proper words in proper places'. *ELT Journal* 47/4. 1993. Reprinted in T. Hedge and N. Whitney. (eds.). *Power, Pedagogy, and Practice*. Oxford: Oxford University Press. 1996.

Chapter 4
'The ownership of English'. *TESOL Quarterly* 28/2. 1994. Reprinted in V. Zamel and R. Spack. (eds.). *Negotiating Academic Literacies. Teaching and Learning Across Languages and Cultures*. Mahwah, N.J.: Lawrence Erlbaum Associates. 1998.

Chapter 5
'EIL, ESL, EFL: global issues and local interests'. *World Englishes* 16/1. 1997.

Chapter 6
'Communication and community: the pragmatics of ESP.' *ESP Journal* 17/1. 1998.

Chapters 7, 8, and 9
'The relevant conditions of language use and learning' in M. Krueger and F. Ryan. (eds.). *Language and Content: Discipline and Content-Based Approaches to Language Study*. Lexington, Mass.: D. C. Heath. 1993.

'Communication, community, and the problem of appropriate use'. 'Perspectives on communicative language teaching: syllabus and methodology'. Both in J. Alatis. (ed.). *Language, Communication and Social Meaning.* Georgetown: Georgetown University Press. 1993.
'The pedagogic relevance of language awareness'. *Fremdsprachen Lehren und Lernen.* 1997.
'Context, community and authentic language'. *TESOL Quarterly* 32/4. 1998.
'Skills, abilities and contexts of reality'. *The Annual Review of Applied Linguistics* 18. 1998.
'Object language and the language subject: on the mediating role of applied linguistics'. *ARAL* 20. 2000.

Chapter 10
'Metalanguage and interlanguage' in R. Hickey and S. Puppel. (eds.). *Language History and Linguistic Modelling. A Festschrift for Jacek Fisiak. Trends in Linguistics, Studies and Monographs 101.* Mouton de Gruyter. 1997.

Chapter 11
'Bilingualization and localized learning' in V. Crew, V. Berry, and J. Hung. (eds.). *Exploring Diversity in the Language Curriculum.* Hong Kong: The Hong Kong Institute of Education. 1999.
'The monolingual teaching and bilingual learning of English' in T. L. Cooper, E. Shohamy, and J.Walters. (eds.). *New Perspectives and Issues in Educational Language Policy. A Festschrift for Bernard Dov Spolsky.* 2001.

Chapter 12
'Communicative language testing: the art of the possible' in C. Elder, A. Brown, E. Grove, K. Hill, N. Iwashita, T. Lumley, T. McNamara, and K. O'Loughlin. (eds.). *Experimenting with Uncertainty. Essays in Honour of Alan Davies.* Cambridge: Cambridge University Press. 2001.

Although I appear as the sole author of this book, there are many people who have made contributions to it, directly by their particular comments on earlier drafts, indirectly and more generally by the continuing stimulation of their ideas and support of their friendship. Among the main contributors are old colleagues and collaborators: Christopher Brumfit, Guy Cook, Simon Murison-Bowie, Cristina Whitecross, who have kept me company over so many years. I should also like to thank more recent, and younger colleagues at the University of Vienna for helping me with this book in various ways: Katharina Breyer, Julia Hüttner, Barbara Mehlmauer-Larcher. And then there is my rather special colleague, Barbara Seidlhofer. But the ways in which she contributes to my work, and to everything I do, can never be adequately acknowledged.

The authors and publisher are grateful to those who have given permission to reproduce the following extracts and adaptations of copyright material:

A. P. Watt Ltd. on behalf of Michael B. Yeats for an extract from 'The Second Coming' by W. B. Yeats from *Collected Poems* (Macmillan).

Curtis Brown on behalf of the A. D. Hope Estate for an extract from 'The Bed' from *The Wandering Islands* by A. D. Hope (Edwards & Shaw).

David Godwin Associates for an extract from 'A Martian Sends a Postcard Home' by Craig Raine.

David Higham Associates for an extract from *Ridley Walker* by Russell Hoban (Jonathan Cape).

Faber and Faber for extracts from *The Inheritors* by William Golding and *The Palm-Wine Drinkard* by Amos Tutuola.

Heinemann, part of Harcourt Education Ltd., and Random House, Inc. for an extract from *A Man for All Seasons* by Robert Bolt.

Independent Newspapers (UK) Limited for extracts from 'Review of Salman Rushdie' by Bhikhu Parekh © The Independent 11 February 1990; 'It takes bottle to cross channel' © The Independent 30 November 1995; and a review by Mark Lawson of *Through my eyes* by Lindy Chamberlain © The Independent on Sunday 4 February 1991.

International Creative Management, Inc. for an extract from *The Bluest Eye* by Toni Morrison © 1970 Toni Morrison.

The Provost and Scholars of King's College, Cambridge and the Society of Authors as the Literary Representatives of the E. M. Forster Estate for an extract from *A Passage to India* by E. M. Forster.

Smith/Skolnik Literary Management for an extract from Vladimir Nabokov Speak, Memory: An Autobiography by arrangement with the Estate of Vladimir Nabokov. All rights reserved.

W. W. Norton & Company Ltd. for an extract from 'pity this busy monster, manunkind' from *Complete Poems 1904–1962* by E. E. Cummings, edited by George J. Firmage © 1991 by the Trustees for the E. E. Cummings Trust and George James Firmage.

1 The theory of practice

There is a good deal of distrust of theory among English language teachers. They tend to see it as remote from their actual experience, an attempt to mystify common sense practices by unnecessary abstraction. They seem often to show the same kind of impatience with theoretical questions as Boswell records Dr Johnson expressing:

> We talked of the education of children; and I asked him what he thought best to teach them first. JOHNSON Sir, it is no matter what you teach them first, any more than what leg you shall put into your breeches first. Sir, you may stand about disputing which is best to put in first, but in the meantime your breech is bare. Sir, while you are considering which of two things you should teach your child first, another boy has learnt them both.

Teaching is common sense; it's just like putting on your trousers. So why do we stand about disputing? Why waste time enquiring into the nature of language, the psychological process of learning, or the relative effectiveness of different approaches to teaching?

If teaching is seen as commonsensical, something that anybody can turn their hand to if they feel so disposed, then, of course, not much prestige attaches to it, and not much respect is accorded to teachers. And language teachers are particularly vulnerable to disregard: everybody who has been through schooling knows what teachers do, and everybody knows what a language is because everybody knows at least one language. If you are going to teach physics, or biology, or history, then you clearly do need specialist knowledge: you have to be a physicist, a biologist, a historian. But English? French? Surely no specialist knowledge is called for here. You have to be a physicist to be a physics teacher, but you do not have to be a linguist to be a language teacher. All you need is a knowledge of the language and common sense.

This view of the language teacher is quite widespread, even among language teachers themselves, and this makes it all the more important to establish what kind of specialist expertise teachers need to have to claim professional authority. It is somewhat paradoxical that the very success of universal education in equalizing access to knowledge leads to a diminishing regard for those who provide it. Once knowledge becomes common property, and common sense, its mystery disappears, and there is no need to hold it in special regard. Familiarity breeds contempt. It was, of course, not always so. Here, for example, is another literary reference. A contemporary of Dr Johnson's, Oliver Goldsmith, in his poem *The Deserted Village*, describes the village schoolmaster, and the awe he inspired among the locals:

> The village all declared how much he knew;
> 'Twas certain he could write, and cypher too;
> Lands he could measure, terms and tides presage,
> And even the story ran that he could gauge.
> In arguing too, the parson owned his skill,
> For even tho' vanquished, he could argue still;
> While words of learned length, and thundering sound,
> Amazed the gazing rustics ranged around,
> And still they gazed, and still the wonder grew,
> That one small head could carry all he knew.

The schoolmaster's prestige is based on knowing what the others do not know. He is not just a proponent of common sense. None of the village parents here, not even the parson himself, would venture to tell this teacher what to teach, or how to teach. This is not to say that teachers need to stun people into wonderment by words of learned length, and baffle them into reverence. There should be no need for such ostentation: their authority should surely be acknowledged without it. But if you do not have specialist knowledge or expertise of some kind, you cannot claim the authority.[1]

Teachers who insist that they are simply practitioners, workers at the chalkface, not interested in theory, in effect conspire against their own authority, and against their own profession. They have authority as teachers only to the extent that they carry in their heads (small or otherwise) specialist knowledge and distinctive expertise, to the extent that they are intellectually fine-tuned to their task.

The invocation of common sense has a seductive democratic appeal: it has the effect of establishing solidarity among 'ordinary', 'down-to-earth' people against the elitism of academics. It deflates their pretensions, pricks the bubble reputation. But although an appeal to common sense is a good polemical tactic, the concept itself, on closer scrutiny, is not at all straightforward. To begin with, what is common about the sense only applies within a group of like-minded people. Common sense is essentially *communal* sense: a set of socially constructed assumptions which constitute the conventional wisdom of a particular community. As such it has two distinctive features which we need to take note of. In the first place, it has no warrant in other communities, which may have very different ideas about what is self-evident and what is not. Secondly, it is necessarily retrospective, based on situations in the past. It is thought that it has become set in its ways and which deflects critical enquiry. But things change and thinking needs to change accordingly. So when somebody says that teaching is based on common sense, we need to know whose common sense, which communal values it expresses, and how far these values are relevant to the situations we are currently concerned with. The first thing to do about common sense is to question it; the last thing to do is to accept it as valid. It *may* be valid, but then the validity has to be argued for and demonstrated. It cannot just be taken as self-evident.

But language teachers, we can argue, do not just follow the common-sense assumptions of ordinary non-teaching people, but develop their own, based on the received wisdom and well-tried ideas of their own pedagogic communities which find expression in established practice. It is widely supposed that the most effective kind of preparation for novice teachers is to develop this common sense or 'know-how' by following the example of teachers who have already become expert by experience (for example, Freeman and Richards 1996). This we might say is a process of initiation by imitation, and it sounds reasonable enough. There are problems about it, however, which it would be as well for us to take note of.

To begin with, it would seem to underplay the imperatives of current reality in that it presupposes that the past experience of teachers, and the expertise they have derived from it, are necessarily relevant to the present. But this does not follow at all, of course, for societies change and students and classrooms change with them. If novice teachers are to have an expertise attuned to changed circumstances, then they will have to discriminate between what it is about the experienced teachers' ideas and practices that is of current relevance and what is not. It is obvious that if novice teachers are to learn from their more experienced colleagues, it cannot just be by means of uncritical imitation. They need to abstract from the behaviour of their colleagues what they feel is significant for their own practices. But this abstraction necessarily involves interpreting particular activities as examples of more general principles and then enquiring into their validity. So even if one accepts that novice teachers can be initiated into their profession by the transfer of know-how, this know-how has to be abstracted from experience and theoretically constructed. Acquiring expertise is not a matter of reflecting what other teachers do, but reflecting on why they do it.

To reflect on practice in this way is to theorize about it, to abstract and make explicit the principles that inform certain ways of doing things. And such abstraction allows for adaptation. Once you have identified the idea about language or language learning that lies behind a particular classroom activity, then you are in a position to make a judgement about how valid it is from your point of view, and if it is how it might be put into practice by an alternative activity more suited to your own teaching/learning situation. The ability to do this constitutes pedagogic expertise which goes beyond experience. For experience itself teaches you nothing directly: you have to learn *from* it, indirectly, and this means discovering something beyond appearances, abstracting something general from particulars. Learning from something necessarily means going beyond that something and abstracting common features beyond common sense that are relevant to other and different situations.

To say this is not to say that personal experience is only of value in language pedagogy to the extent that it can be converted into theoretical principle by the process of rational analysis. On the contrary, what is personal, intuitive, and beyond such analysis is more clearly recognized and more highly prized as a result, for it is only when you have exhausted the resources of explanation that you realize the true value of what is beyond its range. So of course there will always be individual personality factors in teaching which cannot be explained or controlled, and which bring about rapport with students, or lack of it, beyond reason. Teaching, we might acknowledge, is ultimately an art. But it is also a craft. Although the practice and effect of art may, in the last analysis, be ultimately inexplicable, it is nevertheless based on the principles and conventions of craft which can be made explicit.

So to theorize about language teaching is to subject common sense assumptions to critical reflection. You may, as a result, reject or accept them, but either way, you will have some rational basis for your decision. Thought of in this way, theory is not remote from practical experience but a way of making sense of it.

But if theory is so beneficial and indeed so crucial to good practice, as I am claiming it is, why, one must wonder, is it treated with such distrust, not to say disdain, in the language teaching profession, even by those (indeed, it seems, especially by those) who insist that teachers should be 'reflective practitioners'? One reason is that it is associated with the academic discipline of linguistics, and this is seen to be an abstruse field of enquiry at several removes from the reality of the language classroom. Furthermore, in perverse defiance of this obvious limitation, there are claims by people calling themselves applied linguists that this arcane discipline can nevertheless yield insights of practical pedagogic relevance. What makes matters worse is that applied linguists, exploiting the prestige of the discipline they seem to serve, assume an air of superior wisdom and impose these insights unilaterally on an all too deferential teaching profession. In short, as Thornbury has recently put it, language teaching is 'at risk of being hi-jacked by men in white coats' (Thornbury 2001: 403).

This suspicion and resentment of theory are widespread, and misconceived. The misconception is grounded in a misunderstanding of linguistics and its relationship with applied linguistics, and of the nature of theory itself. In respect to the last of these, it is interesting to note that even those who are strident in their opposition to theory are not averse to making theoretical claims themselves. Consider the following text, which appears as a general preface to a series of resource books for English teachers.

A letter from the Series Editors

Dear Teacher,
This series of teachers' resource books has developed from Pilgrims' involvement in running courses for learners of English and for teachers and

teacher trainers. Our aim is to pass on ideas, techniques and practical
activities which we know work in the classroom...
(Lindstromberg and Rinvolucri 1990)

This Preface is couched in the form of a letter, a device designed to reduce the
usual formal distance between author and reader. But authority is nevertheless retained in this first paragraph by the presentation of credentials: the
series is underwritten by extensive experience running courses at this persuasively named institution *Pilgrims*, not only for learners of English, but also for
teachers and teacher trainers too. And the use of the plural of course carries the
implication of generality. But we need to ask *which* learners, *which* teachers,
which teacher trainers are being referred to here, and the extent to which it is
reasonable to suppose that they are representative of *all* learners, teachers,
teacher trainers. The implication of generality is carried over into the second
paragraph. The use of the definite article is significant here: *the* classroom,
that is to say, the generic classroom. The assumption appears to be that what
works in one classroom will be generalizable to all others.

In short, the authors are extrapolating from what has happened in their
particular classrooms with particular groups of learners and teachers and
are, in effect, making a global claim for a local experience, backed up by the
persuasive assertion of authority: they *know* what works. So although the
authors talk about things working in actual practice, what they are doing is
abstracting from this actuality and making a theoretical statement about
how things work in general. Furthermore, we might note, it looks as if the
authors are transmitting their influence unilaterally: they are passing on ideas
and practices which bear the mark of their authority. There is no suggestion
that these need to be critically examined and their relevance worked out in
consideration of local conditions, which will in many cases be completely different from those which obtain in the classrooms from which these generalities have been derived. Knowing how things have worked in particular
circumstances is thus taken as know-how in general. What we seem to have
here is, in effect, the assertion of theoretical authority disguised as practical
down-to-earth advice based on an appeal to illusory shared experience.

To point this out is not to say that one cannot or should not infer general
methodological principles from particular practices but only that we need to
recognize that in doing so we are making theoretical claims; it is misleading to
suggest otherwise. Furthermore, we need to exercise a little caution in making
such claims, recognize that they may be based on limited empirical evidence,
and resist the temptation to transmit them as the truth. And this applies to *any*
theoretical statement, whether it comes from linguists, educationists, teachers, teacher trainers, and whether it comes covertly in the guise of practical
down-to-earth advice, or overtly in the idiom of an academic discipline.

Theory is concerned with the abstraction of generalities from particulars
(which is why the statement we have just been considering is a theoretical one

in spite of appearances). As such it is bound to disregard certain differences in order to establish commonalities. Theory then allows us to identify something as an instance of a more general category of things, and this requires us to ignore other features which are incidental and not categorial. But the essential point to note is that theory is always, and inevitably, *partial*. The abstractions of theory can never match up with the actualities of experience. When theory is referred to practice, it is bound to get caught up in the complexities of the real world from which it has been abstracted. The question always is: how can theory, no matter how global its claims, be interpreted so as to be relevant to local circumstances?

There is a well-entrenched belief among many in the language teaching profession that theory is necessarily opposed to practice. It is ironical that this belief is so often encouraged by those who themselves make theoretical pronouncements about how and what to teach in classrooms under the guise of practical advice. But there is no opposition between theory and practice, and to set them up against each other is, wilfully or not, to misrepresent the nature of both. Instead of setting up a pointless polarity and dismissing the relevance of theory out of hand, what we need to do is explore how it can be *made* relevant and turned to practical advantage. And this is where applied linguistics comes in.

Another persistent belief in some language teaching circles is that not only is theory *opposed* to practice, but is *imposed* upon it by so-called applied linguists who, by a process of transmission, seek to apply linguistic ideas and findings directly and unilaterally into language pedagogy. Such a belief is based on a misconception about the nature of applied linguistics, which is aided and abetted by its very name.

For applied linguistics as it relates to language education does not just take linguistics and apply it. To see why this is so, we need to be clear about the nature of linguistics as a disciplinary enquiry, and the extent to which it is applicable to the concerns of everyday life, including those of the practising teacher.

Linguistics makes statements about language in general or languages in particular, but these statements are necessarily abstractions from the actuality of language as experienced by its users. From their different theoretical perspectives or positions linguists will map out language in different ways, giving prominence to some aspects (deemed to be essential) at the expense of others (deemed to be incidental). All models of linguistic theory, and the descriptions based on them, will be inevitably partial and limited in scope. Of course linguists will always find grounds to prefer one to another and claim validity for their own; and, like everything else, linguistic ideas and attitudes are subject to changing fashion. What needs to be recognized is that what linguists represent is a particular version of reality, abstracted and analysed out of the data of actually occurring language. Such representations are necessarily remote from everyday experience, and from the immediate awareness of ordinary language users.

In some people's minds, of course, this is just what is wrong with them, and when looking at the complex algebraic formulations of generative grammar, one might be inclined to agree. But the remoteness and partiality of linguistic descriptions does not invalidate them. On the contrary, such descriptions are revealing precisely *because* they are partial and informed by a particular perspective. If linguistics could provide us with representations of experienced language, it would be of no interest whatever. Linguistic accounts of language only have point to the extent that they are detached from, and different from, the way language is experienced in the real world.

And this particular version of linguistic reality needs a means of expression that is correspondingly at a remove from the way actual language users talk about their language. It has been suggested that linguists, and other academics, deliberately develop a specialist terminology to keep ordinary people in the dark and sustain the mystery, and the mastery, of their intellectual authority. Edward Said in his Reith lectures some years ago made this observation:

> Each intellectual, book editor and author, military strategist and international lawyer, speaks and deals in a language that has become specialized and usable by other members of the same field, specialist experts addressing other specialist experts in a lingua franca largely unintelligible to unspecialised people.
> (Said 1994a)

But fields of enquiry are necessarily delimited and plotted by their specialist terminology. It is, of course, true that specialist terminology, in common with any other uses of language, can also serve to exercise power, to sustain group solidarity, and exclude outsiders. But this does not warrant condemning it as a kind of conspiracy to corner specialist knowledge, and sustain superiority by keeping ordinary people in a state of exploitable ignorance. For specialist terminology can also have the entirely legitimate use of expressing conceptual distinctions which define different ways of thinking. And it is not just intellectuals, military strategists, lawyers, or linguists, who develop specialist modes of expression. Everybody does it. Said does it himself. All communities do it because all communities develop distinctive ways of talking about things from their own sociocultural perspective. In this sense there *are* no unspecialized people but only people who are specialized in different modes of thought associated with different uses of language which are bound to be, in some degree, unintelligible to others. And if you are an outsider, one of the others, you call it jargon.[2]

The point to be made, then, is that the linguist's representations are not replications of language as it occurs in the real world—the terminology they use, their metalanguage, will be correspondingly remote from everyday usage. What linguists do is to formulate their own version of linguistic reality *on* their own terms and *in* their own terms.

But what good are they, then, to people who live in the real world? What use can they possibly be to people like language teachers and learners who have to come to terms with realities which linguists, it would seem, have conveniently distanced themselves from? The answer is, I think, that these representations can be used as frames of reference for taking bearings on such realities from a fresh perspective. This involves a process of mediation whereby the linguist's abstract version of reality is referred back to the actualities of the language classroom. And this essentially is what applied linguistics seeks to do.

In this view, applied linguistics is not a matter of the application but the appropriation of linguistics for educational purposes. Its aim is to enquire into what aspects of linguistic enquiry can be made relevant to an understanding of what goes on in language classrooms. And this cannot be a unilateral process, for relevance is obviously conditional on particular pedagogic circumstances. And these circumstances are obviously affected by educational as well as linguistic considerations. Language teachers are teachers, and what they teach is not just a language but a subject on the school curriculum.

Mediation, then, involves neither opposition nor imposition, but the realization of interdependency: practice makes reference to theory only to the extent that theory has relevance to practice. Not everybody would see things in this way, of course. John Sinclair, for example, is sceptical of the idea of mediation:

Applied linguists, I have the impression, see themselves as mediators between the abstract and heady realms of linguistic theory and the humdrum practical side of language teaching.
(Sinclair 1998: 84)

But from my own point of view, it is entirely correct that applied linguists should see themselves as mediators. From the perspective of outsiders, linguistic theory may indeed be a heady realm, and language teaching humdrum practice. And this is just the kind of difficulty that mediation has to deal with by showing that what is commonly dismissed as heady, and abstruse can also be interpreted as providing a legitimate intellectual perspective, and that this can be relevantly related to language teaching to make it more meaningful and less humdrum. Without mediation, the heady just remains heady, the humdrum, humdrum.[3]

Mediation as I have described it here is a way of making linguistics useful, and this, I have argued, is made necessary by the very abstract nature of linguistic enquiry. But what if we make it less abstract? What if we build usefulness into the design of the enquiry and instead of going to the bother of making theories useful, just make useful theories instead? We could then cut out the mediating middleman. This would appear to be the position that Labov takes. He first expresses the view that linguistics, far from dealing with abstractions, should be involved in the facts of the real world.

A sober look at the world around us shows that matters of importance are matters of fact. There are some very large matters of fact: the origin of the

universe, the direction of continental drift, the evolution of the human species. There are also specific matters of fact: the innocence or guilt of a particular individual. These are the questions to answer if we would achieve our fullest potential as thinking beings.
(Labov 1988: 182)

I do not myself feel competent to judge the factuality of the origin of the universe and the evolution of species, but my own sober look at the world around us shows that matters of fact are frequently extremely elusive because they are essentially relative. And this is especially the case with specific ones. People have a way of constructing their own facts to suit themselves, figments of their particular sociocultural values and beliefs, and this is surely particularly true of such matters as innocence and guilt. These are not facts: they are value judgements. To treat them as facts is to subscribe to one set of values and disregard others. You may believe you have good moral reasons for doing this, but that is another matter. There are, of course, certain things about the world we live in we can be fairly sure about, and which we can reasonably call factual: population statistics, for example, gross national product, the Dow Jones index. But these are hardly matters which applied linguistics is likely to influence. The kind of issues we are confronted with are not matters of fact of this kind but matters of opinion, attitude, prejudice, point of view. These are the important things which determine the way people think and act. But they are not matters of *fact*. They are matters of *perspective*. And it is for just this reason that mediation of some kind is called for: to see how far these different perspectives, these different fixes people take on the world, can be related, and perhaps reconciled.

As Thomas Gradgrind discovered to his cost in Dickens' *Hard Times*, one should be wary of being too fixated on facts, particularly in educational matters. Not infrequently they turn out to be projections of prejudice. 'Everybody knows that...' but what everybody knows is a social construct; a matter not of fact but convenient belief sanctioned by a particular community. As I said earlier, common sense is always communal sense. So it would be unwise to take such facts as given in advance and then design a theory to account for them. For the theory will then simply confirm partiality, and sustain beliefs without substantiating them. And yet Labov does seem to be speaking in favour of devising theories to fit the preconceived facts. He goes on:

General theory is useful, and the more general the theory the more useful it is, just as any tool is more useful if it can be used for more jobs. But it is still the application of the theory that determines its value. A very general theory can be thought of as a missile that attains considerable altitude, and so it has much greater range than other missiles. But the value of any missile depends on whether it hits the target.
(Labov 1988: 182)

Useful theory, a tool for doing jobs, hitting the target: all this sounds very down-to-earth, even humdrum—certainly no heady realms here. And yet, the missile analogy is a misleading one, and a disturbing one as well. For how can you be so certain in advance what targets you want to hit? What if the targets change, as they are prone to do, so that your fixation on certain particular targets makes it impossible to aim at others? And, crucially, who decides on what is a target and what is not? Missile makers have no say in the matter—they just follow orders, and theory makers would presumably do the same. But whose orders? On this account, theorists would design theories defined as useful for hitting targets determined by all manner of motives: the dictates of commercial profit, perhaps, or political expediency, or whatever. Make me an economic theory which I can use to justify the ruthless exploitation of market forces. Make me a social theory which I can use to justify racism, genocide, ethnic cleansing. Of course, people who talk about useful theories are thinking of benevolent uses. But equally theories can, and have been, made to measure to match malevolent designs as well.

The application of a theory determines its value, says Labov. Well that, it seems to me, depends on what you mean by value. If you mean its practical use, that is one thing. If you mean its theoretical validity, that is surely quite a different matter. Einstein's theory of relativity turned out to be extremely useful for the construction of the atom bomb. But I doubt if anybody would seriously propose that the validity of the theory was in any way determined by the dropping of the bomb in 1945. That, we can agree, was a pretty large matter of fact. But what, we might ask, of the more specific 'facts' of guilt and innocence in this case? These are not so easy to decide.

Increasingly these days, academics are called upon to justify what they are doing in the name of usefulness. The idea of scholarship itself sometimes seems anachronistic and quaint, and intellectual enquiry for its own sake is something we feel calls for some kind of apology. In such a climate, notions like reality, factuality, usefulness sound particularly appealing: they can be invoked in the cause of accountability, and to counter the charge that linguistics is an elitist academic discipline, an abstract and heady realm remote from the everyday world. But this populist appeal is suspect, and can, I think, undermine the integrity of academic enquiry.[4] Linguistics as such only exists by virtue of its specialization as a disciplinary discourse in its own right, and only has validity to the extent that it presents reality on its own intellectual authority and in its own specialist terms. If it starts producing theories and descriptions to specification and their validity is measured by their utility value, then its authority, it seems to me, is bound to be compromised. This does not mean that linguists should set out to be deliberately useless. Nor does it mean that particular problems in the world should not stimulate enquiry; rather, the course of enquiry should not be determined in advance to come up with expedient solutions. To my mind, then, it is not within the brief of linguists to make useful theories. On the contrary, as soon as they start doing that, they lose their scholarly independence and with it their value to the non-scholarly world. This value depends not on making useful theories but on making theories useful. But this is not within the linguists' brief either. For it requires a distancing from their disciplinary perspective and the recognition of its possible relationship with others. This is what I mean by mediation. So the linguist, qua linguist, is not in a position to judge what use might be made of linguistic theory and description. Their usefulness potential is for others to realize. One linguist at least has recognized this well enough. I refer to Chomsky, and his often cited comments to the effect that he is sceptical about the significance for pedagogy of insights from pyschology and linguistics.

> Furthermore, I am, frankly, rather sceptical about the significance, for the teaching of languages, of such insights and understanding as have been attained in linguistics and psychology.
> (Chomsky 1966/71: 152–3)

Chomsky's comments, however, were made in an address to the Northeast Conference on the Teaching of Foreign Languages, and his scepticism is prefaced by an explicit disclaimer to any expertise in language pedagogy. He recognizes that the significance he refers to, and is sceptical about, is not actually for him to decide, and later in the lecture from which these comments come, he makes the following (rather less often cited) remarks:

> It is possible—even likely—that principles of psychology and linguistics, and research in these disciplines, may supply insights useful to the language teacher. But this must be demonstrated, and cannot be presumed. It is the language teacher himself who must validate or refute any specific proposal. There is very little in psychology or linguistics that he can accept on faith.
> (Chomsky 1966/71: 155)

What Chomsky is talking about here is not the applications but implications of his linguistics and these, as he makes clear, it is not his business to work out. It is not the business of any linguist, for no matter how close they may seem to come to terms with reality, they can only come to terms with reality on their *own* terms. The domains and discourses of linguistics and of such practical activities as language teaching remain as distinct as ever. And Chomsky's comments are as relevant now as they were then.

The usefulness of insights that linguistics supplies must be demonstrated. But a little close analysis of Chomsky's text will reveal a difficulty or two. Note the passive and the deleted agent. The usefulness must be demonstrated. But who is it that does the demonstrating? Who is to be the agent? The teacher. But how do teachers recognize these insights in the first place? Linguists, as I have already said, develop their own specialist discourses to suit their own disciplinary perspective on language, and so they should. So whatever insights might be forthcoming cannot simply be *supplied*, retailed from one discourse to another. For one thing, as Edward Said points out, the insights will be couched in an idiom 'largely unintelligible to unspecialised people'. And language teachers are unspecialized as far as linguistics is concerned. So we need a third party, a mediating agent whose role is to make these insights intelligible in ways in which their usefulness can be demonstrated.

So linguistic insights for the purposes of the language teacher are created by mediation. But, equally, so is the usefulness. Applied linguistics is often said to be concerned with the investigation of real-world problems in which language is implicated. But this seems to suggest that problems, like insights, are somehow already there as well defined entities, that somebody in the real world supplies a problem, the linguist supplies an insight and the applied linguist matches them up. But things are not like that. To begin with, problems are perceived and formulated in culturally marked ways; in other words, they belong to particular discourses. So it is likely that they will need to be reformulated so as to make them amenable to investigation. It may indeed be the case that what people identify as a problem is simply the symptom of another one that they are not aware of. In a sense then, investigation, which of its nature belongs to a discourse other than that of the problem, will necessarily reformulate it, and change it into something else, which in turn may create problems that were not perceived at all in the first place. So just as linguistic insights are a function of the mediation, so are the problems they are related to. The process brings together two discourses or versions of reality and this requires an adjustment of fit whereby an area of convergence is created, compounded of elements of both discourses but belonging exclusively to neither.

Since the area of convergence belongs to neither discourse, proponents of both are likely to be somewhat ambivalent about it. Thus language teachers, for example, may, and indeed often do, think of it as an unwanted, and unwarranted, intrusion on their domain. And it is true that there are times when it is: when we get linguistics applied, as distinct from applied linguistics, the process whereby linguistic findings are foisted on pedagogy on just the presumption of relevance that Chomsky warns us against. Conversely, linguists may feel that the area of convergence is a misrepresentation that distorts their discipline. Applied linguists thus find themselves in an anomalous position, in a no-man's land they have made for themselves, and not infrequently under fire from both sides. They could withdraw from the middle ground, of course, and leave the two sides of language teaching and linguistics to get on with their own business without reference to each other. After all, it is the meddling of applied linguistics, one might argue, that has created the conditions of conflict in the first place. But since the business of both sides is with language, there should surely be *some* common ground, some areas of convergence to be explored.

Mediation, then, as I have described it, seeks to identify insights from the linguistic disciplines of potential relevance to the language subject. Its purpose is to stimulate the theorizing process whereby teachers assume the role of reflective practitioners. But it cannot replace that process, nor can it establish relevance in advance, for that clearly must take the local teaching/learning context into account. There has been much emphasis over recent years on the importance of acknowledging the legitimacy of language teachers' own 'cognitions', their own structures of knowledge and ways of thinking (Woods 1996). Nothing I have said about applied linguistic mediation denies that legitimacy. On the contrary, it is these cognitions that constitute the pedagogic discourse that insights from linguistic discourse need to be reconciled with for relevance to be realized. There are, however, two points to be made about such cognitions. Firstly, it would obviously be a mistake to suppose that they are general to all teachers. As with the generic reference to classrooms mentioned earlier, talking about teachers has a down-to-earth appeal, and the danger is that it might be taken as carrying of itself a guarantee of practicality. But we should recognize that such ideas can be just as theoretical as any that come from linguistics, and need just as much to be validated as relevant by reference to local conditions. Teachers' cognitions—which teachers?[5]

Secondly, the recognition of the importance of teacher cognitions, even giving them priority, does not surely preclude the possibility that they might be extended, modified, even changed out of all recognition by influences from outside, including appropriately mediated linguistic insights. There has sometimes been the suggestion that taking account of teacher cognitions is an *alternative* to applied linguistics, in that it is an encouragement of self-realization rather than an imposition of transmitted ideas. But as I have argued, applied linguistics (as distinct from linguistics applied)[6] is not such an imposition, but a way of encouraging theorizing, in which the teachers' own thinking would be necessarily involved. There is no reason why teachers should be deprived of the opportunity to develop their cognitions with reference to other ideas, and it is surely the purpose of teacher education to provide such an opportunity.[7]

Applied linguistics, as conceived of here, is, then, a mediating process which explores ways in which the concerns of linguistics as a discipline can be relevantly related to those of the language subject. There are two features of this process which it is important to stress. In the first place, in this view of applied linguistics, it is indeed linguistics that is taken as the disciplinary point of reference. Though not linguistics applied, it is linguistics mediated. And the mediation is not across disciplines, different academic discourses, but across the divide between the disciplinary domains of detached enquiry and that of practical experienced reality, between expertise and experience. The very nature of the problem being addressed is, of course, likely to involve taking bearings from other disciplines as well. But if applied linguists were required to have expertise across the whole range of potentially relevant academic disciplines, they would be in no position to say anything at all. Applied linguistics is routinely referred to as interdisciplinary, as if this were its distinguishing feature. Though this may lend it a certain academic prestige, it is, to my mind, misleading. The interdisciplinary expertise that is evident in most of the work that is carried out in its name is, not surprisingly, very limited indeed. It seems to me preferable to accept that what we are doing in applied linguistics is exploring the relevance of *linguistics* (bearing in mind that this itself covers a wide range of interdisciplinary enquiry) and to recognize that what we have to say is therefore necessarily partial and provisional. We are pointing things out from a particular and necessarily limited point of view.[8]

The second essential feature of applied linguistic mediation is that the process is necessarily a critical one in that it involves following through the implications, and questioning the validity of accepted ideas. What is applied in applied linguistics is a kind of positive and enquiring scepticism which seeks not so much to provide solutions as to propose how problems might be reformulated. I should make it clear, however, that when I say that mediation is necessarily critical, I am not using that term in the more specific, politically committed sense that is assigned to it in recent work in linguistics and sociology, and taken up in Pennycook (2001). For Pennycook, the kind of mediation I am proposing here amounts to what he calls 'liberal ostrichism', in that it ridiculously fails to engage with, or even recognize, the social injustice that lies at the heart of the problems it addresses. To counteract the bland complacency to the world's evils that such ostrichism implies, Pennycook proposes a critical applied linguistics which not only seeks to expose inequality and prejudice but is politically committed to their eradication. His book is a manifesto for an applied linguistics with a mission, with a cause, or, as he puts it 'with an attitude'. As will be readily imagined, I have some reservations about the Pennycook position. In the first place, mediation does not, as he appears to suppose, imply any indifference to moral or political issues. The work of many a so-called ostrich has been informed and inspired by the belief in social justice without feeling it necessary to give it the label 'critical' and put it on polemical display. And, more crucially, without imposing it unilaterally as a preconceived doctrine. What Pennycook seems to be proposing is that no matter how locally particular a problem might be, it must be cast in the same ideological image and subjected to the same process of sociopolitical interpretation. This is politics applied. Now, of course, the cause of social justice that Pennycook proclaims is one that everybody, overtly and in principle, would espouse. But it is interpreted in local practice in many different sociopolitical ways, some of which may seem to be at some variance with this principle. And what if the cause is not so worthy? We come to the same issue as was discussed earlier in this chapter in relation to Labov's proposal for devising useful theories. So long as Pennycook is on the side of the angels, all is well. But what if his mission is malevolent, or even well meaning but misconceived? Promoting an applied linguistics with an attitude may not be a very wise thing to do. It all depends on the attitude.[9]

The applied linguistics that informs the kind of enquiry I undertake in this book does not impose a way of thinking, but points things out that might be worth thinking about. Pointing out leaves open the question of what action might be appropriately taken, and is in this respect different from recommendation. There is a moment in Robert Bolt's play *A Man for All Seasons*, which nicely illustrates the difference. Richard Rich has been pleading with Sir Thomas More to employ him. More, not trusting him, refuses. A subsequent exchange with the Duke of Norfolk runs as follows:

> MORE: Oh, your grace, here is a young man desperate for employment. Something in the clerical line.
> NORFOLK: Well, if you recommend him...
> MORE: Oh, I don't recommend him; but I point him out.

There is no shortage of people recommending what language teachers should do, whether they call themselves methodologists, teacher trainers, or applied linguists, whether they base their recommendations on practical experience, empirical evidence, or theoretical expertise. But they are in no position to recommend particular courses of action though they can, of course, point out possibilities it might be profitable to explore.

Notes and comments

1 As I have pointed out elsewhere (Widdowson 1997a) the term 'teacher' is traditionally used to refer to somebody with privileged access to wisdom: a sage or savant, whose teaching (or teachings) inspire reverence. Goldsmith's schoolmaster is obviously a figure of this kind who can count on people recognizing the authority of his special knowledge. The problem is, of course, that his authority rests on the ignorance of the gazing rustics. The challenge for teachers today is to establish legitimate grounds for their authority now that Goldsmith's village rustics have disappeared, and education has become democratized.

2 We should note, however, that, as with any other community, those of academic disciplines also develop an insider language for solidarity purposes, to express their distinctive identity. So it is that insights from a discipline like linguistics are often closed off from outsiders and their potential benefits left unrealized. Hence the need for the kind of cross-cultural interpretation that applied linguistics engages in.

3 Sinclair is not the only linguist to express reservations about applied linguistics as a mediating area of enquiry. In a recent article, de Beaugrande expresses the view that applied linguists have no business taking the initiative to bring theoretical considerations to bear on practice. (See de Beaugrande 2001.) What they should do is just 'wait and see' what teachers think will work or not and then come in on the discussion if and when necessary 'on a level they (i.e. the teachers) prefer'. So, according to de Beaugrande, it would seem, an applied linguist is somebody who waits for teachers to react to whatever theoretical ideas or empirical findings happen to come their way and then has a word or two about them if called upon. There is

no room for mediation here. Indeed, it is hard to see any principled role for applied linguistics at all. The applied linguist simply becomes a linguist who descends from the heady realms of theory to talk to teachers about their humdrum concerns from time to time. For further discussion of de Beaugrande's position, see Widdowson 2001.

4 We touch here on complex issues concerning academic objectivity and ideology. It is often said that all enquiry, no matter how rationally conducted, is informed in some degree by ideological belief, and that hence there is no such thing as objectivity. This point obviously relates to the necessary partiality of linguistic descriptions that I argue for in this chapter. Difficulties arise, however, when a particular position or sociopolitical motivation seems to interfere with the rationality of the process of enquiry itself. The work of Labov himself provides an interesting example. In 1969, he published a paper entitled 'The logic of non-standard English' (1969), in which he set out to demonstrate that the English of working-class African-Americans (called Black English Vernacular at the time), then stigmatized as inferior and deficient, was actually more to the point, more logical in fact, than that of a middle-class black speaker who had adopted a more prestigious but actually more verbose and less logical manner of speaking. At the time of writing, Labov's paper was of great sociopolitical significance and highly influential. Subsequently, it has been argued, however, particularly by Bernstein, that Labov's analysis and the conclusions he draws from it, are very questionable (Bernstein 1990: 114–18). If one accepts Bernstein's argument, it might be suggested that what has happened here is that Labov, too, in his entirely laudable concern to remove the stigma from one form of speaking, in effect shifts it unfairly on to another. One might also argue, however, against this objection, that even if the paper is shown to be flawed in academic terms, this matters less than its positive influence on social and scholarly attitudes; that it is the ideology of the cause that matters, not the rationality of the case. The essential issue is the proper relationship between advocacy and argument, and it admits of no easy solution. As I have suggested earlier in this chapter, in the last analysis (to use a particularly apt phrase in this context) it all depends on what cause is being promoted.

5 Just how difficult it is to generalize about such cognitions is well illustrated in a recent article by Breen and his colleagues (Breen *et al.* 2001). They conducted a thorough enquiry into how a group of experienced teachers of English 'conceptualized their classroom practice'. This was, the authors stress, 'a particular investigation' of 'a particular group' in 'a particular teaching situation'. So whatever more general applicability their findings might have is necessarily a matter of speculation. There is always the danger, of course, that the very precision with which data is collected and categorized can beguile the reader, and the researcher, into thinking that it represents compelling evidence of wider significance. Even in this chapter,

which is very cautious in its claims, there is the occasional slippage from particular to general reference with the implication that this particular, small, local and disparate group is generically representative of English teachers (or even language teachers) as a whole. What is most valuable about this article is that it reveals just how diverse and complex teachers' cognitions can be, even within a small group, and therefore how elusive they are of definition. So what I would conclude from this study is not that further research along similar lines is needed to establish what teacher conceptualizations are, but that such conceptualizations will always be particular and will need to be locally accounted for.

6 Linguistics applied is the process of unilateral and unmediated application of the concepts and descriptive findings of linguistics to language teaching and other practical domains. Unlike applied linguistics, as defined in this chapter, it sets out to provide solutions to problems that are taken as self-evident, and does not enquire into the nature of the problems themselves. For further discussion, see Widdowson 1984: Chapter 2, Widdowson 2000a, and Chapter 7 of this present book.

7 There is a good deal more to be said about language teacher education, of course. Readers interested in my own views might refer to Widdowson 1990, 1992a, 1997a.

8 To talk about mediation across domains of the academic expertise of linguistics on the one hand and lay experience of language on the other presupposes that these are distinct and different, and I believe they are. For me, as I argue in this book and have argued elsewhere, linguists only have something of interest to say about language to the extent that they assume a position of disciplinary detachment. Their very detachment from the reality of language as immediately experienced means that what they say is only a partial version of such reality. My view is that it is precisely this partiality that provides a fresh perspective and makes us see our familiar reality in a new light. But others think differently. According to them, this detachment amounts to aloofness, the taking up of a prestigious position of authority. To their mind, disciplines are social constructs which have become unduly privileged and need now to be demolished and replaced by a more democratic representation of opinion, whereby knowledge is not informed by disciplinary principle, but emerges, socially constituted as a function of free interaction. In such a postmodernist view, no special status is accorded to the procedures of intellectual enquiry; disciplines become democratically levelled and in effect the distinction I have drawn between experience and expertise disappears. For an expression of this view, and my reactions to it, see Rampton 1997, 1998; Widdowson 1998.

9 There seems to be a certain ambivalence in Pennycook's own attitude. In the conclusion to his book, Pennycook provides what he calls 'Critical Notes for the Fridge Door', and then appends an apologetic footnote in acknowledgement that this presupposes cultural assumptions that are not

shared by readers whose way of life does not include writing notes on a fridge door, or even having a fridge door at all. The attitude that this indicates would appear on the face of it to be at odds with the position Pennycook takes up in the rest of his book. It is certainly antithetical to the kind of mediation that I am proposing.

For a perceptive review of Pennycook, see Breyer 2002. For other views of applied linguistics (more compatible with my own), see Brumfit 1997; Cook 2003; Davies 1999.

2   Parameters in language pedagogy

What applied linguistics does is to facilitate the process of theorizing, whereby the ideas that inform practice, often assumed as self-evident common sense, are made explicit and reformulated so that they might then be acted upon. This is what I have been arguing. To theorize in this way is not to undermine established custom but to establish its rational credentials and the extent of its current relevance. It follows, too, that to theorize in this way is to avoid allegiance to any particular set of theoretical ideas. Practice which is informed by theory in general is very different from practice informed by a theory in particular. The former opens up enquiry by pointing out possibilities, the latter closes it down by making recommendations. A particular theory applied to practice is a method, the formulation of a solution imposed *proactively* on the learning process. Theory-informed practice, on the other hand, is an approach to methodology: one that seeks to define problems as explicitly as possible so that they are amenable to solution *reactively* in the teaching/ learning process. The distrust of theory and the denial of its relevance in favour of teacher cognitions that I referred to in the last chapter arise from a failure to make this distinction. Teachers often talk about being eclectic, as if this were opposed to being theoretical. But I do not see that it is. Eclecticism is not the same as random expediency, an ad hoc reaction to immediate circumstances, but a matter of choosing from a range of options. This obviously presupposes that you have some idea of what that range might be, and some reason for deciding on one option rather than another.

What kind of options are there in language pedagogy, and how might we theorize about them? Language teaching is carried out in all kinds of different ways and in all kinds of different circumstances, but the very notion of difference presupposes a framework of likeness. We could not talk about one kind of teaching as distinct from another unless we have some general concept of teaching in relation to which they differ. Any statement about difference is coherent to the extent that it implies some similarity in common at some level. We can propose any number of random statements: the Indian Ocean is different from an artichoke, a brick is different from Beethoven's Fifth Symphony, but they are meaningless unless we can discern some principle of comparison which gives point to the contrast. We can say that comparison provides the dimensions or parameters of similarity, and that we recognize contrasting instances as different settings of this common parameter.

The term 'parameter' is associated with a particular linguistic theory and refers to the features of universal grammar, but it can be taken to apply in a wider sense to the relationship between human language in general and languages in particular.[1] All languages are instances of language and so differ in respect to their settings of common parameters. We might suggest, along similar lines, that all kinds of language teaching are different, but relatable as different settings of a set of general parameters which characterize the process of language teaching in general. Let us pursue this idea. Granted that language teaching is done in all manner of ways and is influenced by innumerable and interacting variables associated with different teacher and learner cognitions, classroom conditions, social contexts, and so on, we might nevertheless be able to establish a parametric framework which defines the language teaching enterprise in general as a way of making sense of this variation, and in reference to which differences in practice can be related in a principled way. What kinds of parameter might be proposed?

Since language teaching is concerned with language, one would expect it to be referable to ideas in linguistics. But since it is also a kind of teaching, one would expect it to be referable to ideas about education as well. So it would seem reasonable to take parametric bearings from both areas of enquiry.

Consider education first. We can, broadly speaking, distinguish two parameters here. One relates to the ends of learning, the educational purpose. What is this language subject doing on the curriculum? What are we teaching it *for*? What objectives are we directing the learners to achieve? The second relates to the different roles that are taken up by those who participate in the pedagogic process by which the purpose is to be achieved: the teacher and the learner.

The purpose parameter has to do with the philosophy of education and the ideology which informs policy making. One can conceive of education as the initiation of students into an established culture of knowledge and belief, a continuation of heritage. In this view, the setting is retrospective, past-oriented and dedicated to the maintenance of traditional social values on the assumption that they will be of continuing relevance. Alternatively, one might give the purpose parameter a prospective setting, future rather than past-oriented, focused on initiative rather than initiation, and, one which, in both senses of the term, anticipates change by representing education as the means whereby individuals are prepared to cope with unpredictable eventualities.[2]

With regard to process, the parameters have to do with teacher and learner roles. One can think of education as a matter of teacher direction or learner discovery. On the one hand, there is transmission under the control of the teacher whose task is essentially to make students receptive so that there is as close a convergence as possible of intake with input. Here, teacher authority is given primacy and learning accommodates to teaching. On the other hand, students are encouraged in individual enterprise and approval accorded to divergence. Learner autonomy is given primacy, and teaching accommodates to learning.[3]

Now of course these settings are not absolute and disjunctive alternatives, fixed once and for all to apply with complete consistency for each subject across the curriculum. They are likely to vary at different educational levels and with different subjects. But this does not invalidate them; on the contrary, it gives them a point in that they serve as an explicit framework for decision making as to which aspects of which subjects need to be given one parametric setting rather than another.

Take the subject English literature, for example, as taught in mother tongue classrooms. The conventional setting for purpose is usually retrospective and students are initiated into the canon of privileged texts which represents established literary heritage. The argument for this is that such texts have stood the test of time and so carry their relevance with them into the present. The process is generally given a transmissive setting: students are not expected to engage experientially with the texts on their own initiative, but to understand them at second hand via the received wisdom of critical commentary. But what if it turns out that students do not themselves recognize this relevance, if it no longer has any bearing on their lives, or on the changed social realities of the communities they come from, so that the experience of literature is not only second-hand, but confined to the classroom and not projected into the future beyond schooling? This might suggest to makers of educational policy that the setting for at least some aspects of literary study should be adjusted towards a more prospective curriculum and the canon replaced by texts which are more immediately and obviously relevant to the students' lives. Such a suggestion might well be resisted on the grounds that to alter the criteria for relevance in this way inevitably results in the erosion of educational standards.

Similar considerations apply to how language is educationally conceived in first language settings. Consider, for example, how grammar figures in defining the subject English in the National Curriculum in Britain. The argument for giving it explicit attention is based on an ambiguity: it is associated with both standards in English and Standard English. Thus maintaining standards is equated with the teaching of Standard English, and since you can only maintain something that is already established, there is retrospective reference to accepted norms of correctness which it is assumed can, and should, be projected unchanged into the present and the future. In this view, any reappraisal of Standard English as the suitable setting on the purpose parameter would necessarily constitute a decline in standards. But one can also see an alternative setting as being an adjustment not to declining but to different standards based on changing criteria of appropriateness, with priority given to intelligibility rather than correctness.[4]

With regard to the process parameter, the settings here can also be regulated as required, no matter how rigidly they may seem to be fixed by custom. It seems obvious that some aspects of some subjects, and some teaching/learning contexts, will call for teacher control and the limitation of learner initiative. The question is: which aspects, and which contexts? It has become fashionable in some circles over recent years to talk about teacher intervention as if it were synonymous with interference. Let the learners learn, has been the cry: let nature take its course. Here the process parameter is well and truly fixed at learner autonomy and discovery learning. But there is obviously no point in giving the initiative to people who cannot take it, and if you prepare them to take it you necessarily impose limitations on it. Giving and taking are converse terms in a way that teaching and learning are very definitely not. Teaching must adapt to learning in certain respects, but in other respects the adaptation must be reversed. Natural learning, we need to note, is generally speaking inefficient and slow, and dependent on fortuitous circumstances which favour some and not others. Education is based on the belief that natural learning can be improved upon by creating more favourable circumstances by teacher contrivance and control. With regard to language education, it is precisely because the natural learning of another language is so much a matter of chance and accident that language subjects are designed in the first place. This is not to say that learners should be denied the opportunity for initiative, but only to note two things. Firstly, there are aspects of language learning, and kinds of language learner where direction is crucial and lack of it simply results in needless confusion or diffusion of effort. Secondly, learner initiative is always ultimately under teacher control, no matter how subtly the control may be concealed. The teacher may choose to set the parameter so as to allow it to be exercised, but always within limits, for it is the teacher, and not the learner, who sets the parameter and regulates classroom interaction.

So far I have talked about educational parameters in general which are relevant for the definition of any subject. What of the subject which is concerned with the teaching of a particular language, English as a foreign or second language, for example? What aspects of the language should we be concerned with? What would seem to be of obvious relevance here is the distinction that Chomsky has made between Externalized or E-Language linguistics, which is concerned with contextualized language behaviour actualized in the social process, and Internalized or I-Language linguistics whose business is with the abstract knowledge of decontextualized linguistic properties. On the one hand, we have language conceived of in terms of its indexical functions which can only be realized in use as utterances, spoken or written, appropriate to some context, and motivated by some communicative purpose or other. On the other hand, we have language conceived of in terms of its symbolic forms, as an abstract system or code, which can only be manifested as usage by the citation of words and sentences.

This distinction serves to characterize two broad ways of setting the purpose parameter of the language subject. One way is to set it along I-Language lines and concentrate on encoded forms to be internalized as linguistic knowledge. The other is to to follow E-Language lines and define the objective in terms of communicative functions to be realized as social behaviour. In both cases, the assumption is that the other aspect of language will be learnt incidentally as a contingent consequence and calls for no direct teaching attention. But although these general parameter settings can be said to characterize different strategic objectives in broad terms, the tactics of actual teaching may involve a continual readjustment of settings with both aspects of language focused on at different times and combined in different ways as thought appropriate to the process of achieving these objectives. Thus the setting of an E-language objective for a course does not preclude the use of I-language on the way, or vice versa.

What I am suggesting, then, is that we might take theoretical bearings on the practice of language teaching by reference to three general parameters. One relates to educational purpose and broadly provides for options in regard to retrospective initiation and prospective needs. Another relates to process, which provides for options in regard to teacher authority and learner autonomy. The third has to do with the way language is defined as subject content, providing options in regard to code knowledge and communicative ability in respect both to purpose and process.

The crucial question for pedagogy is how different settings interrelate. To what extent, for example, does a setting on one parameter have implicational consequences on how the others are set? In the design of English teaching, there has been a tendency for certain settings to co-occur in preferred or unmarked combinations and such occurrence can be said to characterize different approaches to language pedagogy. Thus what I have referred to as retrospective purpose would seem to combine most readily with a transmission process based on teacher authority and with content specified in formal linguistic terms. Prospective purpose, on the other hand, seems to go along with a deference to learner initiative and an emphasis on communicative function. So it is that the purpose of communicative language teaching to develop the ability to cope with naturally occurring language in context would seem to call for a content which is drawn from such natural and therefore 'authentic' occurrences, and the devolvement of responsibility to learners themselves working together in groups. A specification of content in terms of the encoded properties of the language, on the other hand (the so-called focus on form) is generally seen as necessarily implying a transmission mode of instruction closely regulated by teacher control.

It is not clear, however, that such combinations are implicationally determined, rather than coincidental.[5] It would appear to be perfectly reasonable, for example, to devise activities at a particular point in a course which focused on encoded features of the language being learnt but did so by inviting learners to make explicit comparisons with their own language. Such a procedure can be seen, furthermore, as integrating two settings on the purpose parameter, for this kind of language awareness activity may not only be a factor in the development of practical proficiency for some learners, but may also promote a sensitivity to cultural differences encoded in the different languages. It is often said, as if it were self-evident, that the learning of a foreign language has the effect of promoting cross-cultural understanding, but this seems unlikely with the kind of rudimentary transactions frequently set as the objective of communicative language teaching. There can be communication of a kind without any sense of community, and developing this sense may well need to be explicitly provided for. I shall have occasion to return to this issue later in the book (in Chapter 11).

A course the purpose of which is to develop communicative competence is not necessarily best served by setting the process parameter in ways which favour learner discovery. A degree of direct transmission under teacher control may prove to be effective in certain cases. One of the reasons why the communicative objective is often so closely tied in with activities which give full rein to learner initiative is that communication itself is defined in very restricted terms. It is quite commonly supposed that communicative language teaching just means getting learners to participate in spoken exchanges in simple social and service transactions of the kind they are most likely to encounter in the context of native-speaker use. But there is more to spoken communication than that. There are complex sociocultural factors involved and we cannot assume that these will be understood and acted upon as a simple function of fluency practice. And communication is not only a spoken phenomenon of course. Coping with written language is also a communicative objective, and this can, with varying degrees of discovery and direction, be brought about by a retrospective focus, by initiating learners into an understanding of writing, literary and otherwise, of the past. It is currently fashionable to suppose that if objectives for a language course are to be realistic, then they must be tied to content which represents real language, and that the only real language is that which is attested as of contemporary currency. It is this assumption of implicational fixity of setting across parameters that needs to be questioned.

There may be implicational relations across different settings, but they cannot, I think, be taken as self-evident, a matter of common sense. How particular parameters are set, and how they can most effectively interact, are issues to be tactically decided in the light of the local educational and pedagogic context. Teaching, we might say, can be defined as the art of appropriate parameter setting, and effective methodology is a matter of continual online adjustment of settings as the course proceeds.

Over recent years, there has been a proliferation of recommendations as to how language teachers should proceed: a bewildering assortment of persuasive ideas and proposals: communicative language teaching, humanistic and natural approaches, process and procedural syllabuses, authentic language, task-based learning. An understandable reaction to all this is to take refuge in common sense and reject the lot. A preferable alternative, I would suggest, is to try to impose some kind of conceptual order on it by theorizing. For it is when particular theories multiply that the need for theory in general becomes most urgent, but theory understood as points of reference to take bearings from, theory that activates and facilitates enquiry into what is appropriate for particular aspects of language, for particular learners, for particular contexts. I have suggested that we can conceive of these reference points as parameters, to be given different settings as locally required. It might be objected that the parameters I have identified here are too general, too simple, or too few, and that may well be the case. I do not recommend them as a definitive scheme or model for analysis; I point them out as possibilities for reflecting on practice in a principled way.

Notes and comments

1 Parameters in generative linguistic theory are those abstract properties of universal grammar, which are innate in the human mind and therefore properties of language in general. The features of particular languages are seen as different settings of these general parameters brought about by various local environmental conditions. For a clear and accessible account of the theory, see Cook and Newson 1996.

2 These brief comments are meant to be only suggestive of the relevance of such educational considerations. They give little indication of the complex philosophical and ideological issues they give rise to, and which have been the concern of educationalists for many years. Just how complex these issues are might be gauged from the recent publication of an *Encyclopedia of Language and Education*. The first of its eight volumes (Wodak and Corson 1997) is devoted entirely to questions of how political issues impinge on matters of policy in language education.

3 Obviously, it is not a matter of making an absolute decision between either learner autonomy on the one hand or teacher authority on the other, but of regulating the most effective relationship between them. Even those who favour allowing maximal initiative to learners will generally agree that the teacher needs to give them some explicit guidance as to how to take it, so that, in practice, learner independence is always in some degree under teacher direction. (For a succinct account of different positions on self-directed learning, see Wenden 2002.) It is worth noting that the idea that the teacher's main task is to develop a capability for self-directed learning does not only affect *how* the contents of a particular course are pedagogically dealt with, but also leads to a reconsideration of *what* these contents should be if they are to provide an investment for subsequent learning after the course is over.

4 Issues concerning the privileged status of Standard English, its relationship with other varieties of the language, and its role in the maintenance of educational standards have been the subject of much controversy. See, for example, Bex and Watts 1999; Fairclough 1995.

5 In the description of different approaches to language teaching, this distinction is usually not made explicit. What we tend to get is a list of attributes, with little indication as to which are taken to be essential as defining features, as matters of pedagogic principle, and which are only incidental as various techniques for implementing them. It is interesting, for example, to see what common features emerge from a comparison of the way communicative language teaching (CLT) is characterized in Larsen-Freeman 2000 and Richards and Rodgers 2001. Neither of them would appear to correspond with Howatt's view of what is distinctive about this approach. Whereas they represent it as a quite radical break from traditional approaches, Howatt takes a very different view:

> Most of the essential features of direct method and structural language teaching have remained in place in CLT, largely unexamined and undisturbed, just as they have been for a century or more. CLT has adopted all the major principles of 19th century reform: the primacy of the spoken language, for instance, the inductive teaching of grammar, the belief in connected texts, and, most significant of all, the monolingual (direct method) principle that languages should be taught in the target language, not in the pupils' mother tongue.
> (Howatt 1987: 25)

For Howatt, the most distinctive feature of CLT is that it has, incidentally, extended the repertoire of practice exercises to include communicative activities.

3 Proper words in proper places

Language teachers do not teach language in general, they teach particular languages: Arabic, German, Japanese, English, and so on. But they teach these as *subjects*, and so, as was argued in the preceding chapter, we need to consider what kind of language is to be specified for the subject to fulfil its educational objective. Our concern is with English. So the question arises as to what kind of English it is appropriate to specify. If you are teaching English it seems obvious that it should be proper English and not some distorted or deviant version of it. What then is proper English, and what is not?

This chapter takes its title from a letter written by Jonathan Swift in 1720 to a young clergyman of his acquaintance: 'Proper words in proper places, make the true definition of style'. But then what, we might ask, makes the true definition of 'proper'? And who is it that does the defining? And is it only style that can be defined in this way? These are the kinds of questions I want to consider here in reference to English. As we shall see, we shall come across a number of current, and contentious issues in English language education: issues concerning linguistic propriety and linguistic property, Standard English and standards of English, and standard bearers and native speakers. To be brisk, the theme of this chapter is: what is proper English, and who says so?

When, to begin with, is a word in its proper place? One answer is: when it finds its niche in a grammatical pattern, when, suitably adjusted by morphological modification, it fits snugly into syntax. Propriety in this sense has to do with the internal relationships of words as determined by the linguistic code. In this case we can talk about proper English in terms of conformity to encoding convention. But this is not the only answer. We can also think of words being in their proper place with reference to their communicative purpose. Here we are concerned not with the internal relationship of words as encoded forms, but with the external relationship of words with the context of their actual occurrence, and propriety is not now a matter of their correctness of form in a sentence, but of their appropriateness of function in an utterance.

To give a simple illustration. If, in the course of a routine interaction, a woman were to ask her husband:

Have you put out the small domesticated furry feline animal?

he would undoubtedly find the expression unusual, stylistically strange, an improper use of language. It would be out of place: contextually out of place.

But it is a perfectly proper English sentence: the words all combine to make a correct syntactic fit. If, on the other hand, the wife were to say:

Have you out the cat put?

there would be reason to suspect that, for some reason or another, she had not quite got a secure grip on the syntax of the language. This time the words are grammatically out of place. The utterance would, in all likelihood, pose no communicative problem: the husband would know what his wife meant. The words relate appropriately to the context but they do not relate properly to each other as the code requires. They are just not English. All this seems obvious and straightforward enough. But as we shall see presently, things are not quite so simple when we consider them more closely. Meanwhile, we turn from proper places to proper words themselves.

Again, the distinction between code and context propriety is relevant. It enables us to distinguish between concepts of *the* proper word and *a* proper word. Suppose (to take another scene from domestic life), at the funeral of an aged relative, I were to make the remark:

Well the old soak has finally snuffed it.

I might well be accused of a lapse in taste, a lapse in propriety indeed in failing to observe accepted decorum. But nobody would say that my words were not English ones. If, on the other hand, I were to come out with the utterance:

Well the old man has perspired at last.

this would be taken as a linguistic lapse, a malapropism, a miscue for 'expired', a slip of the tongue occasioned perhaps by an excess of grief, or finding too much solace in the sherry.[1] 'Perspire' and 'snuff' are not the proper words to use: one is semantically mistaken and the other is pragmatically misplaced. But although they are not the proper words on these occasions of use, they are nevertheless both proper words of English, just as, for example, 'despire' and 'smuff' are not.

But they could be, of course. There is nothing in the formation of these words as such which is un-English. The language has the necessary phonological and morphological resources for making them should the need ever arise. They are in this respect available as a potential or virtual presence in the code, in reserve, so to speak, and ready for actual realization as and when required for active service. It is this potential that Lewis Carroll draws on in inventing his so-called portmanteau words like 'frabjous' and 'frumious' and 'chortle'. Of these, 'chortle' has been taken on as a proper English word and appears in the dictionary. The others have not. They remain lexical curiosities.

So we might define proper words as those which are sanctioned by conventional usage, and we might suppose that confirmation of this is to be found in the dictionary. But here we run into difficulties. To begin with, of course, it depends on which dictionary you choose to consult. But let us turn to one which claims to be the most comprehensive of them, the *Oxford English Dictionary* (*OED*). Within its vast archive are to be found large numbers of words which are historically attested, but now no longer in use: words, for example, like 'depertible', 'depredable', and 'deprehend'. Unlike the Lewis Carroll cases, these are lexical *has-beens*, not *might-have-beens*. But although they are obsolete, and are marked as such, they do not seem to have lost their status as proper words: history, we might say, gives them a certain presence.

But what actually is the difference between the *has-beens* and the *might-have-beens*? The *has-beens* are attested as having been used in the past. How often, though, and by whom? It must presumably be on more than one occasion and by more than one person, otherwise the words remain in the perpetual possibility of the *might-have-been*. But then how do we explain the curious case of Shakespeare?

Shakespeare was, of course, a keen coiner of new words and a great number have, as they say, 'entered the language' and have become conventional and commonplace: 'assassination', for example, 'barefaced', 'laughable'. But he also came up with quite a few words which never took on. 'Appertainments' is one (from *Troilus and Cressida*) and 'exsufflicate' is another (from *Othello*). They are marked in the *OED* as 'rare', but they are not just rare, they are non-existent, apart from one single idiosyncratic instance, which, for all we know, might have been a printer's error anyway.[2] They are, in fact, *might-have-beens*. So why do they take on the status of proper words in the dictionary? And apart from these words there are numerous others which have a record of more than a single occurrence—but only just.

So why does Shakespeare get this privileged treatment? Why are *all* his words counted as proper, whether they are taken on and made current or not? The reason in a word (another word from *Othello*, as it happens) is: reputation. He is, after all, the Bard, and as Aldous Huxley's character Mr Tillotson was fond of saying: 'The Bard is always right'; and, we might add: always right and proper.[3] These idiosyncratic words appear in the dictionary on Shakespeare's authority, and, as we shall see, his is not the only authority that is adduced when deciding on what is proper English and what is not.

So it would appear, then, that we cannot establish whether words are proper or not simply by invoking the criteria of frequent usage or common currency. There are factors to do with prestige and authority which come into play. And there is a further and related factor to take note of, one which is related to range of usage.

Consider the word 'deprehend', the *has-been* I mentioned earlier, and the word 'depurate'. The first is marked as obsolete in the *OED* and the second is not. But I personally do not recognize either of them: they are not proper words of English as far as I am concerned. If I did not have the *OED* to hand, I might suspect that both are fake coinages. They are both beyond my lexical range, one of them, 'deprehend', because it belongs to a remote domain of use in the past, the other because it belongs to a (for me) remote domain of use in the present, it being a specialist term in medicine.

It would seem, then, that what we identify as a proper word of English depends on the necessary limitations of our own lexical knowledge. Propriety is relative. So for some people, for example, those who know about sailing boats, 'strake' and 'trunnion' are proper English words like 'steak' and 'onion', but for others they are not, because they do not have them as part of their vocabulary. The words are not proper because they are not possessed. Propriety is relative. And it is also closely related to a sense of property.

Proper English words, but proper *for* whom and *to* whom? The same considerations arise when determining the proper *places* of words as well: different dialectal codes will have different rules of internal arrangement, and different communities will have different conventions of external use in context. A word which is properly placed as correct in one code or as appropriate to one social custom, will be regarded as misplaced in others.

All of this clearly has relevance to the pedagogic issue raised at the beginning of this chapter: whose usage are we to take as the model for language learners to aspire to? Those who make policy statements or plan language programmes often express objectives in terms of mastery of the language, or native-speaker competence, as if these were coherent and well-defined concepts. But they clearly are not. Which native speakers are we talking about, and what does mastery mean? As I have already indicated there are numerous English words that I have not myself mastered, and never can; and numerous possible placements I am ignorant of, and always will be. And I count myself as competent in the language. I am indeed a native speaker of English. So whose English do we try to get the student to master, if indeed 'master' is itself the proper word in this context?

This question is of obvious relevance for the design of learners' dictionaries. The selection of words to be included should presumably be based on some notion of which lexical range constitutes a suitable objective to set for learners. This would be a very tricky matter for any language, but it is particularly so for English, given the extent and variety of its diaspora, and its widespread use as an international means of communication within and across communities.

Consider the case of the *Collins COBUILD English Language Dictionary* (*COBUILD Dictionary*) (Sinclair 1987), for example. It says on the dust cover and in its publicity, that it is 'helping learners with *real* English' (emphasis in the original). Real English, that is to say, proper English, as distinct from the invented language which has traditionally been presented in language classrooms. The dictionary does not include the words 'depurate', or 'strake', or 'trunnion', on the reasonable assumption that these words, being highly infrequent, are remote from any future need for the language that English learners in general might have. They could well be real, however, for students following certain courses of English for specific purposes (medicine or marine engineering, for example), so their omission would clearly reduce the helpfulness of the dictionary in this case. So we obviously need to ask: real (or proper) English for what kind of communication?

Or for what kind of community? The usage that is represented as real in the dictionary is necessarily selective and restricted in range. There is little representation of what is real language for very large numbers of native speakers: the informal, colloquial, insider speech variously marked for difference of generation, region, and social class. And there are other omissions in the *COBUILD Dictionary* of a rather different kind. We find 'goon' for example, but not 'goonda', 'warehouse' but not 'godown'. But these words would be real enough for innumerable speakers of English outside what Kachru (1985) refers to as the Inner Circle,[4] in India and elsewhere, and would figure quite naturally in their daily discourse. They are, one might suggest, part of the lexis of English as an international language. Or are they? What does it mean to talk about English as an international language anyway? This is a question I shall take up in a later chapter, but meanwhile there is a more delicate difficulty to deal with.

Consider the word 'prepone'. This does not occur in current British usage and never has occurred in the past. Not surprisingly, therefore, it is not to be found in the *COBUILD Dictionary* or the *OED*. It does, however, appear, in a handbook of Indian and British English published by Oxford University Press in New Delhi (Nihilani, Tongue, and Hosali 1979), and it is apparently quite commonly attested in India. Is it proper English?

In one respect it could not be more proper, for it is impeccably well formed according to the standard rules of English morphology. It is indeed a good example of the productive exploitation of the generative power of grammar which is said to be a defining feature of linguistic competence, and this presumably applies as much to the morphological formation of words as to the syntactic formation of sentences. 'Prepone', then, is properly formed. It is also semantically apt in that it contrasts precisely with 'postpone' to denote the advancing as distinct from the deferring of an event. A meeting can obviously be brought forward, preponed, just as it can be put back, postponed. The word neatly fills a lexical gap. All that standard British English has to offer instead is the rather cumbersome phrase 'bring forward' which (to the confusion of learners) does not even allow the entirely reasonable contrasting phrase 'take backward'.

So is 'prepone' to be recognized as real English? After all, not only does it, like the Lewis Carroll verbal inventions referred to earlier, conform to the encoding rules of English, but, unlike those of Carroll, has actually been coined to meet a communicative contingency and is given the sanction of social use. In this respect it is like the innumerable other examples of lexical coinage that have been devised to deal with new technology over recent years, and which have been readily received into the language. What is more, it might be pointed out, in its innovative use of linguistic resources, it resembles the kind of language which Shakespeare wrote, and this is usually highly commended; indeed, as we have seen, it is considered proper by definition. But there is an obvious difficulty and this can, appropriately enough, be illustrated by reference to E. M. Forster's novel *A Passage to India*.

The Nawab Bahadur is pondering on which of God's creatures might be admitted to the mansions of heaven. He has discussed the matter with the Christian missionaries, the old Mr Graysford, and the young Mr Sorley. What about monkeys, for example? Are they to be allowed a place in paradise? Mr Graysford said no, but the progressive Mr Sorley 'saw no reason why monkeys should not have their collateral share of bliss'. And the jackals? He agreed, though with some hesitation, that, yes, jackals and indeed perhaps all mammals would be eligible. The Nawab continues to press him:

> And the wasps? He became uneasy during the descent to wasps, and was apt to change the conversation. And oranges, cactuses, crystals and mud? And the bacteria inside Mr Sorley? No, no, this is going too far. We must exclude someone from our gathering, or we shall be left with nothing.

Similarly, we must exclude *some* linguistic creations from the canon of proper English or we shall be left with nothing of the language. Creativity cannot itself be a qualification for inclusion. Indeed in a way it is a *dis*qualification, since what counts is conformity to some norm or other. Monkeys and perhaps all mammals are admitted to the divine presence because they are relatively close to the human norm, but wasps are altogether too remote. And similarly, one might say, some instances of language creation are considered close enough to conformity to be allowed the status of proper English, but others just go too far and must accordingly be excluded. But excluded on whose authority? Who decides? In the case of the heavenly mansions, it is the missionary. The monkeys are not consulted. But in the case of proper English, who is the authority here?

The English, perhaps. The language is after all labelled with their name, so one might suggest that they should have a decisive say in the matter. If in doubt about proper usage, we could consult the original native speakers. Well, not the original native speakers, of course, but their indigenous descendants. But not *any* of them, not indeed the majority of them, but a carefully selected subset, those who are educated, or of a certain social class and whose testimony on what is proper can be relied upon. Thus stockbrokers from Surbiton in Surrey might be taken to be fairly reliable informants, but not, let us say, bricklayers from Burnley in Lancashire, whose English is likely in some respects to be considered quite improper.

But what of native speakers of English who, through no fault of their own, are not English at all, and for the most part never have been: all those millions of people on the other side of the Atlantic, for example, getting up to all kinds of things with the language without referring to the authority of its original speakers? It may be true that if we include everything in our gathering we are left with nothing, but if we exclude too drastically we are not left with much either. The Americans pose a problem, even those who are cognate with Surbiton stockbrokers. Is their English proper or not?

More, it would seem, than used to be the case. More so than in 1946, for example. That was the year of the first appearance of the journal *English Language Teaching* sponsored by the British Council. One of its features was a section about correct usage, and in response to a query from a reader about the expressions 'fry-pan' and 'frying-pan', we find the following reply:

> 'Fry-pan' is not accepted as standard English and is considered incorrect by most grammarians. It is probably an American form.

Not accepted by whom? On whose authority is this judgement made? The agent is conveniently deleted. Considered incorrect by *which* grammarians? Presumably American ones (Charles Fries in Michigan, for example, or Leonard Bloomfield in Yale) had not been consulted.[5] So who decides? The editor of *English Language Teaching* decides, assuming the authority as a representative of a particular group of British native speakers of English. Nowadays, of course, it would not do to be so dismissive of American words like 'fry-pan'. Apart from the fact that it is because of the United States that the language has become so dominant in the fifty intervening years, we cannot afford to cause offence. We might still feel free to be dismissive of Indian words like 'prepone', because it does not matter if we cause offence in this case. And anyway, we might think, the Indians are not real native speakers, so they don't need to be consulted.

An enquiry into the notion of proper English leads us, as we have seen, to a consideration of what is appropriate for particular uses in communication, and for particular users in different communities. And this in turn leads us to the question of ownership, and the extent to which this gives authority for taking custody of the language and determining its norms of propriety. Who are the real owners of English, and its effective custodians? This is the question that will be taken up in more detail in the following chapter.

Notes and comments

1 Mrs Malaprop, a character in Sheridan's *The Rivals*, has the habit of producing impressively sounding words which make no semantic sense, but which bear a phonological resemblance to those that do. Thus she speaks of 'an allegory on the banks of the Nile' and refers, with some pride, to her own speech as 'a nice derangement of epitaphs'. This kind of lexical derangement as a so-called slip of the tongue is of fairly common occurrence in ordinary speech and can be accounted for as a performance error, a short circuit in the brain across different connections in the online processing of spoken language. (See Aitchison 1994.) With Mrs Malaprop, however, it is not just an occasional lapse but a regular feature of her particular idiom. And whereas a malapropism may occur as an inadvertent confusion in ordinary speech, there is the

suspicion with Mrs Malaprop herself that she is not confusing two words in her mental lexicon, but accessing the only one she knows.

2 Shakespeare's plays were written as scripts and put into print at second hand. Hence the possibility of textual corruption. For an account of the process of producing texts from scripts, see Maguire 1996.

3 In 'The Tillotson Banquet', a story that first appeared in the collection *Mortal Coils* (1922).

4 The relevant quotation from Kachru is:

> The spread of English may be viewed in terms of three concentric circles representing the types of spread, the patterns of acquisition and the functional domains in which English is used across cultures and languages. I have tentatively labelled these: the Inner Circle, the Outer Circle...and the Expanding Circle...
> (Kachru 1985: 12)

Though tentative at the time, these labels have now stuck. The Inner Circle refers to areas in which English is acquired as a mother tongue and functions as an established first language in the community. These are what Kachru calls 'the traditional bases' of the language and include Britain and the United States. The Outer Circle refers to areas in which English is acquired as an additional language and has an established institutional function. These are typically countries where English was originally imported and imposed by colonial power. The Expanding Circle refers to places where English is a foreign language and has no established social role in the community concerned but functions rather as a means of international rather than intranational communication. All countries within the European Union (with the obvious exceptions of Britain and Ireland) are in this circle, as indeed are most other countries in the world (including those colonized by means of a language other than English). Kachru talks about this circle expanding rapidly, but the expansion is not in the number of areas in which English has this function but in the domains of its use, particularly, of course, with the development of electronic communication.

5 It was just such xenophobic claims to linguistic ownership on the part of the British that prompted Noah Webster to compile a dictionary of English which would be distinctively American. *An American Dictionary of the English Language* (1828) introduced new lexical items of North American origin (like 'skunk') and the now familiar American spelling conventions ('center' for 'centre', 'plow' for 'plough', and so on). He also proposed changes that did not take ('tung' for 'tongue', for example) and which were, therefore, in the terms used in this chapter, *might-have-beens*, though his reasons for coining them were very different from those of Lewis Carroll. Webster's innovations, motivated as they were by nationalist sentiment, were in fact an early exercise in language planning. (See Kaplan and Baldauf 1997.)

4   The ownership of English

The enquiry of the last chapter into what might be meant by proper English led us to the question of ownership. We might put the point by making play with the form of these words, saying that the two morphologically derived nouns *propriety* and *property*, are not only etymologically related but still retain an implicational connection, as indeed is made explicit in the term *proprietor*.

It is generally assumed that in setting the objectives for English as a subject we need to get them to correspond as closely as possible to the competence of its native speakers. This raises two questions: who are these native speakers, and what is it that constitutes their competence?

As was mentioned in the preceding chapter, we could (again playing with the formal resemblances of words) suggest that the native speakers of English are the English. Such an idea is likely to be dismissed as untenable, but it is worth asking why. They were, after all, the original speakers and the language and the people, bound together by both morphology and history, can be said to represent a common heritage. So they can surely legitimately lay claim to this linguistic property as their own. It belongs to them, and they are custodians. So if you want real or proper English, this is where it is to be found, preserved, and listed, rather like a property of the National Trust.

Of course, it is not *exclusively* their own. English, of a kind, is found elsewhere as well and still spreading, a luxuriant growth from imperial seed. Seeded among other people, but not ceded to them. At least not completely. For the English still cling tenaciously to their property and try to protect it from abuse. Let us acknowledge (let us *con*cede) that there are other kinds of English, offshoots and outgrowths, but they are not real or proper English, not the genuine article.

As an analogy, consider a certain kind of beverage. There are all kinds of cola, but only one which is the real thing. Or consider a beverage of a very different kind. Until quite recently, the French have successfully denied others the right to use the appellation Champagne for any wine that does not come from the region of that name where Dom Perignon first invented it. There may be all kinds of derivative versions elsewhere, excellent no doubt in their way, but they are not real or proper Champagne, even though loose talk may refer to them as such. Similarly, there is real English, *Anglais real*, Royal English, Queen's English, or (for those unsympathetic to the monarchy) Oxford English, the vintage language.

Such a view, as I have expressed it here, would seem on the face of it to be absurd—indeed, patently absurd, since it is based on the idea that one can take out a patent on the language, and claim the right to exert control over it to keep it exclusive. But if we ignore all the rhetorical flourishing, and strip the argument down to its essentials, it looks rather less absurd. Let us return to the patent idea. One reason for taking out a patent is to retain exclusive rights to a profitable formula and prevent other people from exploiting it to their own commercial advantage. It is clearly in the interests of the British to suggest they have the patent on proper English because it is good for business, and this is indeed suggested in the promotional literature of language schools and publishers.

But there is another justification for taking out a patent. Take the example of Champagne. One argument frequently advanced for being protective of its good name has to do with quality assurance. The label is a guarantee of quality. If any Tom, Jane, or Harry producing fizzy wine is free to use it, there can be no quality control. Some years ago an English firm won a court case enabling it to put the name Champagne on bottles containing a non-alcoholic beverage made from elderflowers. Elderflowers! The Champagne lobby was outraged. Here was the thin end of the wedge: before long the label would be appearing on bottles all over the place containing concoctions of all kinds calling themselves Champagne, and so laying claim to its quality. The appellation would not be controlled. Standards were at stake. The same point can, of course, be made, and is made, about Coca-Cola. There is only one. This is it: the real thing. Be wary of other brands of inferior quality.

And the same point is frequently made about English. In this case, you cannot, of course, preserve exclusive use of the name and indeed it would work against your interests to do so, but you can seek to preserve standards by implying that there is an exclusive quality in your own brand of English, aptly called Standard English. What is this quality, then, and what are these standards?

The usual answer is: the quality of clear communication and standards of intelligibility. With Standard English, it is argued, these are assured. If the language disperses into different forms, a myriad of Englishes, then it ceases to serve as a means of international communication; in which case the point of learning it largely disappears. As the language spreads, there are bound to be changes out on the periphery; so much can be conceded. But these changes must be seen not only as peripheral but as radial also and traceable back to the stable centre of the standard. If this centre does not hold, things fall apart, mere anarchy is loosed upon the world, and we are back to Babel.[1]

So the patenting of English can be represented as a way of preserving its integrity and preventing its decline. There is thus a happy coincidence of commercial interest and the common good. The promotion of the English brand of English guarantees its quality as a means of communication. But although such a view is quite widely held, it does have a chauvinistic ring which even those who hold it would wish to disguise. Why only this brand, after all? The English may have first claims on the language historically speaking, but they are, of course, by no means the only proprietors of it now. So we need to extend our reference group of owners beyond the English, beyond even the British, to include Americans, Australians, and others in Kachru's Inner Circle of native speakers of the language. We might then propose, more generally (and acceptably) that the ownership of English is not just in the hands of the English, but of its native speakers whoever they are, and that it is they who can claim the authority to be its proper promoters and custodians.

But a moment's reflection makes it clear that we do not actually mean native speakers, whoever they are. Most speakers of English, even those who are to the language born, speak non-standard varieties of the language and have themselves to be instructed in the standard at school. We cannot have any Tom, Dick, and Harriette claiming authority, for Tom, Dick, and Harriette are likely to be speakers of some regional or social dialect or other. So the authority to maintain the standard language is not consequent on a natural native-speaker endowment. It is claimed by a minority of people who have the power to impose it. The custodians of Standard English are, in effect, self-elected members of a rather exclusive club.

Now it is important to be clear that in saying this I am not arguing against standard English. You can accept the argument for language maintenance, as indeed I do, without accepting the authority that claims the right to maintain it. It is, I think, very generally assumed that a particular subset of educated native speakers in England, or New England, or wherever, have the natural entitlement to custody of the language, and the right and the responsibility to preserve it. It is this assumption, I think, that is open to question.

Consideration of who the custodians are leads logically on to a consideration of what it is exactly that is in their custody. What, then, is Standard English? It is that variety which has been socially sanctioned for institutional use and as such the only one which has been extensively described in grammars and dictionaries. It is often said that such descriptions are not prescriptive in that they tell us what the usage of the language is and not what it should be, but we should note that since this standard variety is represented as *the* language (there being no descriptions of other varieties readily available) descriptions of it do in effect prescribe what is acceptable as proper English and what is not. And this is particularly the case with learners of English as a foreign or second language, for they have no other reliable source of reference. For them, clearly, the standard descriptions do not just provide information about what native speakers do but they also present norms to be conformed to. In practice then, whatever principle is invoked, the description of the standard is the version of the language that is taken as officially prescribed.

Being so documented as the institutional language the standard is particularly well suited to written communication, and as we shall see later, there is an argument for accepting it as a written variety. But there is a certain ambivalence in its description. The usual way of defining it is in reference to its grammar and lexis, as a kind of superposed dialect which, however, in its spoken form can be manifested by any accent. So it is generally conceded that Standard English has no distinctive phonology.[2] A glance at any learners' dictionary, however, will make it clear that the standard is associated with a particular phonology, namely that which approximates to Received Pronunciation (RP): variant pronunciations are not provided. One might say that in theoretical principle the lexico-grammar of the standard language is independent of any phonological realization, but in descriptive practice it is not. We should note too that the same concession to variation is not extended to its graphology. On the contrary, here no allowance is made at all: spelling is either right or wrong, and that's that. It is true that there is a recognition, sometimes grudgingly given, of certain written variants (centre/center, traveller/traveler, programme/program, and so on) but these are matters of consistent convention associated with different standards (British versus American). Otherwise, tolerance for variation is more or less non-existent.

There is something of a contradiction here. If Standard English is defined as a distinctive grammatical and lexical system which can be substantially realized (or realised) in different ways, then what does spelling have to do with it? It is true that some spelling has a grammatical function (like the *s* which, in British if not American English at least, distinguishes the verb *practise* from its noun homophone *practice*, or the *'s* which marks the possessive as distinct from the plural) but most of it does not. If you are going to ignore phonological variation, then, to be consistent, you should surely ignore graphological variation as well and overlook variations in spelling as a kind of written accent.

The reason why spelling is standardized is, as was indicated earlier, because Standard English, unlike other dialects, is essentially a written variety, mainly used for institutional purposes (education, administration, business, etc.). Its spoken version is secondary, and typically used by those who sustain or control these institutions. Institutions are not designed to deal with individuality: they call for conformity. This means that although it may not matter too much how the standard is spoken, it emphatically does matter how it is written. Furthermore, because writing, as a more durable medium, is used to express and establish institutional values, deviations from orthographic conventions undermine in some degree the institutions which they serve. They can be seen as evidence of social instability: a sign of things beginning to fall apart. So it is not surprising that those who have a vested interest in maintaining these institutions should be so vexed by bad spelling. It is not that it greatly interferes with communication: it is usually not difficult to identify words through their unorthodox appearance. What seems to be more crucial is that good spelling represents conformity to convention and so serves to maintain institutional stability.

Similar points can be made about grammatical features. Because language has built-in redundancy, grammatical conformity is actually not particularly crucial for many kinds of communicative transaction. What we generally do in the interpretative process is to edit grammar out of the text, referring lexis directly to context, using lexical items as indexical clues to meaning. Attention to grammar might well interfere with processing efficiency, and we only edit it back when we need it to fine-tune our interpretation, or to subject what we are reading to critical analysis for one reason or another. Focusing on the linguistic features of the text, we might say, can distract us from the communicative function of the discourse. But then, if the reason for insisting on Standard English is because it guarantees effective communication, the emphasis should logically be on vocabulary rather than grammar. But the champions of Standard English do not see it in this way: on the contrary, they focus attention on grammatical abuse. Why should this be so? There are, I think, two possible reasons.

Firstly, it is precisely because grammar is so often redundant in communicative transactions that it takes on another significance, namely that of expressing social identity. The mastery of a particular grammatical system, especially perhaps those features which are redundant, marks you as a member of the community which has developed that system for its own social purposes beyond the transaction of ordinary mundane matters. Conversely, of course, those who are unable to master the subtleties of the system are excluded from membership of the community. They do not belong. In short, grammar is a sort of shibboleth.

So when the custodians of Standard English complain about the ungrammatical usage of the populace, they are in effect indicating that the perpetrators are outsiders, non-members of the community, and bent, perhaps on undermining it. The only way they can become members, and so benefit from the privileges of membership, is to learn Standard English, and these privileges include, of course, access to the institutions which the community controls. Standard English, from this perspective, is an entry condition and the custodians of it the gatekeepers. You can, of course, persist in your non-standard ways if you choose, but then do not be surprised if you find yourself marginalized, perpetually kept out on the periphery. If what you say is not expressed in the grammatically approved manner, it is likely to be less readily attended to and assigned less significance. And if you express yourself in writing which is both ungrammatical and incorrectly spellt, you are not likely to be taken very seriously.

Standard English, then, is not simply a means of communication but the symbolic possession of a particular community, expressive of its identity, its conventions, and values. One can see why it should be thought to be in need of careful preservation, for to undermine Standard English is to undermine what it stands for: the security of this community and its institutions. Thus, it tends to be the communal rather than the communicative features of Standard English that are most jealously protected: its grammar and spelling.

I do not wish to imply by this that this communal function is to be deplored. Languages of every variety have this dual character: they provide the means for communication and at the same time express a sense of community, represent the stability of its conventions and values, in short its culture. All communities possess and protect their languages. The question is which community, and which culture, have a rightful claim to ownership of Standard English?

For Standard English is no longer the preserve of a group of people living in an offshore European island, or even of larger groups living in continents elsewhere. It is an international language. As such it serves a whole range of different communities and their institutional purposes and these transcend traditional communal and cultural boundaries. I am referring to the business community, for example, and the community of researchers and scholars in science and technology and other disciplines. Standard English, especially in its written form, is their language. It provides for effective communication, but at the same time it establishes the status and stability of the institutional conventions which define these international activities. These activities develop their own conventions of thought and procedure, customs, and codes of practice; in short, they in effect create their own cultures, their own standards. And obviously for the maintenance of standards it is helpful, to say the least, to have a standard language at your disposal. But you do not need native speakers to tell you what it is.

And indeed in one crucial respect, the native speaker is irrelevant. What I have in mind here is vocabulary. I said earlier that the custodians of Standard English tend to emphasize its grammatical rather than its lexical features. I have suggested that one reason for this is that grammar is symbolic of communal solidarity. 'Ungrammatical' expressions mark people as non-members. What you then do is to coax or coerce them somehow into conformity if you want to make them members (generally through education) or make them powerless on the periphery if you do not. So much for grammar. What then of lexis?

As was pointed out earlier, Standard English is generally defined by its lexis and grammar. In fact, when you come to look for it, standard lexis is very elusive; so elusive that one wonders if it can be said to exist at all.[3] And on reflection it is hard to see how it could exist. To begin with, the notion of standard implies stability, a relatively fixed point of reference. So if I invent a word, for example, it is not, by definition, standard. But people are inventing words all the time to express new ideas and attitudes, to adjust to their changing world. It is this indeed which demonstrates the essential dynamism of the language without which it would wither away. So it is that, as was pointed out in Chapter 1, different groups of users will develop specialist vocabularies, suited to their needs but incomprehensible to others. When I look at my daily newspaper, I find innumerable words from the terminology of technology, law, fashion, financial affairs, and so on which I simply do not understand.

They may claim to be English, but they are Greek to me (as indeed, etymologically, many of them are). Are they Standard English?

One way of deciding might be to consult a standard reference work, namely a dictionary. But as was pointed out in our discussion of proper words in the preceding chapter, we would find that most of these words of restricted technical use do not appear. As we noted earlier, this is because, reasonably enough, the dictionary only contains words of wide range and common occurrence. If these are to be the criteria for deciding what is standard (or proper) English, then these words of restricted use do not count by definition. Yet they are real enough, and indeed can be said to represent the reality of English as an international language. For the reason why English is international is precisely because its vocabulary has diversified to serve a range of institutional uses.

As I indicated earlier, the custodians of Standard English express the fear that if there is diversity, things will fall apart and the language will divide up into mutually unintelligible varieties. But things, in a sense, have already fallen apart. The varieties of English used for international communication in science, finance, commerce, and so on are mutually unintelligible. As far as lexis is concerned, their communicative viability depends on there *not* being a unified standard lexis, but on the development of separate standards appropriate to different domains of use.

The point then is that if English is to retain its vitality and its capability for continual adjustment, it cannot be confined within a standard lexis. And this seems to be implicitly accepted as far as these domains of use are concerned. Nobody, I think, would describe the abstruse terms used by physicists or stockbrokers as non-standard English. It is generally accepted that communities or secondary cultures which are defined by shared professional concerns should be granted rights of ownership and allowed to fashion the language to meet their needs, their specific purposes indeed. And these purposes, we should note again, are twofold: they are communicative in that they meet the needs of in-group transactions, and they are communal in that they define the identity of the group itself.

The same tolerance is not extended so readily to primary cultures and communities, where the language is used in the conduct of everyday social life. Lexical innovation here, equally motivated by communicative and communal requirement, is generally dismissed as quaint regional deviation. In the last chapter mention was made of the two words 'depone' and 'prepone'. The first is a technical legal term and the second a commonly used expression in India. The first has a status that the second lacks, and the reason for this lies in their origin. 'Depone' is attested in the use of native-speaker lawyers, 'prepone' is a curious coinage by non-native speakers. So it is not a proper word—not pukka. And of course the word 'pukka' itself is only pukka because the British adopted it.

Where are we then? When we consider the question of Standard English what we find, in effect, is double standards. The very idea of a standard implies stability, but language is of its nature unstable. It is essentially protean in character, adapting its shape to suit changing circumstances. It would otherwise lose its vitality and its communicative and communal value. This is generally acknowledged in the case of specialist domains of use but is not acknowledged in the case of everyday social uses of the language. So it is that a word like 'depone' is approved as proper, and a word like 'prepone' is not.

But the basic principle of dynamic adaptation is the same in both cases. And in both cases the users of the language exploit its protean potential and fashion it to their need, thereby demonstrating a high degree of linguistic capability. In both cases the innovation indicates that the language has been learnt, not just as a set of fixed conventions to conform to, but as an adaptable resource for making meaning. And making meaning which you can call your own. This, surely, is a crucial condition. You are proficient in a language to the extent that you possess it, make it your own, bend it to your will, assert yourself through it rather than simply submit to the dictates of its form. It is a familiar experience when one is learning a language to find oneself saying things in a foreign language because you can say them rather than because they express what you want to say. You feel you are going through the motions, and somebody else's motions at that. You are speaking the language but not speaking your mind. Real proficiency is when you are able to take possession of the language, turn it to your advantage, and make it real for you. This is what mastery means.

So in a way, proficiency only comes with nonconformity, when you can take the initiative and strike out on your own. Consider these remarks of the Nigerian writer, Chinua Achebe:

> I feel that the English language will be able to carry the weight of my African experience ... But it will have to be a new English, still in communion with its ancestral home but altered to suit its new African surroundings.
> (Achebe 1975: 62)

Achebe is a novelist, and he is talking here about creative writing. But what he says clearly has wider relevance and applies to varieties of English not only in his own country, but elsewhere, including its ancestral home. Achebe is here referring to a very general linguistic phenomenon. English, like any other vital language, is continually being renewed and altered to suit its surroundings. All uses of language are creative in the sense that they draw on linguistic resources to express different perceptions of reality.

The new English which Achebe refers to is locally developed, and although it must necessarily be related to, and so in a sense in communion with, its ancestral origins in the past, it owes no allegiance to any descendants of this ancestry in the present. And this point applies to all other new Englishes which have been created to carry the weight of different experience in different surroundings, whether they are related to the contexts of everyday life or to specialist domains of use. They are all examples of the entirely normal and necessary process of adaptation, a process which obviously depends on nonconformity to existing conventions or standards. For these have been established elsewhere by other people as appropriate to quite different circumstances. The fact that these people can claim direct descent from the founding fathers has nothing to do with it. How English develops in the world is no business whatever of native speakers in England, the United States, or anywhere else. They have no say in the matter, no right to intervene or pass judgement. They are irrelevant. The very fact that English is an international language means that no nation can have custody over it. To grant such custody of the language is necessarily to arrest its development and so undermine its international status. It is a matter of considerable pride and satisfaction for native speakers of English that their language is an international means of communication. But the point is that it is only international to the extent that it is not their language. It is not a property for them to lease out to others while still retaining the freehold. Other people actually own it.

But this poses a problem for pedagogy. The issues we have been discussing over the last two chapters arose from the initial question about how we might define English as a subject, what we should take as its objective. So long as we specify this objective by direct reference to descriptions of the language attested and ratified as proper on educated native-speaker authority, then there is no difficulty. There is still the question of which kind of proper English to favour and much is made of the difference between standard Inner Circle varieties (American versus British English, for example). But this is a relatively minor matter compared with the dilemma that our discussion now seems to confront us with. For if instead of one or two varieties of English to choose from we have a diverse plurality of them, then how are we to decide on which represents a suitable setting for our purpose parameter? There may be reasons in principle for rejecting the concept of proper English as determined by native-speaker communities in favour of English that has been appropriated by communities of all kinds all over the globe, but how would this work out in practice? One might agree that English is now an international language, but from a pedagogic perspective, so what?

Such questions require us first to take a closer look at the nature of English as an international language, and this brings us to the next chapter.

Notes and comments

1 Consider, for example, how Standard English is equated with standards in the following remarks by Randolph Quirk. The implication seems to be that any deviation from one constitutes a decline in the other.

> I believe that the fashion of undermining belief in standard English has wrought educational damage in ENL [English as a native language?] countries, though I am ready to concede that there may well have been

compensating educational gains in the wider tolerance for an enjoyment of the extraordinary variety of English around us in any of these countries. But then just such an airy contempt for standards started to be exported to EFL and ESL countries, and for this I can find no such mitigating compensation. The relatively narrow range of purposes for which the non-native needs to use English (even in ESL countries) is arguably well catered for by a single monochrome standard form that looks as good on paper as it sounds in speech.
(Quirk 1985: 6)

Many would question the assumption here that the range of purposes for which non-native users of English in ESL and EFL countries (i.e. in Kachru's Outer and Expanding Circles) need the language is narrower than for native users in ENL (i.e. Inner Circle) countries, and can be served by 'a single monochrome standard' provided and preserved as a norm on ENL authority.

For further elaboration of the Quirk position, and other views on this issue, see Seidlhofer 2003. For a critical view of the prescription of Standard English in British schools, see Fairclough 1995: Chapter 10. I discuss the role of English as an international language and what implications this has for maintenance of native-speaker norms in the following chapter of this book.

2 The following can be taken as expressing the generally accepted (indeed the standard) view:

> ...*Standard English* [is] the variety of the English language which is normally employed in writing and normally spoken by 'educated' speakers of the language. It is also, of course, the variety of English that students of English as a Foreign or Second Language (EFL/ESL) are taught when receiving formal instruction. The term Standard English refers to grammar and vocabulary (*dialect*) but not to pronunciation (*accent*).
> (Trudgill and Hannah 1994: 1)

For a particularly clear discussion of the nature of Standard English, see Trudgill 2002: Chapter 15.

3 Trudgill also argues that 'there is no necessary connection between formal vocabulary or technical vocabulary and Standard English; that is, there is no such thing as Standard English vocabulary' (Trudgill 2002: 169). He does, however, go on to argue that one might distinguish standard from non-standard words by reference to their range of dialectal usage.

5   English as an international language

The spread of English as an international language has been extensively documented and discussed (in, for example, Crystal 1997; Graddol 1997). It is a fact which few would dispute, though some might deplore, and one which, as we have noted in the preceding chapter, is a matter of considerable satisfaction, not to say profit, for those of the Inner Circle who speak it as natives, including, of course, those who belong to its country of origin—its ancestral home, as Chinua Achebe puts it. I have already suggested that such satisfaction is actually misplaced, and it prompts me to enquire further into what it actually means to say that English is international. What, more generally, does it mean to talk about language spread?

Take the word 'spread' itself. As a verb it is ergative: its object can become a subject. And this means that it can be used to disguise causation. So we can say that a rumour spread rather than somebody spread a rumour, and so avoid specifying an agent. It just spread under its own steam, so to speak. Similarly, we can say English has spread, like a growth or infection, driven by some internal causative force, or that it has been spread by some outside agency or other. So you can take up one of two positions on the matter: either that the spread of the language just happened in the natural way of things, or that somebody, some persons known or unknown did the spreading. If you take the second position, it is but a step to argue that the spreading was deliberate, that people conspired to spread it, motivated by colonial ambition. This view is at present in vogue. It has been vigorously argued of late that English was used, is being used, as an instrument for imposition of power. In other words language spread is tantamount to linguistic imperialism (Phillipson 1992). Now one may accept that attempts were indeed made, are being made, to exploit the language in this way in the exercise of commercial and political power, but this is not the whole story. For language is a very unreliable instrument for this purpose. And to see why this is so, we need to consider another feature of the word 'spread'.

If you spread something, or something gets spread, the assumption usually is that it remains intact. Start spreading the news (as Frank Sinatra sings), and everybody is supposed to get the same news. Spreading is transmitting. A disease spreads from one country to another and wherever it is it is the same disease. It does not alter according to circumstances; the virus is invariable. But as was discussed in the last chapter, language is not like this. It is not transmitted without being transformed. It does not travel well because it is fundamentally unstable. It is not well adapted to control because it is itself adaptable. One might accept the conspiracy theory that there was an *intention* to use English to dominate, but the assumption that the intention was successful, which is often taken as a necessary corollary, is based on a concept of the language as an invariant code with communication as the simple transmission of encoded messages by ideal speaker-listeners in homogeneous speech communities.[1]

The point about the control of people by language is that it is bound to fail because as soon as the language is used it cannot be kept under your control. People appropriate it. Shakespeare's *The Tempest* provides us with a nice illustration of the point. Prospero is a colonialist if ever there was one, having taken over the island and placed its original inhabitant, Caliban, under his autocratic rule. Caliban is enslaved. Like so many others under colonial rule, however, he does get to learn English. Miranda, like a well meaning missionary, has taught it to him:

MIRANDA:
                                    I pitied thee
Took pains to make thee speak, taught thee each hour
One thing or other. When thou didst not, savage,
Know thine own meaning, but wouldst gabble like
A thing most brutish, I endow'd thy purposes
With words that make them known.
The Tempest Act 1, scene 2 lines 351–8

Whatever good intentions she might have had, however, Miranda's efforts are not entirely successful:

CALIBAN:
You taught me language, and my profit on't
Is, I know how to curse. The red plague rid you
For learning me your language.
The Tempest Act 1, scene 2, lines 363–5

Caliban, it would seem, resists the control of the colonial language. Instead he masters it himself and exploits it to express his resistance. The moral of this story is that attempts at linguistic imperialism fail, and are doomed to do so from the very start because of the very nature of language.

It is not only language which has this intrinsically changeable character, of course. The same is true of ideas, beliefs, values, and indeed anything which has its origins in the mind. Including news, of course. Frank Sinatra may suppose that what he says will be transmitted intact, but we all know what happens to news once it is spread abroad. Diseases are transmitted unchanged into human bodies and brains. But other things are transformed in human minds, formed and reformed by a multiplicity of social and psychological influences. Of course it might be convenient to reduce the variety and arrest the change, to get minds organized and fixed into established patterns of religious or political belief. But these patterns never seem to stay in place. They too shift and divide, sects and parties break away, reform, divide again. 'Things fall apart'. But then they get reassembled. 'The old order changeth, yielding place to new.'[2] Only in time to fall apart again. And so on. And since language is inextricably implicated in these things of the mind—these ideas, beliefs, values—it is naturally subject to the same process.

But if English does not get spread as a fixed pattern, as a linguistic entity, artificially kept unitary and stable like a set of regulations, then what does language spread actually mean? What is it that spreads so changeably? And how does the change come about?

When we talk about English, French, Chinese, Arabic as different languages, the very use of this countable noun inclines us to think of them (of *them*) as things, relatively complete and well defined entities. This is because we conceive of them in terms of what has been conventionally encoded. So English is contained within the covers of dictionaries and grammars which, as we noted in the previous chapter, record the usage which is deemed to be proper on the authority of a particular group of its users. In this context, whatever does not conform to this preferred encoding is not English.

But, as we have seen in previous chapters, the linguistic forms that have actually been encoded by no means exhaust the resources of the code. So it is that the morphological resources of English can be exploited to bring new lexical items (like 'chortle' or 'prepone') into existence. The motivation for devising such lexical innovations will, of course, vary. Sometimes, it may be the expression of individual creativity, as with the Lewis Carroll coinages, or the many lexical curiosities to be found in James Joyce's *Finnegan's Wake* ('museyroom', 'excheck', 'twoddle', 'robulous',...). It may be to provide a term for a new concept ('radar', 'heliport', 'genome', 'spin doctor',...) or to label a new product with a brand name ('Oxo', 'Oxydol', 'Metadent', 'Weetabix',...). New expressions, as we noted earlier, may be motivated by perceived communicative convenience within a group, but then, as Edward Said observed (see Chapter 1), they can be used to define the group and exclude outsiders.

Whatever the motivation, all these are examples of how the potential for meaning inherent in the code, but as yet unrealized, can be exploited to meet communicative or communal needs. So far we have been considering the formation of new words as lexical items, but the same process of creative exploitation can be seen at work in grammar too. At the beginning of this chapter, for example, I made mention of the grammatical feature of ergativity. This is a property of the verb which signifies a certain kind of agentless process. Thus the verbs 'spread', 'open', 'close', 'break' are said to be ergative verbs in that they all allow the object in a transitive sentence to figure as the subject in a corresponding intransitive one, so that the second can be read as denoting the same process as the first but without an agent. 'Somebody spread the rumour/The rumour spread', 'Somebody opened the door/The door opened', 'Somebody broke the window/The window broke', and so on. Now although only certain verbs have been conventionally encoded as ergative in this way, and would be marked as such in a dictionary or grammar of Standard English, the potential exists for making other transitive verbs ergative along similar lines. So, alongside expressions that have become standard like 'The shirt washes well', 'The steak cuts nicely', 'The book reads agreeably', and so on, we might propose 'The cake eats well', 'The garden weeds easily', 'The meeting postpones (*or even* prepones) regularly', and so on.

This exploitation of the ergative potential does not, one might suggest, lead to usage that is deviant to any great degree. But more extreme examples are not difficult to find. Consider the following, the first line of a poem by E. E. Cummings:

pity this busy monster manunkind
not...

Syntactically speaking, 'pity this monster not' is bad enough, being a violation of the normal encoded word order. But not content with this, Cummings also decomposes the two words 'mankind' and 'unkind' into their morphological components and then proceeds to fuse them, in disregard of the fact that the words belong to distinct grammatical classes, to produce (appropriately enough) a linguistic monster: the grammatically and morphologically aberrant hybrid 'manunkind'.

We might allow some leeway for linguistic initiative, but this, we might decide, goes too far. This is not English. But then we are back with the problem of Nawab Bahadur and the missionaries (see Chapter 2): how much leeway, and on what criteria do we decide how far is too far? We may say that Cummings is not writing English (certainly not the English we would wish to encourage in our teaching), and to the extent that he is not conforming to code conventions, this is perfectly true. But he is nevertheless writing *in* English (not in French, Arabic, or Chinese). But he is writing a poem, one might object, and everybody knows that poets are prone to oddity. The point to be made here, however, is the one made in the last chapter in reference to Chinua Achebe: in both cases, though these writers may be seeking to achieve a literary effect, the process of exploiting the inherent resources of the language to suit their purposes is the same in kind, if different in degree, to the other instances we have considered. What the author has done is to exploit the resources of the language to produce a novel combination, not allowable by the conventional code, but nevertheless a latent possibility which is *virtual* in the language though not actually encoded.

We cannot just dismiss all examples of nonconformist usage as aberrations or oddities, no matter how appropriate to purpose they may be. It would be preferable, I suggest, to consider them as evidence of the existence of what I shall call the *virtual* language, that resource for making meaning immanent in the language which simply has not hitherto been encoded and so is not, so to speak, given official recognition. If we did not recognize this virtual reality, we would not be able to make any sense of these nonconformities at all.

This exploitation of the latent possibilities in virtual language is a very general phenomenon: it is not something that only verbal artists do. Language learners do it all the time. Children learning their first language invent new grammatical rules and coin new words, much to the delight of their parents. Pupils in school do the same thing with a foreign language, much to the exasperation of their teachers. In these cases, the actualization of the virtual language is generally taken as as a transitory and transitional phenomenon, evidence of developmental stages in learning: a pre-language on the one hand, an interlanguage on the other. They occur because learners do not know better: the conventional codings are not yet internalized, and so they are different from the deliberate exploitations of poets, who already know these conventions and consciously violate them. Learners are creative in spite of themselves and their nonconformities are taken as evidence of incompetence, for all their appealing inventiveness. Learners are, by definition, not in control of the language. The nonconformities of literary writers are, on the contrary, generally attributed to linguistic control of a very high order. Nobody would suggest that Chinua Achebe or E. E. Cummings needs English lessons. Nevertheless, I would argue that the language of learning and literature are both exploitations of the virtual resource.[3]

But they are exploitations which generally do not get adopted as conventions within a wider community. But there are cases when a similar exploitation does stabilize as conventional usage. These are cases of language spread: when a language diversifies into varieties of different kinds, varieties which are established by common custom as the mode of communication appropriate to particular communities. This is not to say that literary exploitations of the virtual language may not sometimes become part of conventional idiom, nor, more importantly, that they may not lend legitimacy and status to the very process of exploitation itself. But we need to be cautious, I think, in assuming that individual literary writers are representative of their communities. Achebe refers to 'my African experience' but this may not, of course, be shared by all Africans. Consider the following remarks about the work of the Indian author Salman Rushdie:

> Determined to give the Indian sensibility an authentic voice, Rushdie stands up to English language as an equal—and relentlessly plays with its grammar, syntax and spellings until it becomes pliable enough faithfully to express the way an Indian thinks, feels, talks, laughs, jokes and relates to language.
>
> He does to English what the English have done to India. He deconstructs the language, colonises it, reclaims it for the Indian with Promethean courage, and amply avenges imperial history.
> (Bhikhu Parekh: *The Independent on Sunday*, 11.2.90)

Rushdie uses English, I would suggest, to express *his* Indian sensitivity, just as Achebe uses it to express his African experience. One can accept that his writing lends prestige to what Kachru refers to as the 'Indianization of English' (Kachru 1983), but this process does not depend on him. It is not, I think, that Rushdie has made the language more pliable: it is—as are all languages—virtually pliable already. And so Indians are able to appropriate English without Rushdie's assistance. In thinking, feeling, talking, laughing, and joking with it, they have naturally adapted it to their own surroundings and purposes.

Everybody is creative in the sense that everybody exploits the virtual language. It is, as I have suggested, misleading to claim such innovation as being an especially literary phenomenon. This is not to deny that in literature the creativity may be more controlled and directed, that the verbal artist may have a heightened awareness of the virtual potential in language, and may be particularly adept at exploiting it. But I think it is important to recognize that literary writers do not devise a unique process in their writing; what they do is to make unique use of the very general process whereby the virtual language is exploited. And this is the process that brings about language spread.

What I am proposing, then, is that we might think of English as an international language not in terms of the distribution of a stable and unitary set of encoded forms, but as the spread of a virtual language which is exploited in different ways for different purposes. If one accepts this notion of spread, as distinct from distribution, then it is difficult to maintain the conspiracy theory that the language itself has powers of suppression, that it is the English language which colonizes, using the English people simply as a medium, as a means of transmission. By the same token, if you want to avenge imperial history you do not do it by taking vengeance on the language. If you object to what people are doing with English, your quarrel is with the people not the language. In this respect, Caliban got it right: he curses the colonizing power, and does so by exploiting the very language it taught him.

When we talk about the spread of English, then, it is not that the conventionally coded forms and meanings are transmitted into different environments and different surroundings, and taken up and used by different groups of people. It is not a matter of the actual language being distributed but of the virtual language being spread and in the process being variously actualized. The distribution of the actual language implies adoption and conformity. The spread of virtual language implies adaptation and nonconformity. The two processes are quite different.

And they are likely to be in conflict. Distribution denies spread. So you can think of English as an adopted international language, and then you will conceive of it as a stabilized and standardized code leased out on a global scale, and controlled by the inventors, not entirely unlike the franchise for Pizza Hut and Kentucky Fried Chicken. Distribution of essentially the same produce for consumers worldwide: English not so much a lingua franca, but rather a franchise language. There are no doubt people who think in these conveniently commercial terms, and if English as an international language were indeed like this, there would be cause for concern. But it isn't. It spreads, and as it does it gets adapted as the virtual language gets actualized in diverse ways, becomes subject to local constraints and controls.

What I am suggesting, then, is that the virtual language spreads through different actualizations, various encodings of the same basic resource. The question arises as to how this variety comes about, what it is that gives particular encoded shape to this intrinsically mutable resource? Is there perhaps something in the emergence of language varieties comparable to the process of natural selection?

Let us begin by considering the concept of language variety more closely. It is convenient, and indeed customary, to define language variety along two dimensions: time and space. With reference to time, it is usual to talk of change across different *periods*, of stages of a particular language, making the simplifying assumption that originates from Saussure that the language is stabilized, held in suspended animation like the state of play in a game of chess. So historical linguists will refer to Middle English, Early Modern English, and so on. Each is seen as an actual encoded state of what is virtually the same language. So Chaucer's *Canterbury Tales*, for example, is English, but Middle English.

With reference to space, it is usual to talk of variation across different *regions*. At any one time, the virtual resource of the language is encoded in a range of various ways. These different encodings coexist. So the English spoken in Norfolk, for example, differs from that spoken in Lancashire, and, more specifically, that spoken in Norwich is different from that spoken in Liverpool. But they are acknowledged to be variants of the same language, alternative actualizations. We refer to them as dialects. All this seems straightforward enough. But what if we go further afield, move metaphorically from Kachru's Inner to his Outer Circle, cross the ocean and arrive, for example, in Africa. Here too we find the language variously encoded: Nigerian English, for example, or more particularly that spoken in Lagos. Are these dialects too? Well...the question gives us pause. The answer does not seem to be so straightforward. Dialects? It all depends...Depends on what? Why the ambivalence?

There are two reasons which come to mind. Firstly, when we talk of dialects of English we tend to think of forms of speaking, different encodings which, to use Achebe's phrase again, are not far from their ancestral home. Indeed they have the same heritage and can trace their history back to the same ancestors. They have developed concurrently over time within the same larger community. So the term does not, in fact, only refer to variation across regions, but to variation which has a pedigree in that it has also developed as change over periods of time. The concept of dialect necessarily has a diachronic dimension to it. But the varieties to be found in far-flung regions have not developed like this. They have sprung up in a relatively extempore and expedient way in response to the immediate communicative needs of people in different communities with quite different ancestors. There is no comparable developmental continuity. The status of dialects in England as variant actualizations of the same virtual language is confirmed by their common history. To the extent that other varieties do not have such a history, one may hesitate to call them dialects.

The term dialect, I suggest, implies some common communal development which links them to the same history. It also implies dependency. We come to the second reason for being ambivalent about the nature of Outer Circle varieties of English. A dialect presupposes a language it is a dialect *of*. A code which declares independence is no longer a dialect but a language in its own right. People in Durham or Norfolk have not declared independence, and are not (in the foreseeable future at least) likely to do so. People in Ghana and Nigeria have done so, and as part of the process may well wish to appropriate the language and make it their own. In this case, one might say that what they speak is another English, not a variant but a different virtual language. And this is what is implied by referring to Englishes in the plural and not English in the singular: several virtual languages, not several variants of the same one. Different linguistic species.

This discussion of the appropriate use of the term dialect raises a number of issues. To begin with it makes it clear, I think, that the varieties of English that have sprung up on a global scale cannot be equated with the gradual evolution of dialects through socially related communities. They are essentially displaced and discontinuous encodings, brought about relatively abruptly by outside intervention and motivated in the main by communicative expediency. In this respect, the varieties we find globally scattered throughout the world are phenomena unique to our time. They are not dialects, they are something else. Something less dependent.

And yet it does not seem satisfactory to give them the status of separate languages either and say they are different Englishes. For this is to imply, as I have already suggested, that they are developments of different virtual languages: not Ghanaian or Nigerian English but Ghanaian, Nigerian, *tout court*. And why not, one might ask. After all, in the United States, some people do at times refer to their language as American rather than American English, thereby assigning it independent national status.[4] But there are difficulties here, and again these become apparent by considering the relationship between regional variation over space and periodic change over time. A particular virtual language gets variously actualized over a period by communities adapting it to their changing needs. If these communities have reason to assert their own independent identity, they will gradually generate their own norms dissociated from previous coding conventions. They will be oriented inwards rather than outwards, and their actual language then ceases to be exonormative as a dialect and becomes endonormative as a separate language. And once a community invests its separate social identity in its language in this way, conditions are naturally created for it to become different as a virtual resource. Once a new linguistic species has been brought into being, so to speak, it becomes increasingly distinctive under its own momentum. The change in pyscho-sociological attitude to the language triggers off linguistic change. So it is that varieties evolve into autonomous languages ultimately to the point of mutual unintelligibility. One might suggest that just as members of different species do not, on the whole, mate, so speakers of different languages do not, on the whole, communicate.

If, however, English is to be an international means of communication, the evolution of different and autonomous Englishes would seem to be self-defeating. And yet, it seems only right and proper to grant that regional varieties do not have the dependent status of dialects. We have something of a dilemma here. We want independence without autonomy. How then do we resolve this paradox?

We begin, I suggest, by considering another distinction at this point, one made by Halliday, between dialects and registers (Halliday *et al.* 1964). The first is said to be a variety with reference to user and the second a variety with reference to use, so we can talk about, say, Liverpool English as a dialect and Legal English as a register. Put another way, dialects are associated primarily with different kinds of community, and registers primarily with different kinds of communication. The distinction would seem to provide us with an escape from our dilemma. For we can say that the varieties we have been considering can be seen in similarly different terms. To the extent that they are user-oriented and serve the needs of the community, then they are dialect-like, but, as we have seen, endonormative and independent. They are likely, therefore, to take their own natural course and in time evolve into separate species of language, adapted to the needs and expressive of the identity of separate communities, gradually becoming mutually unintelligible. The very adaptations which make the language suited to local communal requirement disqualify it from service as a global means of communication. This should cause us no concern. And anyway, even if it did, we could not do anything about it since there is no way of imposing any exonormative control to arrest such development. We should in other words, expect that English will divide up into different languages in the natural evolutionary process just as others have done in the past, quite simply because it is the very virtual nature of language so to do. As French and Italian develop from Latin, so Ghanaian and Nigerian develop out of English.

But we also want English as an international language for global communication. Does this not imply that there must be some exonormative control to prevent this diversification into different species of language, this linguistic speciation, so to speak? Does it not mean that there must be some custodians of the common code to keep it global, to regulate, legislate, set the standard? Even if we allow diversification for local communities, we must surely deny it in the interests of global communication. It is this view which insists on the importance of maintaining the standard language, for if this linguistic centre cannot hold, things do indeed fall apart.

There is, however, another possibility and this is suggested by the second kind of variety that Halliday distinguishes, namely register. Register is said to be a variety of language which has developed to serve uses *for* language rather than users *of* it. So it is that we can talk of the English used for business, banking, commerce, various branches of science and technology. This is English for professional and academic activities: English for specific purposes. These are generally represented as relatively neutral, transactional uses of language which do not get entangled in the kind of social issues that we have been considering. The emphasis here is on communication and information rather than community and identity. So one way of resolving our dilemma is to let English diversify into kinds of independent dialect, but keep it in place as a range of registers. Speciation in the one case is counter-balanced by specialization in the other.

That is all very well, you may say, but how does a focus on register keep the language in place? If this is a variety of language, how do you prevent it becoming diverse? This too is surely just as subject to change as the local varieties we have been discussing. This is true. But there is a difference. Registers relate to domains of use, to areas of knowledge and expertise which cross national boundaries and are global of their very nature. You learn the register of scientific enquiry or medicine or commerce or computer technology in order to communicate with like-minded people in other parts of the world. What distinguishes a register from a dialect is not, in fact, that it relates to *uses* rather than *users*, to *communication* rather than *community*. Registers have their users too, and indeed define different communities. But these communities are not in this case local ones which we belong to by upbringing, the shared sociocultural experience of everyday life, usually mediated through the spoken language. They are global communities which we have to qualify to belong to through the secondary socialization of education and training, involving a heavy investment in the written language. They are defined not so much by experience as by expertise. We are taught to become doctors, engineers, academics, or whatever by explicit instruction. And learning to become members of these communities necessarily involves learning the variety of language, the register, which has become established as conventional for their communication. Learning the language used for medicine is an entry condition on membership of the medical community, and in many parts of the world this language happens to be a register of English.

Registers as the varieties used by these secondary expert communities as exploitations of the resources of the virtual language do indeed, and necessarily, change over time, particularly, as previously noted, with respect to lexis. But the change is naturally and endonormatively controlled from within by the requirements of communication across the international community of its specialist users. So scientific English changes, for example, as the communicative needs of the community of scientists changes. It remains an internationally intelligible means of communication quite simply because the community that uses it is international. Notice too that professional and academic registers are, for the most part, essentially written varieties, and tend to retain a written mode even when spoken, and writing is always likely to exert a stabilizing influence. It follows from this that registers will regulate themselves in the interests of global communication. There is no need of native-speaker custodians.

Of course, if it serves the purpose of a particular expert community to develop a register as an in-group language, this will inevitably lead to some loss of more general intelligibility. There are indeed registers which are inaccessible to outsiders, and this raises an ethical question concerning the unequal distribution of knowledge and power, as was indicated by the remarks of Edward Said which were commented on earlier (Chapter 1). This is a matter I shall touch on again in the next chapter. For the present, however, the relevant point to note is that these outsiders are just as likely to be people who would claim competence in English as those who would not. Thus, as I pointed out earlier (Chapter 3), as a native speaker of English I freely confess that the English registers of computer science, finance, stock exchange reports, genetics, and many more, are largely incomprehensible to me. As far as these uses of language are concerned, I am incompetent. But the crucial point is that there are innumerable people all over the world, speaking all kinds of primary language, from all kinds of primary sociocultural backgrounds who have become competent in these varieties of the language. And as they have achieved this competence, they become full members of these global communities with equal rights to initiate innovation. Whether you are a native speaker of the language or not is irrelevant. It is what you now are that is important, not where you have come from.

My argument, then, is that English has spread to become international by the exploitation of the resources of the virtual language, and that this has resulted in two kinds of development. One of them is primary and local and takes the form of varieties which are dialect-like in that they serve the immediate everyday social needs of a particular community. The other is secondary and global and takes the form of registers associated with particular domains of institutional and professional use.

The distinction I am making cuts across those in the Kachru scheme of things. The local 'dialectal' varieties clearly belong exclusively to the Outer Circle, where English is typically characterized as a second language. The global registers, however, are by no means exclusive to the Expanding Circle, where English is usually said to be a foreign language, for they are taken up by Outer Circle people as well, and have to be as a matter of economic and sociopolitical survival. It is in these uses of the language as a lingua franca that the dynamism of international spread is to be found, and as users of these varieties all speakers of English, whether as a first, second or foreign language are in the same Expanding Circle.[5]

Kachru's scheme is in this respect oversimplified. But then so, in some respects, is the distinction that I have been making. I have talked about the spread of English as resulting in two kinds of variety, but it would be a mistake to suppose that its spread is confined to such varieties, or that such varieties are clear-cut and well defined. Although it is possible to identify particular features as salient and distinctive in certain ways of using language, and so characteristic of this local dialect or that global register, we should also note that English spreads into all kinds of general uses of language as well, particularly in recent years with the development of telecommunications and information technology. As the electronic network has spread, so English has spread with it. Its traces are to be found everywhere, sometimes in the most unlikely places. The varieties that I talked about are cases where it has settled into conventional encodings, but the virtual language will continue to be exploited in all manner of innovative and unpredictable ways.

So what implications does all this have for pedagogy?[6] The enquiry in these chapters into the nature of English was prompted by the question as to how we might specify objectives for teaching the language. In the course of the discussion we have considered the notions of proper and standard English, English as an international language, the virtual language, local varieties, and global registers. With reference to which of these, then, if any, can we set our purpose parameter in defining our subject?

Clearly the purpose for including English as a subject on the curriculum will vary from place to place, but in their general rationale, statements of educational policy usually invoke the importance of its role as a means of international communication. Since, as we have seen, this takes the form of different global registers whereby expert communities conduct their internal affairs, in science, technology, business, and so on, it would seem reasonable to suggest that one way of defining purpose would be in reference to these specialist domains of use. English is included in the curriculum because it promises to provide its learners with the necessary qualification they need to be members of these expert communities. This promise is in some ways a delusion, but nevertheless it is represented as a primary objective and motivation for millions of English learners all over the globe, whether they belong to Outer Circle or Expanding Circle countries. They are not learning the language primarily to interact with native speakers as such, but only those who are themselves qualified to be members of these global communities. It is hard to see why otherwise the language should figure so prominently and so pervasively in curricula all over the world. It seems only logical to suppose the way objectives for the subject English are set should embody the rationale for including it on the curriculum, which in turn should correspond with the reasons why it has spread, and continues to spread, as an international language. Such reasoning might lead us to propose that objectives should be specified in reference to specific purposes. In the next chapter I will pursue this proposal and see where it takes us.

Notes and comments

1 There is an intertextual reference here, of course, to Chomsky's well-known, not to say notorious, definition of the scope of linguistic theory:

> Linguistic theory is concerned primarily with an ideal speaker-listener, in a completely homogeneous speech-community, who knows its language perfectly...
> (Chomsky 1965: 3)

Such an idealization leaves out of account what real speaker-listeners actually do with their language. In effect, it eliminates the variable of human agency altogether in order to identify the invariant properties which are intrinsic in language itself. The idea of linguistic imperialism would seem to depend on the same idealization since it represents imperialism as an intrinsic linguistic property of a language, and does not allow for the variable ways it might be appropriated and modified by actual users. One might make the point that if one holds that English is *per se* imperialistic, then this rather lets imperialists themselves off the hook. They are, so to speak, simply carriers of a linguistic infection. But either way, whether you believe the infection was spread accidentally or by deliberate intent, the belief depends on an idealization, like Chomsky's, which detaches language from its variable contexts and conditions of actual use.

There is, however, another perspective on the negative effects of the spread of English. Leaving aside the question of deliberate imperialistic motive, the very nature of this spread poses a threat of domination. For as English is adopted and adapted in different contexts of use, it may well infiltrate the social domains previously the preserve of local languages. The encroachment of the language is a natural consequence of its appropriation. Thus English becomes a threat not because it is imposed from outside but because it is integrated from within, made dominant by domestication. Hence the concern that its spread is fatal to linguistic diversity. (See Skutnabb-Kangas 2000.) And there seems little doubt that it is. The question is how such a concern can be effectively addressed. The fate of languages is a function of socio-economic and political circumstances, and to change their fate is to change these circumstances, and this may not be to the advantage of the communities concerned. The conservation of languages comes at a cost, which people may, or may not, be prepared to pay.

I take up this issue again in Chapter 11. The point I would make here, consistent with the argument in this chapter, is that this threat to linguistic diversity is minimized if English is dissociated from primary sociocultural contexts of use, and its appropriation as lingua franca restricted to institutional domains of international use which do not, to any great extent at least, encroach on these contexts.

The linguistic imperialism issue has been widely, and heatedly, debated over recent years, prompted by the publication of Phillipson 1992. It is one of the controversies that appears in Seidlhofer 2003. Brutt-Griffler 2002 presents a more measured and carefully reasoned account of the complex factors that have influenced the historical development of English as an international language.

2 These two quotations can be read as representing two positions on language change.

> Things fall apart; the centre cannot hold;
> Mere anarchy is loosed upon the world.
> (W. B. Yeats: *The Second Coming*)

Here, we might say, the centre can be taken as the Inner Circle, and the assumption is that if it cannot hold the language in place, linguistic anarchy will be loosed upon the English-speaking world.

> The old order changeth, yielding place to new,
> And God fulfils himself in many ways,
> Lest one good custom should corrupt the world.
> (Alfred Tennyson: *The Idylls of the King*)

Here, whether you attribute it to some kind of divine intervention or not, the old established order of Inner Circle English changes and yields place to new varieties of the language.

3 I have pointed out elsewhere (Widdowson 1984: Chapter 10) the formal resemblance between the inadvertent errors of language learners and the deliberate manipulations of literary writers. It raises all kinds of problematic questions, of course, about creativity and intentionality, some of which are addressed in Widdowson 1992b, which explores ways in which the virtual language is exploited in poetry.

4 Noah Webster would have approved of this since his dictionary was designed to give American English its own distinctive identity. (See Note 5 in Chapter 3 above.) We should note, however, that the United States is an Inner Circle country which has the power to dictate terms, so for its people to brand the language as distinctively their own is to assert their independence and dominance. So the status of the language is retained, and may indeed be enhanced. For varieties of English in the Outer Circle the case is different. To give the language a distinctive brand name here (Nigerian rather than Nigerian English) might well diminish its status by suggesting that it is not worthy of the name of English at all. In reference to Chinua Achebe's remarks, quoted in the last chapter, no matter how new the English may be, it still needs to be associated nominally, it seems, with its ancestral home. It would appear that you can only afford to dispense with the prestige attached to the name if, as in the case of the United States, you have compensating sources of prestige and power to call upon.

This is one issue (among several) that Brutt-Griffler touches on when she challenges the position I take in the paper upon which this present chapter is based. (See Widdowson 1997b, 1998; Brutt-Griffler 1998.)

5 Phonological features of English as an international language are discussed in Jenkins 2000, 2002. She identifies what she calls a 'lingua franca core' and argues for its pedagogic relevance as a basis for the teaching of pronunciation. The concept of English as a lingua franca and the case for compiling a corpus for the description of its lexical and grammatical features are discussed in Seidlhofer 1999, 2001, 2002. For a consideration of the pragmatic aspects of lingua franca English, see also House 2002.

6 The implications I am concerned with in this book are those which bear on my particular line of argument. A wider ranging discussion of pedagogic issues arising from the spread of English as an international language is to be found in McKay 2002.

6 English for specific purposes

In the last chapter, I argued that the global spread of English as an international language has come about, and continues apace, because it operates in a range of institutional and professional domains of an academic, economic, and political kind. These domains transcend, and may indeed undermine, national boundaries and the more particular concerns of primary communities. As the language has spread, so it has necessarily diversified into different registers, different encodings of the virtual code potential, particularly with respect to lexis, specifically adapted to communicative requirement. It was suggested that since this is the reason for the continuing spread of English, it should logically provide the principal reason for learning it, in which case we might propose that the objectives of the subject English should be formulated in reference to the registers that serve these global purposes.

The picture presented so far is of well defined domains and purposes which correspond in a straightforward way with different patterns of encoding. In such a view, the S of ESP expresses a direct correlation between two kinds of specificity: a specific purpose is directly matched up with a specific variety of English. I have already suggested, however, that such a picture is an oversimplification. We now need to look at these issues more closely.

Perhaps the first point to be made is that in one sense *all* uses of English, as of any other language, are specific. All uses of the language serve particular purposes. Whenever I indulge in utterance, I fashion the form of my message according to communicative requirements. I open my mouth to speak, or take up my pen to write (or, nowadays my keyboard to type) and I thereby make a bid to focus the recipient's attention on what I mean in the most effective way possible. I am doing just that at this present moment. I am being as specific as I can about the point I want to make. My English at the moment is designed to serve a specific purpose and it is that which makes it communicative. In a sense, English for specific purposes is what communication in English in general is all about.[1]

All language use is specific in a sense. But in what sense exactly? When discussing the notion of proper words in proper places in Chapter 3, we considered three kinds of propriety: that of words in themselves ('prepone', 'depone', etc.); their proper places in grammatical constructions; and thirdly, their appropriate placement in context. In the chapters that followed our concern has been with the first two of these, with what is taken as proper or conventional in respect to the language code. The varieties of English we have been considering are different kinds of encoding. The difference in the case of local 'dialectal' varieties is evident in both the grammatical and lexical features, whereas with global registers, the difference would seem to be predominantly lexical. So we can talk about specificity in terms of encoded linguistic features. Thus we can identify 'depone' as a lexical item specific to the register of legal English. But when I say that all uses of language are specific to purpose, I am referring not to what is specific about the language itself as a code, but what specific use it is put to on particular occasions. What is at issue here is not what is proper in terms of encoded properties but how these are put to appropriate contextual use. In a word we are concerned now with specificity in a pragmatic sense.

People make specific use of the resources of a language to design utterances, spoken or written, which will achieve their intended purposes. And they do this in accordance with the principles of cooperation and least effort. Thus they design utterances which will key into the context of recipient knowledge in the most economical way. It is for this reason that what we mean is generally not recoverable from what we say. We use language *indexically*, to point to aspects of knowledge assumed to be shared between us and our interlocutors. (See Widdowson 1983, 1990.) What we suppose is known already we do not refer to; all we need to do is to activate it and indicate its relevance. All this is simply to say that the meaning of a language as semantically encoded is not at all the same as what people mean *by* language when they put it to pragmatic use.

This can be illustrated in an obvious way by public notices. If I see the word 'TRAINS' on the wall in the Russell Square station of the London Underground, I read it as a complete text and interpret it as a *reference* to the trains on the District Line, and interpret its *force* as an indication as to where I should go to catch one. The designer of this single word text, confident that he (or she) can assume shared knowledge of the Underground, in placing the text in this particular location thus directs me to a quite specific meaning. This is not what the word itself means; it is what it means to me, not what it denotes but what I take it to refer to. The word itself is actually very unspecific: a plural noun, a lexical item. As the dictionary has it:

> TRAIN: railway engine with several carriages or trucks linked to and pulled by it.

The text can, of course, be taken as the manifestation of the linguistic code. I can, if I am so inclined, simply identify its formal features: 'trains'—a word consisting of six letters, five sounds, a noun morphologically marked as a plural, or a verb morphologically marked as third person singular present, and so on. But I would not normally process this notice as a word in this way. I would refer it to context, assume a communicative intent, and realize it pragmatically, thereby assigning it significance as discourse. The point is that the text serves only to make a connection between two states of mind or projections of reality, that which informs the intention of its first person producer and that which informs the interpretation of the second person at the receiving end. What the first person intends the text to mean and what the second person interprets it to mean are, in other words, different discourses. If a text does not mediate, or textualize a discoursal relationship between first person intention and second person interpretation then it remains inert as a linguistic object.

The text we have been considering mediates this relationship effectively by a minimal use of linguistic means. The single word is enough to key us into the relevant context. No further use of the code is called for. Indeed linguistic elaboration would mark the text as unconventional and so make it less pragmatically effective. But most texts, of course, are not so simple, but draw on linguistic resources more extensively to mediate meaning. Even so, texts may fail to mediate effectively.

Consider the following text, for example:

In homes, a haunted apparatus sleeps,
that snores when you pick it up.

If the ghost cries, they carry it
to their lips and soothe it to sleep

with sounds. And yet, they wake it up
deliberately, by tickling with a finger.
(from Craig Raine: *A Martian Sends a Postcard Home*)

What, you might ask, is all this about. It is an obscure text. But what is the reason for its obscurity? The text is in English after all, and there is nothing difficult about the syntax or the semantics. It is cohesive enough: the pronoun 'it' makes a clear anaphoric connection with the noun phrase 'a haunted apparatus', which is lexically linked with the following phrase 'the ghost'. It is easily processed in this respect and we can indeed use it for the posing of comprehension questions in the conventional way. 'What happens when the apparatus is picked up?' 'It snores.' 'How is the ghost woken up?' 'By tickling it.' Good: full marks to the students even though they may not really understand what the text is actually about. It is cohesive as text, but incoherent in that it fails to textualize. Why is this so? The title of the poem provides the clue. It represents the impressions of a Martian, unfamiliar with earthly things. There is therefore no convergence on shared knowledge, no common frame of reference. If I provide you with a frame of reference, by telling you that what is being described here is a telephone, then things fall into place and you begin to make sense of the text. You accommodate it into your familiar world: the text now mediates pragmatically and is made coherent by activating a relevant discourse. Consider another example:

The man turned sideways in the bushes and looked at Lok along his shoulder. A stick rose upright and there was a lump of bone in the middle. Lok

peered at the stick and the lump of bone and the small eyes in the bone thing
over the face. Suddenly Lok understood that the man was holding the stick
out to him but neither he nor Lok could reach across the river... The stick
began to grow shorter at both ends. Then it shot out to full length again.
   The dead tree by Lok's ear acquired a voice.
'Clop!'
His ears twitched and he turned to the tree. By his face there had grown
   a twig.
(from William Golding: *The Inheritors*)

Another mysterious text. What is going on here? What is this curious stick
and how is it related to the bizarre immediate growth of a twig on a tree?
What on earth is all this about? Is it indeed on earth at all? In a way it is not,
at least not on the earth that we are familiar with. What we have here again is
the representation of how things which are familiar to us might look to an
alien eye, an eye not schooled in shared perceptions of the world. Lok is a
Neanderthal man, and this text describes his first encounter with Homo
sapiens, the naked ape. He has never seen hairless humans before, so their hands
look like bones. He has never seen a bow and arrow before, so the bow is seen
as a stick which behaves in an incomprehensible fashion, and the arrow shot
into the tree can only be seen as a twig suddenly growing from it.

   As before, there is cohesion without coherence. Again, there is nothing difficult about the language of the text as such. In a way, indeed, it is the very
simplicity of the language which causes the problem. The conclusion is clear:
simplicity of language is not to be equated with accessibility of meaning. This
is obvious enough, you may say. But it does not seem to be always so obvious
to those who advocate a simple defining vocabulary for dictionary definitions, or the use of simplified texts in language teaching.

   As before, what causes the problem, of course, is that there is a disparity in
perceptions of the world. The Martian and the Neanderthal man do not see
things in our terms, so their terms are indexically defective: they do not
engage shared schematic knowledge. They are outsiders looking in, making
sense of things *in* their terms and *on* their terms. This is common sense to
them, because it is *communal* sense: the reality which is sanctioned by their
particular social community. So we have problems coming *to* terms with it.

   Communication is then clearly closely related to community and culture. If
you do not share a communal view, a common culture, and the linguistic cat-
egorization which goes with it, then communication will prove difficult.

   All this is obvious enough, and might indeed seem rather trivial. But it
raises a number of issues of some significance. To begin with, we should note
that although there is nothing specific about the linguistic forms that are used
in these texts, there is something specific in the way they are used. So the first
is not an example of Martian English, but of how a Martian might use it, and
in the case of *The Inheritors*, we do not get a Neanderthal dialect, but the

representation of how a Neanderthal might use Standard English to express his perceptions of reality. (For a particularly perceptive discussion of this, see Halliday 1973.)

We might compare these texts with others, where the language itself *is* made specific. Consider the following, for example:

> He said, 'Whats the use of helping qwirys on him that poor simpo I dont think he knows nothing to tel no moren any of them ever do. I do like other Pry Mincers done befor me becaws thats what the Mincery wants. Im terning them frontwards in a woal lot of ways only I cant do it all at 1ce. We aint none of us what you cud cal qwick but mos of them roun me theyre 2ce as unqwick as I am lwl tel you that...'
> (from Russell Hoban: *Riddley Walker*)

Here too we have a fictional representation of a remote world, not this time, as with *The Inheritors*, an imagined projection of the past but of the future. It comes from a novel set far in the future, and here the language itself is indeed specific, quite distinctive in its orthographic, lexical, and grammatical features. Bearing in mind the points raised about proper English in Chapter 3, we might say that this is just not English, even though it is *in* English. In the terms of our discussion in Chapter 5, it does not draw on conventional encodings, but exploits the resource of the virtual language. The same can be said of the following text:

> I was a palm-wine drinkard since I was a boy of ten years of age. I had no other work more than to drink palm-wine in my life. In those days we did not know other money, except cowries, so that everything was very cheap, and my father was the richest man in our town.
> (from Amos Tutuola: *The Palm-Wine Drinkard*)

Here, in the words of Chinua Achebe cited in the last chapter, is a new English 'altered to suit its new African surroundings'. But whereas in Achebe's fiction the alteration is for the most part in the manner in which established encodings are used, as with Golding, in Tutuola's case we have an altered English, an alternative exploitation of the virtual language.

The point to be made, then, is that specificity of pragmatic function does not necessarily call for a corresponding specificity of linguistic form. It will only do so contingently, when existing encodings do not adequately provide for particular conceptual or communicative purposes. But it is important to notice that the innovative encodings are indeed contingent, that it is their pragmatic realization that is primary, the extent to which they textualize discoursal meaning. So it is not enough to know what such encodings signify, one also needs to understand the significance of their use. The problems that the Martian and Lok encounter are not linguistic. It would not help them to understand the phenomena they experience by providing them with the lexical labels 'telephone' and 'bow and arrow'. Their problem is that they cannot grasp a reality which is schematically structured in an unfamiliar way. The reality in their case takes the form of cultural artefacts. But the same point applies to other aspects of culture. Consider, for example, the following text:

> The Chamberlains were Seventh Day Adventists (which, by normal Bruce rules, was peculiar), and Lindy, a rather spiky, intense individual, failed to act out in court the required sub-Neighbours version of the innocent grieving mother. In more than one way, she suffered from cultural insensitivity. The Aborigines at Ayers Rock did not seem surprised that a dingo might have taken a baby, but who gave a XXXX what the Abos thought?
> (from a review by Mark Lawson of Lindy Chamberlain: 'Through my eyes.' *The Independent on Sunday*, 4.2.91)

This text does not represent a fiction but refers to facts. The difficulty is that the reader may not know what the facts are, may have no frame of reference which can serve as indexical bearings and so is in effect cast in the role of outsider. What event is being referred to? Who are the Chamberlains? You have to be in the know to make much sense of this text. And you have to be in the know about a good deal else as well. You have to recognize that the expression 'Bruce rules' refers to the attitudes of stereotypical Australian men, that 'Neighbours' is a television soap opera about Australian life, that 'XXXX' is meant as an intertextual allusion to a popular advertisement for Australian beer, and so on.

But it is not only a matter either of the text failing to mediate reference by a convergence of common knowledge. The writer also positions the reader as a person who not only shares *knowledge*, but *values* as well. So it is that we are invited to adopt the same somewhat superior and contemptuous view of Australian attitudes. The text is designed to be accessible to, and acceptable to, a like-minded reader. And if you can identify with this assigned reader, then you confirm your common communal values, and ratify your role as insider. You then *authenticate* the text as a discourse which is expressive of a particular community which you belong to. There is thus the creation of a solidarity between writer and reader, and a kind of conspiracy against those who cannot fill the position of assigned reader: the writer makes allusions to things which are particular, specific indeed, to a closed community of like-minded people.

If you cannot ratify the role of assigned reader, you become an outsider, excluded, alienated from the text. Either you cannot authenticate it, and no coherent discourse is derived from the text. Or you authenticate it on your own terms, and assert your own discourse, which may have little convergence with that of the writer's original intention.

Communication implies community and membership is mediated with the meaning of the text. It is not just a matter of knowing the semantic meanings of the words. For the words are *schematically connected* to form conceptualizations of reality which define the culture of a particular discourse community (Swales 1990). It would not help the Martian to know that the device he encounters is called a telephone, or Lok that the stick that so baffles him is called a bow. What they lack is insider experience of a whole new way of conceptualizing things, and talking about them. They do not have the culturally determined ideational and interpersonal schemata.[2] Without that they remain outsiders. You do not acquire the conceptual significance of things when you learn their names.

Innumerable people who attempt to interpret the newspaper article about the Chamberlains remain outsiders too, whether they are native speakers of the language or not. For the limits of their ability to authenticate the text as discourse do not correspond with their competence in the language. If they are baffled by this text it is no reflection on their linguistic proficiency. It is not that they do not understand what the English means, but rather that they do not understand what those who are using it on this occasion mean *by* it.

The author of the Chamberlain passage is using English quite specifically to engage a particular discourse community of readers. It would not, however, be taken as a typical example of English for specific purposes. Let us now look at a text that would:

> Leading industrials recorded a majority of falls in the 2p to 8p range. Gilts also kept a low profile, with conventionals down a quarter and index-linked three-eighths lower. Quiet builders provided a firm spot in Ward Holdings, up 17p to 177p following a 63 percent upsurge in pre-tax profits. Golds relinquished 50 cents to a dollar.
> [source]Unknown

Here is a text which is unquestionably *in* English, but for all my native-speaker competence in the language, I can derive little from it in the way of coherent discourse. What are these gilts and conventionals and quiet builders. An explanation would involve induction into (for me) a strange culture of the stock exchange. I could only make sense of these expressions by referring them to the whole schematic complex of international finance. Since stocks and shares are a mystery to me, I have to fall back on what linguistic competence I have to try to make out what the text might mean. So it is, for example, that I recognize the expression 'index-linked' as a past participle, but does it function here as a nominal, like 'conventional', and so a different kind of stock (or share?), or does it refer to a kind of conventional— an index-linked kind, distinct from conventionals in general, or does it refer to all of the conventionals mentioned earlier? I do not know. Those who belong to the discourse community of investment banking would of course be able to use the expression to key them in directly to what they know. In other words, the term 'index-linked' would itself be pragmatically index-linked to their familiar affairs. They would be able to infer the relevant discourse because of their *professional* competence as members of this discourse community. There will be no need for them to analyse the meaning out of the text painstakingly, as I have sought to do as an outsider.

Although this would be taken as a typical ESP text, whereas the Chamberlain text would not, the problems they pose for interpretation arise in both cases from what might be called discourse disparity: the author has designed a text specifically for a discourse community to which the reader does not belong. Communication can only be achieved when there is a measure of convergence between the worlds of the first and second person parties. The first person fashions a message to mediate a relationship with the second person, to establish a sharing. Communication at the best of times can, of course, only be approximate since the convergence can never be complete, and it is always possible to derive some meaning even from the most obscure of texts. Nevertheless, it is obvious that the normal conduct of human affairs must be based on an assumption that convergence is achieved to the degree that satisfies communicative requirement. It may not be complete, but it is adequate to purpose. The participants, even when distanced by print, come to terms, so to speak, and cooperate in the achievement of meaning. Difficulties arise, as we have seen, when participants cannot cooperate, either because there is disparity of linguistic knowledge, but also, crucially, as I have argued, when there is a cultural disparity: when the second person recipient is not a member of the discourse community for whom the text is designed. It is also possible to wilfully decline to cooperate, of course, and to assertively, or resistantly, impose our own discourse assumptions on the text. In this case it is a matter not of *accessibility* but of *acceptability* of the first person discourse that has been textualized. (For further discussion, see Widdowson 1990.)

As I observed at the beginning of this chapter, then, all uses of language are specific to purpose in the sense that they are designed to communicate by keying in to particular contexts of communally-shared assumptions. To the extent that such uses can be identified as typical of particular communities we can talk of distinct varieties. But two matters have arisen from our discussion which we need to note.

Firstly, these varieties can be conceived of in two very different ways. One has to do with the kinds of encoding, the different conventional realizations of the virtual language, which typify different texts. As argued in the last chapter, these can be seen as local dialect-like forms of speaking associated with primary communities of users, or as global registers developed for institutional and international purposes. But texts are only the linguistic produce of the discourse process. Communication, as we have seen, is not simply a matter of issuing semantic tokens of fixed meaning. It involves also using the resources of the language code indexically, to indicate (point out, invoke) specific aspects of shared schematic knowledge of ideational patterns of conceptualization and interpersonal patterns of communication. That is to say, it involves engaging with the shared assumptions, values, beliefs, and conventions of behaviour that define the culture of particular discourse communities. So another way of conceiving of variety is in terms not of *text types* or registers but of *discourse types* or genres, the culturally informed ways of thinking and communicating that are realized by these texts, and motivate their production in the first place. Registers are linguistic constructs, and differences between them can be directly identified as linguistic features from the textual data themselves. Genres are cultural constructs, and differences here can only be inferred indirectly by interpreting the textual data as discoursal evidence.

The extensive work done in the ESP field on genre analysis (for example, Swales 1990; Bhatia 1993) seeks to identify the particular conventions for language use in certain domains of professional and occupational activity. It is a development from, and an improvement on, register analysis because it deals with discourse and not just text: that is to say, it seeks not simply to reveal what linguistic forms are *manifested* but how they *realize*, make real, the conceptual and rhetorical structures, modes of thought and action, which are established as conventional for certain discourse communities. Genre analysis is, therefore, not principally about the English of Engineering, of Medicine, of Business, or Banking, but about the conventions of thought and communication which define these areas of professional activity, and how, *incidentally*, these are given expression, or textualized, in English.

A second matter concerns the extent to which these genres, or the registers which give them linguistic expression, are identifiable as distinctive constructs. They have developed to meet the requirements of particular communities, and will obviously continue to vary as the requirements change. The process that brought them about is not suddenly arrested. It may well suit the purpose of analysts, and users too, to conceive of genres as stable states of communicative affairs: analysts can fix on certain features as typical and disregard others, and users can feel secure in a set of conventions which define their community. But the conception of genres as stable entities is only a convenient fiction: they are in reality sociocultural processes, continually in flux. So it would be preferable to think not of the English *of* computers, or commerce, or whatever, as if it were fixed in advance, but the English *for* computers, or commerce, or whatever, which are changing in all manner of ways as these activities develop. This being so, two further points would seem to follow.

The first takes us back to observations made in Chapter 4 about the ownership of English. Since these generic developments are not controlled by native speakers of English, so neither is the language which is used to realize them. Thus, obviously enough, *business English*, for example, in the present or the future, emphatically (and perhaps fortunately for global commerce) does not correspond with *English business*, nor more generally, with the business conducted by the Inner Circle speakers of the language. Although native speakers have the tendency to assume the responsibility of custodians in maintaining *the standard* to preserve *standards* of international intelligibility, their sense of responsibility is misplaced. For these standards will be internally, endonormatively, regulated by the requirements for international communication. If business English approximates to the standard language it will be because it makes for efficient communication among business people, whatever their primary language. Native speakers of English have no right to pronounce on the matter. In short, it is not their business. Indeed, attempts at exonormative control can only inhibit the very flexibility of the language upon which its effectiveness for global communication depends. (For further discussion, see Widdowson 1994, 1997b.)

The second point concerns the concept of genre itself, and how its descriptive validity is related to its pedagogic viability, and this will, in due course, take us back to the question that motivated our discussion of specificity in this chapter in the first place. If, in thinking of English as used in professional and occupational communities, we need to accept that these uses will change in line with the developing cultures of these communities, then any account of genres as stable sets of conventions which call for conformity is bound to be only partial and potentially misleading. For such conventions are not fixed but in flux. They are affected not only by conceptual and sociocultural changes within discourse communities but also, perhaps more markedly, by developments in the means of transmission.[3] We know that medium has an effect on mode, that development in communications alters communication, that technological advances like the printing press, the telephone, the computer, the fax machine have led to different modes of language use, different genres. Thus the rapid development in electronic communications has radical effects on the way people conduct their communicative affairs. Now the point about genre analysis is that it can only concern itself with what has actually been attested *in the past*, and indeed is only valid to the extent that it does. But this necessarily sets limits on its viability as a basis for specifying pedagogic objectives, for these must be a projection into the future. So even if one knew which particular discourse communities a group of students were seeking to be members of in their learning of English (a crucial proviso, which I will return to presently), it would clearly be unsatisfactory to instruct them in reference to outdated generic conventions. It would seem preferable to present such genres not as specific norms to be conformed to, but as more general points of reference within which room for manoeuvre is possible.

To use the findings of genre analysis in this way has the added advantage that it actually brings pedagogic viability into line with the limited validity of such findings. For not only is genre analysis necessarily past rather than future-oriented, it is also based on impressionistic judgements about distinctiveness. Although genres are commonly presented as if they were well-defined discourse types associated with particular discourse communities, the defining criteria are elusive. Certainly there is no reliable procedure for identifying one genre as distinct from another on textual evidence. What happens is that the analyst takes an impressionistic decision on what constitutes this genre, or that, and then proceeds to abstract certain features which appear to be particularly and regularly prominent, leaving others aside as non-typical stylistic variants. So it is that the distinctiveness of the genres is a function of the analysis itself. People do not generally shift abruptly from one distinct genre into another (except, perhaps, for deliberate comic effect), but rather take their bearings from certain focal points of prominence. The value of analysis is that it makes explicit what these focal points might be. In this respect, genre analysis is descriptively valid, and by the same token pedagogically viable, to the extent that it is not specific to the particulars of actual language use.

So, to return to the question of specifying objectives for learning, it seems clear that we cannot derive them in any direct way from descriptions of the generic conventions associated with global institutionalized uses of English. Even if we were able to predict which of such uses our students would need to be prepared for, we could not prepare them adequately by setting up specific models to conform to.[4] It would seem that we need to define our objectives not in reference to specific domains of use but in more general terms. But as was demonstrated earlier in this chapter, we can also think of specificity in more general terms in the sense that all language use depends on being contextually specific. We might propose then that the kind of objective we are looking for is a more general capability for being specific in this sense, what I have referred to elsewhere as communicative capacity (Widdowson 1983). The question now arises as to where we might look for guidance as to how this capability might be formulated. I have in this chapter pointed out the necessary limitations of genre analysis for our purpose, but there are other areas of linguistic description that we might turn to. What bearing do they have on how objectives might be defined? This question is taken up in the next chapter, and it will involve us too in the more general question touched on in Chapter 1 about the relationship between the discipline of linguistics and the subject of language teaching.

Notes and comments

1 Indeed, ideas about communicative language teaching as a general pedagogic approach had their origin in the design of courses of English for specific purposes in the late sixties. Since such purposes were defined in terms of the learners' current needs and were of their nature pragmatic, courses had to be designed to provide an immediate communicative pay-off. The emphasis, therefore, necessarily shifted from the internalization of encoded features of the language as a long-term investment to the appropriate short-term realization of such features in specific contexts of use. The question then naturally arose as to whether and to what extent such a communicative orientation might be applicable more generally, when there were no specific pragmatic purposes to provide for, and where eventual needs were largely unpredictable. Essentially then the question was, and still is, how far pedagogic proposals appropriate to specific circumstances can validly give rise to general principles for a communicative approach to language teaching. For further discussion of the relationship

between ESP and CLT see Widdowson 1978, 1979, 1983. How different genres are textualized, what we can call their difference of texture, can now be specified with particular precision by the use of computers in corpus analysis. See, for example, the chapters in Part II of Flowerdew 2002.

2 Schemata can be defined as customary ways in which a particular community structures its reality. They represent patterns of expectation which people project on to events. Where these patterns relate to conceptualizations of the third person world 'out there' they can be referred to as ideational schemata. Where they have to do with accepted conventions of communicative behaviour, how people as first and second persons interact with each other, they can be referred to as interpersonal schemata. For further discussion, see Widdowson 1983: 54–9.

3 There is an important caveat to be made at this point. I have been discussing patterns of language use that will naturally adapt themselves to changes in the occupations and professions they relate to. But there are cases where such adaptation leads to fixity, where communicative convention requires a strict control over variation. What we then find are what Firth called 'restricted languages' (Firth 1957). The English of air-traffic control would be an example: here the specific purpose to be achieved confines users to a limited range of expressions in routine exchanges. Seaspeak, the English deliberately devised for maritime communications (what might be called sea-traffic control) would be another example (Weeks *et al.* 1984). These uses of English are not only restricted as code but are reduced in pragmatic range, their purpose being to depersonalize the language in the interests of transactional effectiveness. Over recent years, however, certain uses of English involving interpersonal interaction have been similarly reduced to depersonalized routine. The token ritualized utterances of flight attendants, or hotel receptionists are cases in point. These and other so-called service encounters are often explicitly regulated into standard form by employers with their staff trained into conformity. A particularly interesting example of this kind of phenomenon is the 'call centre'. Here telephone enquiries of every conceivable kind, concerning anything from a gas bill to a flight reservation, are directed to an employee of the centre who will process the enquiry by following a fixed interactional routine with the caller while keying the enquiry into a computer.

Here is a case where advances in communications technology do not, as I have suggested here, have the effect of diversifying generic uses of the language but on the contrary of reducing them to conventional fixity. For a particularly insightful account of this kind of restricted language, see Cameron 2000.

4 One might also make the point, of course, that the use of English for such global institutional purposes is itself a rather limited, even arid, objective, and that even if this is taken as a primary purpose, some allowance must be made for the learner to appropriate the language for a wider range of social

interaction and individual self-expression. Consider the following remarks by Said, made in reference to students of English at an unnamed university in the Middle East:

> The reason for the large numbers of students taking English was given frankly by a somewhat disaffected instructor: many of the students proposed to end up working for airlines, or banks, in which English was the worldwide *lingua franca*. This all but terminally consigned English to the level of a technical language stripped of expressive and aesthetic characteristics and denuded of any critical or self-conscious dimension. You learned English to use computers, respond to orders, transmit telexes, decipher manifests, and so forth. That was all.
> (Said 1994b: 369)

The kind of restricted language that Cameron describes (mentioned above) lends some support to Said's concern.

7   The scope of linguistic description

In Chapter 1, I argued that a definition of the subject English, or that of any other language on the curriculum, calls for mediation whereby educational and linguistic considerations are reconciled, and I discussed such mediation in reference to the general notion of parameter setting. With respect to the parameter of educational objective, the question arose as to what the purposes for learning might be, and what kind of language is to be specified to meet them. This led us into a discussion of varieties of English, and which, if any, of them might be set up as the model for learners to aspire to. We proposed that the purpose for most learners is to engage with English as an international means of communication, and that this is the reason, usually made quite explicit in policy statements, why English figures so prominently in curricula all over the world. We then, in the last chapter, explored whether the international uses of the language for so-called specific purposes, as described by genre analysis, might provide us with our required specification of objectives and concluded that they could not. The discussion of this issue exemplified the process of mediation in that it involved considering the relationship between the descriptive validity of genre analysis and its pedagogic viability, this being a particular instance of how the settings on different parameters relate to each other. The particular case of genre analysis is the cue for a more general discussion about the applicability of linguistic descriptions to the specification of content for the language subject.

In traditional ways of thinking, applicability poses no problem at all. Since languages are both what teachers teach and linguists describe, it would seem self-evident that the findings of linguistics should determine how the content of language courses is to be defined. Linguistics has always in fact been deferred to as the accepted authority on these matters, the assumption being that the language subject is directly derived from the linguistic discipline, and that the units of description constitute the units for learning. On the face of it, this seems reasonable enough: if teachers cannot draw on linguistic descriptions in the design of their instruction, where else, after all, can they turn? But drawing on descriptions is not the same as being determined by them.

The assumption that the content of the language subject should be a direct projection of linguistic description goes back a long way. The following can be taken as a representative statement:

He (the language teacher) is not teaching linguistics. But he is teaching
something which is the object of study of linguistics, and is described by
linguistic methods. It is obviously desirable that the underlying description
should be as good as possible, and this means that it should be based on
sound linguistic principles.
(Halliday *et al.* 1964: 66)

The something that the teacher is teaching, the language subject, is here
equated with the object of study of the linguist, the object language. All
very straightforward, one might think. But the difficulty is that views change,
and change quite radically, about what makes for a good description, and
what sound linguistic principles are. The linguistic methods and principles
employed by taxonomic structuralists, for example, are very different from
those of generativists of the Chomsky stamp, which are, again, very different
from those of functional grammarians, variationists, pragmaticists, and so
on, all of whom would claim that their descriptions are good and their principles sound. As was indicated in the last chapter, the fact of the matter is that
the object of study is, to a considerable degree, constructed by the linguistic
methods and principles themselves and is therefore always only a partial
representation of language as experienced by its users. So the question is:
which construct, which version of linguistic reality can be depended upon to
provide the basis for the language subject?

In practice, it has been the one in current fashion. Thus, when structuralist
linguistics was in the ascendancy and the object language was described in
terms of its formal properties, then the content of language courses was specified along the same lines in terms of sentence patterns. With the shift to the
pragmatic functioning of language, the units of courses were specified in
terms of communicative functions.[1] And in more recent years it is corpus
descriptions of language that appear to dictate what the content of language
courses should be.

It is this assumption of direct and unilateral determination that I want now
to question, taking up the argument outlined in Chapter 1 that the 'something' that the language teacher teaches is *not* the same as the object of study
of linguistics, and that what is deemed to be a 'good' description in reference
to 'sound linguistic principles' cannot be assumed to be a good specification
for the content of the language subject. To understand why this should be so,
we need first to be clear about the nature of linguistic principles, and how
their soundness is decided.

As we saw with Labov in Chapter 1, the principles that linguists adduce for
their enquiry can be motivated by ethical considerations. They routinely say, for
example, that they consider all linguistic systems as equal and treat them all
alike, whatever their status as languages or dialects, with the same even-handed
detachment. Though this axiom may be laudable as an article of linguistic
faith, such an egalitarian attitude does not, of course, by any means always

correspond with that of language users themselves who do make evaluative judgements about relative status in no uncertain terms.[2] All forms of speaking may be counted equal on linguistic grounds, but this equality is a function of the outsider perspective of the analyst. For in reference to the kind of social criteria that insiders go by, they are certainly not. So we need to note that the principle of lingual equality puts the linguist at a remove from experienced reality. It is worth noting too that this egalitarian principle does not extend to other *perceptions* of language. Though there is no discrimination against languages among linguists there is very considerable discrimination against *ideas* about language, whether these are formulated as explicit theories or not. Linguists are not notably hesitant in dismissing ideas held by the uninformed commoner, or by their own academic colleagues, as misconceived, inadequate, or hopelessly wrong.

Linguists, then, typically take up a position, a particular perspective, and this, while giving them insights denied to others, at the same time limits their view. Their vantage point, in other words, is both advantage and disadvantage. So linguists do not tell it how it is, but how, from their particular point of view, it seems to be. This point of view is sustained by eliminating others, and the diversity of experience is reduced in the interests of conceptual clarity.

The position that linguists take up is also one of authority by the very fact that it is intellectually distanced. The descriptions they produce are influential and so while partial in coverage are prescriptive in effect. Linguistic reality is in the eye of the beholder, but certainly as far as language teaching is concerned, it is the eye of the most influential beholders that prevails. As has already been noted, it is the *linguist's descriptions* of language that are taken as authoritative for *pedagogic prescriptions* of language content for teaching.

So it is that Sinclair feels he can identify with teachers and speak on their behalf when he makes the following remarks:

> We are teaching English in ignorance of a vast amount of basic fact. This is not our fault, but it should not inhibit the absorption of new material.
> (Sinclair 1985: 252)

The basic fact that Sinclair is referring to is that which emerges from the computer analysis of a corpus of English that is actually attested as having been produced by its native users. There can be no doubt that teachers have indeed been in ignorance of this basic fact and that developments in corpus analysis that Sinclair refers to do need to be drawn to their attention, but there is also the implication here that such fact has necessarily to be absorbed into pedagogy. And this, I think, is at one with the assumption of necessary determination referred to earlier: now that linguists have discovered this basic descriptive fact, about which teachers (and indeed everybody else) were previously ignorant, it can and should now be prescribed as the content for English courses. Whereas previously we had to depend on the evidence of our own uncertain intuitions about English, or the unreliable responses of informants, we now have a record of actual occurrences. So much is certain. What seems to me uncertain is the conclusion that since we now have samples of real language at our disposal, that is what should constitute data for learning and that there is never a need, or excuse, for invention of examples in the classroom.

Course and reference books for English teaching directly derived from these corpus descriptions have been published, some bearing the slogan 'Helping the learner with *real* English', but it seems to me that there are two assumptions here that we need to examine: the first is that these descriptions are indeed of real English, and the second is that it is this English that should be prescribed as the objective for learning.

First, then, what kind of fact is it that comes out of the computer analysis of a corpus of text, and how far does it account for linguistic reality? Corpus linguistics, of which the COBUILD work under the direction of Sinclair is an impressive example, provides for the description of what Chomsky calls 'Externalized language' or 'E-language', that is to say, the description of performance, the actualized instances of attested behaviour (Chomsky 1986, 1988). This, as we noted in Chapter 1, he distinguishes from the study of 'Internalized language' or 'I-language', that is to say, the enquiry into competence as abstract knowledge or linguistic cognition. In the case of I-language, whether or not a particular expression is actually attested is irrelevant to the model of description since its purpose is to account not only for sentences which happen, incidentally, to have occurred, but also those that never have, and perhaps never will. It is, so to speak, a model of absences for which presences provide only partial and unreliable evidence. In E-language descriptions, on the other hand, presences are the only evidence there is, and knowledge is equivalent to a generalization from behaviour: it is not that performance is an *actualization* of competence, but that competence is an *abstraction* from performance. In this view, the only facts about what people know are those which can be directly inferred from what they have done.

We are talking here about Chomsky's notion of competence as the knowledge of formal linguistic properties. But competence can be more broadly conceived so as to include knowing how to act on this knowledge in actual language use. As is well known, a broader conception has indeed been proposed by Hymes under the name of communicative competence. This, he proposes, can be defined in reference to four aspects of knowledge that a 'normal member of a community' can bring to bear in deciding:

1 whether (and to what degree) something is formally *possible*;
2 whether (and to what degree) something is *feasible* in virtue of the means of implementation available;
3 whether (and to what degree) something is *appropriate* (adequate, happy, successful) in relation to the context in which it used and evaluated;
4 whether (and to what degree) something is in fact done, actually *performed*, and what its doing entails.
(Hymes 1972: 281)

It is clear that I-language study ('I-linguistics') is concerned with the first two of these aspects, the possible and the feasible. 'E-linguistics', on the other hand, is concerned with the other two, with the actualized occurrence of language when it is put to communicative use. But as was pointed out in the preceding chapter in the discussion of the distinction between register and genre, actually occurring instances of language behaviour can be described in two different ways: as discourse and as text. The first of these focuses attention on the third of Hymes' aspects: appropriateness. It deals with the way language keys into context, with the pragmatic use of language in the transaction of social business, the interaction of social relations, the negotiation of indexical meaning of different kinds: reference, force, and effect.[3] The second E-linguistic line focuses attention on the fourth of Hymes' aspects and deals with patterns of the frequency and co-occurrence of linguistic features in texts. It is this textual aspect of E-Language that corpus descriptions capture with such precision.

Traditionally, language descriptions have focused attention almost exclusively on the possible, taking the standard language as the norm. What corpus linguistics does is to shift this focus to the actually performed. The difference is exemplified in two standard reference grammars: *A Comprehensive Grammar of the English language* (Quirk *et al.* 1985) and *Longman Grammar of Spoken and Written English* (*LGSWE*) (Biber *et al.* 1999). The former is essentially descriptive of what the grammarian authors know of English as representative users, and what they know, as grammarians, of other descriptions of English. This is checked out against information in a corpus about actual occurrence but not determined by it. The Quirk *et al.* grammar is essentially an account of their knowledge of what is grammatically possible in English, not of the actually attested behaviour of its users. According to one of them, the corpus was used as a stimulus to enquiry and a source of supplementary evidence. As he puts it:

> The major function of the corpus... is to supply examples that represent language beyond that corpus...
> (Greenbaum 1988: 83)

'Beyond the corpus', let us note. In the grammar of Quirk and colleagues, primacy was clearly given to the possible, and not to the performed. The work of Biber and his colleagues, on the other hand, radically shifts this primacy to the performed. To quote from the introduction:

> The *LGSWE* adopts a corpus-based approach, which means that the grammatical descriptions are based on the patterns of structure and use found in a large collection of spoken and written texts, stored electronically, and searchable by computer.
> (Biber *et al.* 1999: 4)

In this case, it is not that the description is derived from the grammarian's knowledge and then checked against the data as a secondary source. The data represent the primary source.

Biber and his colleagues go on to say that their work:

> ...complements previous grammatical descriptions by investigating the linguistic patterns actually used by speakers and writers in the late twentieth century.
> (Biber *et al*. 1999: 4)

Although it is not made explicit who these speakers and writers actually are, we can reasonably infer that they are native speakers of the standard language, so the collection of texts upon which the description is based, though large, is also quite limited. It is by no means representative of *all* speakers and writers of English. On the contrary, most of them are likely not to be represented.

Biber *et al*. say that their grammatical description complements previous ones and in their introduction they specifically mention that of Quirk *et al*. and say that they have adopted its 'descriptive framework and terminology'. The complementation consists of providing quantitative information about the frequency of occurrence and co-occurrence of tokens of the types of grammatical category identified by the earlier grammar. The categories themselves remain in place. This is not, however, the way that other corpus linguists see it. Sinclair, for example, the most eminent of them, has taken a very different view, and has argued that the evidence which emerges from computer analyses does not 'merely give us a better documented description of the language' but indicates inadequacies in the categories of description themselves, that is to say, the categories of what is possible in the language. He says:

> The categories and methods we use to describe English are not appropriate to the new material. We shall need to overhaul our descriptive systems.
> (Sinclair 1985: 252)

The view here is not that corpus descriptions complement existing systems but conflict with them: new material calls for new categories, and the implication is that they are determined by what has been performed, actualized as overt language behaviour. In this view, you do not represent language beyond the corpus: the language is represented *by* the corpus. In reference to the Hymes scheme, the distinction between the first aspect and the fourth is in effect conflated: there is no category of the possible that is distinct from the performed and by supposing that there is, linguists and language teachers alike have misrepresented the nature of language, failing (through no fault of their own) to present real patterns of common occurrence, and presenting patterns of language which are unreal because they occur very rarely, if at all.

There is no doubt that computerized text analysis does reveal a vast amount of quantitative information, fact indeed, about the frequency of linguistic tokens, the recurrence and co-occurrence of words. It provides a detailed profile of what people do with the language. It is a fascinating revelation and its importance for linguistic description can hardly be exaggerated. Nevertheless, it is surely legitimate to ask just what it is that such analysis tells us about linguistic knowledge and what people do with it. What exactly is this 'vast amount of basic fact' about English that we have hitherto been ignorant of, and that corpus descriptions will now reveal?

I have already, in Chapter 1, had occasion to be sceptical about claims to factuality in linguistic matters, pointing out that what are often taken as matters of fact are frequently matters of perspective. The perspective of corpus linguists is that of the third person observer, not that of the first person experiencer of language. The only facts that they can deal with, therefore, are facts of observable behaviour, facts about the texts that language users have produced. As is often pointed out, these are not infrequently facts that the producers themselves are unaware of. And this is why corpus descriptions can always spring surprises and demonstrate that our intuitions about usage are wrong. But then it follows that what these descriptions represent is not insider first person reality as apprehended by language users but outsider third person reality, a construct of observation. One can readily accept that it is important to point out that people's beliefs about their behaviour do not correspond with what they actually do, but of course it is also a fact that they have these beliefs, and this calls for some explanation. Why then are intuitions so unreliable?

One explanation is that the textual data that corpus descriptions collect for analysis is never experienced *as such* by language users. As was pointed out in the preceding chapter, the textual product is the trace of a discourse process of contextualized interaction and it is this which constitutes reality for the language user. People do not set out to produce texts, and certainly not text fragments: they simply occur contingently as a by-product. So to isolate textual data from the contextual conditions of their production is necessarily to create an analytic construct which inevitably misrepresents language reality *as experienced by its users*. This is quite simply because users do not experience texts or textual fragments in contextual isolation. It is, then, no wonder that users have such unreliable intuitions about them. Biber *et al.* observe:

> Under natural circumstances, texts occur and are understood in their discourse settings, which comprise all of the linguistic, situational, social, psychological, and pragmatic factors that influence the interpretation of any instance of language use.
> (Biber *et al.* 1999: 4)

So when Biber *et al.* talk as they do about their grammar describing not only linguistic structures but their functional use, they are not referring to these factors which come into play in the discourse process, but only to the texts that result from the complex interaction of these factors. They are not talking about the use of language in natural circumstances, but about the unnatural analysis of one aspect of this use taken out of the contextual settings that make them pragmatically significant.[4]

To return to the Hymes scheme once more, what we get in his terms, therefore, is a description of performance or attestedness in dissociation from contextual appropriateness. One of the points that Hymes makes in proposing his scheme is that a description of the possible alone in terms of sentences is inadequate as an account of competence because language use does not involve the contextually unmotivated composition of sentences. But it does not involve the contextually unmotivated composition of texts either. Corpus linguistics, as we have seen, raises questions about the relationship between the possible and the performed (Hymes factors 1 and 4), but it also raises questions of the relationship between the performed and the appropriate (Hymes 4 and 3) which also need to be addressed.

So I would argue that although corpus descriptions do indeed yield a vast amount of fascinating facts, they are limited to one aspect of language use. They do not include the discourse factors that Biber *et al.* refer to. This, I would suppose, is bound to set some limits on their descriptive claims to capture reality. It also sets limits on their pedagogic relevance as a basis for defining the content of language courses. I will return to this matter in the next chapter, but meanwhile there is another issue concerning the relationship between the possible and the performed that calls for comment.

In the Hymes scheme, what is possible has to do with what people know of their language, and this is not directly observable. In contrast, what is performed, what people do with their knowledge, obviously is directly observable. In this respect, E-language linguists, dealing as they do with the actually performed data of language behaviour, are on much safer ground. But the question arises as to how far these data are reliable evidence of knowledge.

As far as Chomsky is concerned, they are not reliable at all:

> I see no reason to deny...that behaviour is only one kind of evidence, sometimes not the best, and surely no criterion for knowledge.
> (Chomsky 1980: 54)

So where, one might ask, is evidence to be found? One answer is: in the mind of the linguist, and made available by introspection. But then, of course, you have to assume that the linguists' intuitions are reliable as typical indicators of common knowledge, that is to say that they can draw on their own competence as representative members of the speech community whose language they are describing. The difficulty is, of course, that, as was pointed out in Chapter 1, they are also members of another community, namely the community of linguists with all its disciplinary subculture of different and incompatible attitudes and values—and this disqualifies them as representative informants.

But intuitive introspection is not the only way of gaining access to knowledge directly. Another is elicitation, which seeks to tap the knowledge of speakers of the language who, it is assumed, are more reliable informants in that they are innocent of any analytic intent. So what does elicitation reveal about insider knowledge and how does this correspond with the observations recorded by corpus descriptions?

Elicitations can be of three kinds. One, which we might call *co-textual elicitation*, focuses on the performed. It would involve finding out how far informants could, suitably prompted, provide information about the occurrence and co-occurrence of words in texts. It would seek to establish the extent to which this textual patterning is indeed inaccessible to intuition. This, though an interesting question, is not our present concern. A second kind is what we might call *contextual elicitation*. Here informants are given a context of some kind and asked what language they would normally produce in the circumstances. This clearly has to do with their knowledge not of the possible but of the appropriate in the Hymes scheme and, again, does not bear on the point at issue we are at present concerned with. The third kind of elicitation does. This is what we can refer to as *conceptual elicitation*. This sets out to reveal how linguistic encodings are mentally organized, how the possible is represented in the mind.

One of the best known examples of conceptual elicitation in this sense is that carried out by Rosch (Rosch 1975; Aitchison 1994: Chapter 5). It is particularly appropriate to the present discussion because it relates to work done in language pedagogy and this will take us back to our central concern about the relationship between description and prescription. What Rosch did was to give subjects a verbal prompt so as to elicit from them the word which sprang most immediately to mind as an example of a particular category. These categories were, in the terms of lexical semantics, superordinate terms (for example, 'vegetable' or 'vehicle'), and the subjects were asked to identify a particular hyponymous word (for example, 'turnip' or 'train') as having some marked mental prominence for them. Lexical analysis in terms of sense relations treats all such words as equal co-hyponyms. It turns out that with cognitive representations, however, some hyponyms are more equal than others. With remarkable consistency, subjects homed in on one hyponym as in some sense representative of the category. This Rosch refers to as the prototype word. Thus, for this group of subjects, the prototypical hyponym for 'bird' was 'robin', for 'vegetable' was 'pea', and so on.[5]

There is an obvious explanation for such findings. When prompted by the word 'vegetable' the word 'pea' comes more readily to mind, rather than, say, 'asparagus' or 'artichoke' because these two words co-occur more frequently in use, or quite simply because 'pea' is generally a more common word than the others. But the obvious explanation does not seem to be tenable. For if this were so, then the prototype word would be directly identifiable from its frequency profile in computer printouts. But it turns out that this is not the case and that prototypical prominence in the mind does not accord with frequency of actual occurrence. The word 'cauliflower', for example, has a higher prototype score than the word 'potato' and in the clothing category 'bathing suit' is more prominent than 'shoe'; but these differences in cognitive representation do not correspond with measures of textual frequency. So it would appear that the mental lexicon is a representation of knowledge, a kind of linguistic knowing, that accords neither with the formal semantic categories of the possible as described by I-Language linguists, nor the patterns of actual textual occurrence as described by corpus linguists.

Prototypical prominence could in fact be considered as one criterion for the identification of what has been called nuclear or core vocabulary (Stubbs 1986; Carter 1987), and therefore to have particular relevance to language pedagogy. Before pursuing this further, there is another point worth pondering. The notion of the prototype relates to lexis, but can it also be applied to grammar? Can we also talk about prototype sentences as well as words? Synonymous with 'nucleus' and 'core' is the word 'kernel' and this word, for anyone acquainted with linguistics, has its own reverberant associations: the kernel sentence. This figured prominently in the early days of generative grammar. It was the elementary syntactic unit generated from phrase structure rules before transformations were applied to bring about structural change ('time passes', 'the dogs attacked the intruder', etc.). It was a central concept in that model of description. With subsequent developments in generative grammar, it disappeared. Chomsky despatched it summarily in 1965, but he seemed to do so with some regret. This is what he says:

> The notion 'kernel sentence' has, I think, an important intuitive significance, but since kernel sentences play no distinctive role in the generation or interpretation of sentences, I shall say nothing more about them here. (Chomsky 1965: 18)

And nothing more is said about them elsewhere either as far as I know. But this begs a tantalizing question. If these kernel sentences have such an important intuitive significance, then why is their importance not reflected in grammatical description? Here, too, it seems, we have a case of something that a community somehow knows about its language which is not reflected in a formal model of language, at least not that proposed by Chomsky. But if these simple sentences do not have any distinctive role in the grammar, then what role do they have? The answer is, surely, that they have a role in the mind, an intuitive role indeed. They are prototype sentences which elude description in much the same way as prototype words do. They cannot be accounted for in analytic models of syntactic structure (on Chomsky's own admission) any more than prototype words can be accounted for in analytic models of lexical structure.

But, like prototype words, not only do they not figure in descriptions of the possible, they do not figure in descriptions of the performed either. Even the most cursory glance at a concordance display will reveal that they hardly ever occur. Where they do figure, however, is in descriptive grammars of the kind exemplified by Quirk *et al.* (1985), which is not surprising since they are based not on observed behaviour but on intuitive knowledge. To that extent, we can can say that such grammars reflect a psychological reality that corpus-based grammars do not.

And such sentences also figure very prominently, of course, in pedagogic prescriptions of language. They are the traditional stock-in-trade of language teaching. Teachers may have been labouring under a descriptive delusion, in ignorance of certain basic facts about actual usage, but they seem to have grasped the intuitive significance of the kernel sentence. Or have they? What is its role in language teaching after all? What is the relevance of the notion of prototypicality more generally? We come now to the question of how all these descriptive matters bear on the issue of what language may be selected as appropriate for the language subject.

We need to note, to begin with, that the notion of the lexical prototype has in some respects been anticipated in work directly concerned with the peda-gogic prescription of language. I refer here to the concept of *disponibilité*, or availability of words. This was proposed thirty-five years ago in the pioneer research which led to the specification of the core or nuclear language to be included in *Le Français Fondamental* (Gougenheim *et al.* 1964). The research involved the analysis of actually occurring data and this revealed certain frequencies, in the same way as does modern corpus analysis, although necessarily without the finesse that modern technology can now provide. At the same time, it was recognized that there was something real to be accounted for which was not actual in the data. French people had a knowledge of words which they did not necessarily act upon in their behav-iour: words which the researchers themselves felt, intuitively, they ought to include in spite of their poor showing in performance. To quote from the description of the research that appears in Halliday *et al.* (1964):

> There remained the problem of words absent from the list which were nevertheless intuitively felt to be necessary. Two of the names of days of the week, for example, *mercredi* and *vendredi*, failed to appear in the texts, yet that could hardly justify their omission from a basic teaching vocabulary. The biggest single group of words that seemed to the researchers to be inadequately represented in the lists was the category of abstract nouns. French people obviously knew a great many words of this kind and there-fore had them available for use, but it seemed that they might not use any particular noun very frequently.
> (Halliday *et al.* 1964: 194)

The researchers therefore then carried out an exercise in conceptual elicit-ation, not dissimilar from that conducted by Rosch. They identified a number of categories: clothing, furniture, animals, occupations, and so on, and elicited responses by questionnaire from thousands of schoolchildren all over France as to which common everyday nouns they thought it would be most useful to know in respect to such topics. To quote Halliday and his colleagues again:

> Under the heading of 'furniture', for example, *table* was universally given, but *vitrine* was rather rare. The quality of being mentioned by a high proportion of those answering the questionnaire for a given topic was termed *disponibilité*, which might be translated as 'availability'; thus the word *table* is more *disponible* as a word relating to furniture than is *vitrine*. (Halliday *et al*. 1964: 195)

The parallels with the Rosch research are obvious. Just as the word *table* is more readily available in the French mind than the word *vitrine* so, for Rosch's group of English-speaking informants, 'pea' and 'robin' come more readily to mind than 'asparagus' and 'ostrich'. In both cases we have cognitive representations which emerge from elicitation but which may not show up in the frequency profiles of actual occurrence. But there is a difference.

The research of Rosch reveals something of the mental lexicon of a group of speakers of a particular speech community. The prototype is a descriptive category of member competence which lurks in the mind beyond immediate awareness. The French research did not elicit user response in the same way. It asked its subjects to make a conscious judgement about words which it would be most useful to know. So availability or *disponibilité* is a *prescriptive* criterion and not a *descriptive* category. Words were identified as *disponible* not because of their frequency of use but because of their usefulness as determined by the informants. But these informants, let us note, were not adult users of the language, but children. And the reason for this was that the research was carried out with the explicit prescriptive purpose of specifying the language for a course expressly designed for children. The assumption was that what was most available in the minds of French children would be an index of what children learning French would need to know. One might question this assumption, but the crucial point is that in the case of Gougenheim and his colleagues, pedagogic appropriacy was a crucial consideration that determined the design of their research. This is not so, of course, with Rosch, and not so with corpus descriptions. Here pedagogic relevance is something that needs to be subsequently inferred. This is a matter I will take up in more detail in the next chapter.

As far as the present chapter is concerned, what I have tried to show is that all linguistic descriptions are necessarily limited. Although it is important to acknowledge that corpus descriptions capture a linguistic reality that others do not, it needs also to be recognized, I think, that the reality they represent is in fact only partial. What they account for is one aspect of language behaviour, namely the texts that language users produce, what, in Hymes' terms is actually attested or performed. This is an impressive achievement in that it reveals patterns of frequency and co-occurrence which are not intuitively apparent, either to user or analyst. The computer analysis of text provides detailed information about the co-textual relations of words in use: how they relate lexically in collocation, and how they relate to particular grammatical features in colligation.[6] Here indeed we have, as Sinclair says, 'a vast amount of basic fact'. But it is basic fact about text, not about discourse. It does not, of itself, reveal facts about the pragmatic aspect of behaviour, how people use language appropriate to context to achieve a particular reference, force, or effect. You cannot read off pragmatic intention or interpretation from a concordance display. You can, of course, speculate about the discourse that gives rise to textual features, and you can follow up hunches by tracing words back to their original source in the texts from which they came (if they are open to access). But these are intuitive inferences, not analytic facts. Of course, computer analyses may encourage an enquiry into pragmatic use, but this can only be because they do not themselves reveal it: their findings only prompt you to find it out for yourself. The facts that a computer program displays are at two removes from the reality of language behaviour as experienced by its users: the analysis into frequencies and concordance regularities is at one remove from the texts from which they derive and the texts are themselves at a remove from the contextual conditions which motivated their production in the first place.

Corpus descriptions are also limited, I have argued, in that there are aspects of linguistic knowledge that they do not adequately account for. It is true, of course, that the patterns of text that they describe are projections of user competence in the sense that if users did not know how to produce them intuitively they would not be there to describe. But these productions do not exhaust the possible. People have more knowledge of their language than they actually realize in a different sense: they know more than is given expression in their overt behaviour. There are, for example, innumerable instances of words which are no longer current, and so do not figure in the data, but which users are capable of understanding, so the present frequency of a word is not a measure of receptive knowledge. Furthermore, as we have seen, this frequency does not either reflect prototypicality, the relative cognitive salience of words and structures. And finally, of course, since corpus descriptions can only deal with attested instances of encodings, and focus attention on normal usage as measured by frequency and regularity of occurrence, they cannot capture what I have referred to as the virtual language, a knowledge of which must be presupposed since not otherwise could the language be put to innovative use. In short, linguistic descriptions based on introspection give an account of the possible in dissociation from the performed; and descriptions based on observation give an account of the performed in dissociation from the possible. In both cases, what is not adequately accounted for is what is appropriate to the context and what is potential in the code.

To say that linguistic descriptions are partial in these respects is not to criticize them as such but only to recognize their necessary limitations. They do not capture the reality of language in its entirety, but only aspects of it. Nor should we expect otherwise. It is only when claims are made that they do capture reality that questions need to be raised. And in the context of the present argument, this is particularly the case when the further claim is made that these descriptions of 'real' language necessarily provide prescriptions for the content specification of the language subject. In the next chapter I consider this last claim more closely.

Notes and comments

1 It is not always clear, however, just which model of linguistic description is being used to take pedagogic bearings from. In their compilation of readings on the communicative approach to language teaching (CLT), Brumfit and Johnson provide extracts from Hymes and Halliday as constituting 'the linguistic background' to the approach (Brumfit and Johnson 1979). We need to note, however, that although both of these scholars reject a formalist view of language in favour of one which focuses attention on the communicative functioning of forms in the expression of meaning, their conceptualizations of function are very different. In Halliday, function refers to what he calls 'the meaning potential' that has been semantically incorporated into the language code. He is concerned with how functions are signified in different encoding options in the grammar of a language. Hymes, on the other hand, as is clear from the discussion later in this chapter, is concerned with pragmatic function, how this potential gets variously realized in contexts of use. This distinction, crucial though it is, has seldom been drawn explicitly in the literature on CLT, and a good deal of confusion has resulted in consequence. Thus, the distinctive feature of CLT was, and still is, said to be that in its concern for communicative function, it focuses on meaning *rather than* on form, and this in some quarters was taken to justify a disregard of grammar. Here it would seem to be Hymes' notion of pragmatic function that is intended. But such a view runs directly counter to Halliday's concept of function where there can be no such disjunction since it has to do with semantically encoded meaning *in form*. This concept of function would lead to a renewed emphasis on grammar, not to its neglect.

There is a similar confusion in the way proposals for a so-called 'notional syllabus' have been interpreted. In its original formulation in Wilkins (1976, 1979), such a syllabus consists of two sets of notional categories. The first are 'semantico-grammatical categories' which include the kind of functions which would be accounted for in a Hallidaian functional grammar. These, as the name indicates, have to do with the signifying of semantic meaning. The second set are 'categories of communicative function' and these are pragmatic in nature, and have to do with functions in the Hymes sense, the contextually appropriate use of language in the performance of communicative activities of one kind or another. Since there are two kinds of communicative content in such syl-labuses, they have often been referred to as 'notional/functional' rather than just 'notional'. In practice, the tendency has been to focus attention on the pragmatic categories as having greater novelty value (the other set bore an obvious resemblance to what teachers were teaching anyway). But what needs to be recognized is that both sets of category are functional, but in different ways, and that the crucial question, in both linguistic descrip-tion and pedagogic prescription, is how the two kinds of function, the semantically encoded and the pragmatically realized, are to be meaning-fully related. I explore how this relationship might be dealt with peda-gogically in Chapter 9. Further discussion of Hymes' account of communicative competence, and how it relates to Halliday's functional grammar is taken up again in Chapter 12.

2 The following can be taken as a representative statement of the linguistic equality principle:

> Every grammar is equally complex and logical and capable of producing an infinite set of sentences to express any thought one might wish to express. If something can be expressed in one language or one dialect, it can be expressed in any other language or dialect. You might use differ-ent means and different words, but it can be expressed. No grammar, therefore no language, is either superior or inferior to any other.
> (Fromkin and Rodman 1998: 14–15)

Two points need to be made about this assertion. One is that it is an expres-sion of belief and not an empirical finding. It is indeed hard to see how one would set about establishing equality of complexity, or the equivalence of expressions across languages. Secondly what empirical evidence we do have from language users rather than language analysts suggests that on the contrary languages are not perceived as equal and expressions in one are not equivalent to expressions in another. One imagines that Lady Bracknell for one would take issue with Fromkin and Rodman on this point:

> French songs I cannot possibly allow. People always seem to think they are improper, and either look shocked, which is vulgar, or laugh, which is worse. But German sounds a thoroughly respectable language, and indeed, I believe is so.
> (Oscar Wilde: *The Importance of Being Earnest*, Act 1)

Lady Bracknell, one might object, is hardly a reliable authority on the mat-ter. But the point is that when it comes to the expression of attitude and the making of value judgements about languages there is no reliable authority. And Lady Bracknell is by no means an isolated example. As Cameron (1995) shows what 'ordinary' lay people think about language is very much at odds with the pronouncements of linguists and, as she argues, needs to be taken into account and not summarily dismissed.

For a similar view of the significance of folklinguistic notions about language see Preston 1991, 1998. The second of these references bears the title: 'Why we need to know what real people think about language'. With regard to the points raised about applied linguistics in Chapter 1, the reason why we need to know this, of course, is that we cannot otherwise engage in mediation. In the first of the papers referred to here, Preston talks about folk ideas about language learning, and concludes:

> What people believe about how they learn, how difficult the target of their learning is, what special talents they have (or lack) for learning, what social outcomes await them, and the host of other matters that only an empirically designed folk-linguistic investigation can lay bare is surely an important matter for applied linguistics. Teacher trainers, national and local curriculum developers, materials developers, and classroom practitioners will surely fare better with knowledge of the speech community's understanding of the language learning process. And as it is with most scientific matters, it is better to find out what those understandings are than to imagine them.
> (Preston 1991: 601)

3 These three aspects of meaning, though particularly associated with speech act theory (as formulated in Austin 1962; Searle 1969) have, as I argue elsewhere (Widdowson 1984, 1990), a more general pragmatic relevance. Reference has to do with the *propositional* meaning that is achieved, what is being talked about in a particular instance of language use, and force has to do with *illocutionary* meaning, what communicative act is performed in making the reference. Thus in talking to you, I might make reference to a particular future state of affairs intending this to have the force of a threat. The (perlocutionary) effect of this might be to frighten you, amuse you, make you angry, call the police, and so on.

4 The lack of concern for the contextual settings and pragmatic significance of the textual facts is evident from the way all the varied domains of language use that provide the textual data are grouped into just four 'registers'. Thus all instances of spoken interaction, whatever the relationship between interlocutors, on whatever topic, in whatever setting, are conflated into the category of conversation. Similarly, everything that appears in a newspaper, from the editorial to the financial pages to the sports reports is all described without differentiation as 'newspaper language'.

5 It should be noted, however, that prototypical values will differ across different discourse communities. Although 'robin' was elicited as the prototype bird from Rosch's group of subjects, for a different group of English speakers it could be 'sparrow' or 'seagull'. So it is not that a particular word is prototypical in a particular language but among a particular group of

language users. One might make the point that there is a similar variation in the textual patterning that corpus analysis can reveal in the genres of different discourse communities (see Note 1, Chapter 6). In this sense, prototypes can be understood as the conceptual equivalent of the co-textual key words that typify the texture of different kinds of discourse. Thus discourse communities might be defined by the patterns of lexical knowledge that can be elicited in the Rosch manner or by patterns of lexical occurrence that can be observed in the texts they produce.

6 I have drawn quite a stark distinction in this chapter between the internal co-textual patterning of language and the external contextual relations it contracts in pragmatic use. But it is an open and intriguing question as to whether some implicational link cannot be established between them. The more specific and precise the corpus analysis of particular genres becomes, the more likely it would appear to be that correspondences can be identified between them, so that pragmatic significance can be inferred from particular kinds of co-textual patterning. (See Hoey 2001; Stubbs 1996.) Certainly it would seem that in certain very restricted genres, of the kind discussed in Cameron (2000) (see Note 3, Chapter 6), co-textual patterning and contextual use are more or less mutually predictive. The question is how far this kind of correspondence can be established in genres of a less restricted kind.

8 The appropriate language for learning

In Chapter 6, I argued that, in a sense, all uses of language are specific in that they are designed to key into a particular context of shared knowledge and assumption. In Chapter 7, I sought to demonstrate that descriptions of language, even those that focus on E-language and claim to capture the reality of language use, do not, and cannot of their nature, account for this contextual specificity. To use a distinction that I made many years ago (Widdowson 1979), what we get from such descriptions are facts about *genuine* texts as attested products of use, but not about the *authentic* discourses which give rise to them, for these depend on the specific ways in which language is made communicatively appropriate to context.

It seems reasonable to suppose that the limitations of linguistic description will have some bearing on their applicability to the prescription of pedagogic objectives for the language subject, and should cause us to call into question the assumption that prescription is necessarily determined by description, which, as I pointed out in the last chapter, has traditionally been taken as self-evident.

This assumption of determination is implied, I suggested, in the slogan 'Helping the learner with *real* English' in that it combines two claims. The first is one that we have been examining in some detail in the previous discussion, namely that these descriptions are indeed of real English. The second we have touched on in passing, but now needs to be given more critical attention, namely that the 'real English' so described is helpful to learners.

In the last chapter, I interpreted this claim as having to do with the specification of what should be prescribed as content for learners to learn. But there is another way of reading it: it could mean that when learners come across real English, such descriptions will help them to cope with it. On this interpretation, this is a *descriptive* claim, and as such seems quite valid: as an account of the properties of actually attested text, they can clearly serve as an invaluable source of reference. In this respect, what COBUILD and other corpus-based descriptions have done is a massive achievement which deserves recognition: there is no doubt that it represents a very important development in the description of English. What is at issue is the claim made on the other interpretation, namely that this real English will help the learner to learn the language. This is a *pedagogic* claim, and the fact that the descriptions have given rise to a whole range of teaching materials suggests that this is the meaning that is intended. The descriptive claim carries no implication for the definition of English as a subject. The pedagogic claim clearly does. And Sinclair, the pioneering inspiration behind the COBUILD enterprise, has himself made it quite clear that he believes that the subject should be reformulated in the light of descriptive findings. There are, he tells us, three clear messages that emerge from corpus-based descriptions of English, two of which we have already had occasion to comment on. The first reads as follows:

> The categories and methods we use to describe English are not appropriate to the new material. We shall need to overhaul our descriptive systems.
> (Sinclair 1985: 252)

What is at issue here is the extent to which descriptive systems should be based on the observation of attested usage rather than on introspection and elicitation, the traditional sources of linguistic data. This, as was discussed in the last chapter, has to do with principles of linguistic description, and has no bearing on language pedagogy as such. The other two messages, on the other hand, decidedly do:

> We are teaching English in ignorance of a vast amount of basic fact. This is not our fault, but it should not inhibit the absorption of new material.
> (Sinclair 1985: 252)

The implication here is that the subject English is misconceived unless it absorbs the newly revealed facts about English as it is actually used: the subject is, in effect, subject to linguistic description. Here we have an assertion of the traditional assumption of determination. The third of Sinclair's messages is a more explicit formulation of the second:

> Since our view of the language will change profoundly, we must expect substantial influence on the specification of syllabuses, design of materials and choice of method.
> (Sinclair 1985: 252)

As we have seen, there is no doubt that corpus descriptions do reveal new facts about the object language—facts about usage which we have hitherto been in ignorance of, and it would be foolish, not to say unprofessional, of teachers to ignore them. There is no doubt either that what corpus linguistics has revealed does provide a new perspective on language, which has implications for principles of linguistic description which, in turn, may well have implications for how we conceive of the subject. There must, obviously, be *some* relationship between the language subject we teach and the object language people actually use, but, as I have argued elsewhere (Widdowson 1991, 2000a, 2000b) it cannot be one of direct determination. It is a relationship that has to be mediated.

As has already been noted in Chapter 1, Sinclair is sceptical of the idea of mediation. For him descriptive facts, it would appear, have a direct and determinate relevance to pedagogy. Thus he has proposed a number of precepts for language teachers to follow, the first of which is:

Present real examples only.

Where do such precepts come from? They are directly derived from corpus analysis. Sinclair himself says:

> The precepts centre on data, and arise from observations about the nature of language. They are not concerned with psychological or pedagogical approaches to language teaching.
> (Sinclair 1997: 30)

It seems reasonable to ask, however, how one can have precepts for teaching which are *not* concerned with pedagogical approaches; though disclaiming any concern with pedagogy, Sinclair nevertheless pronounces a pedagogic precept. Unlike Sir Thomas More (referred to at the end of Chapter 1) he is not just pointing out what the linguistic findings are, but recommending that they should be the exclusive source of examples for language teaching. My view would be that such findings need to be pointed out, but that we also need to address the critical question of their pedagogic relevance. For Sinclair, it would seem, to raise a question of this kind is to encourage teachers to remain ignorant of linguistic facts revealed by corpus descriptions, and so 'endorse their complacency', as he puts it (Sinclair 1997: 30). The innovation of this development in linguistic description is thus tied to the ingrained traditional assumption of necessary determination: the content of the language subject must conform to what is described by linguists.

'Present real examples'. We have already discussed the nature of this reality. But what constitutes an example and how is it to be presented? According to McCarthy it is not a matter of simply 'dumping large loads of corpus material wholesale into the classroom' (McCarthy 2001: 129). This is obvious enough. But what, then, is it a matter of? If not large loads, then perhaps small loads? If not wholesale, then what processes are involved in retailing this material? Such questions inevitably bring pedagogic factors into consideration. So what are these factors?[1]

We might approach these questions by considering in some detail what kinds of problem learners are likely to encounter when presented with an example of 'real' language. Take the following text.

IT TAKES BOTTLE TO CROSS CHANNEL
Bibbing tipplers who booze-cruise across the Channel in search of revelry and wassail could be in for a rough ride. Itchy-footed quaffers and pre-Christmas holiday-makers are being warned not to travel to France, where

widespread disruption continues despite the lifting of the blockade on trapped British lorry drivers.
(*The Guardian* 30.11.95)

Here we have a genuine text taken from a British daily paper: a real example of English in use. What pedagogic considerations might come into play in presenting such a text to a class of students—let us say as an exercise in reading comprehension for fairly advanced learners who have already had several years of formal instruction in the language? We might note, to begin with, that certain expressions are likely to cause difficulties. The headline, which readers might reasonably expect would key them into the content of the passage, creates its own problem of interpretation. What are learners to make of the phrase 'It takes bottle'? If they are familiar with the common convention in headlines that articles are omitted, they might deduce that 'bottle' is an instance of the familiar count noun, in which case they will look for something in the text that 'it' can refer to. *What* takes a bottle? Since there is no cataphoric candidate in the text, students might then take an alternative tack and assume that 'bottle' is in fact an uncountable noun and as such has a meaning they are unfamiliar with. Reference to a dictionary would confirm the assumption. If the one they consult is the *COBUILD Dictionary* they will find among all the meanings of the countable noun the following entry for an uncountable noun:

> In British English, **bottle** is used to refer to courage or boldness; an informal use. *But will anybody have the bottle to go through with it?*

Thus enlightened, the learners can now make sense of the headline: it takes courage to cross the Channel. On, then, to the passage proper. 'Bibbing tipplers who booze-cruise.' Back to the dictionary. The word 'bib', they discover, exists only as a noun, and denotes a piece of cloth or plastic that is put under a baby's chin to protect its clothes from getting soiled when it is being fed. That is not very helpful. On, then, to the next word. The noun 'tippler' does not appear in the dictionary. A tippler is presumably someone who tipples, so they might then look up the verb 'tipple'. But that is not there either, though the noun 'tipple' is:

> In British English, a person's tipple is the alcoholic drink that they usually drink; an informal use.

The learners might then infer from this that tipplers are persons indulging in their habitual alcoholic drink.

On then to the next word. The verb 'booze-cruise' does not figure, as noun or verb, in this dictionary, though the word 'booze', noun and verb, does. So by now our learners are beginning perhaps to get some sense of who these people are that are being referred to here. They read on. 'Revelry' poses no problem: if they do not already know the word, it figures in the dictionary. They then encounter 'wassail', which does not. And they have yet to negotiate 'rough ride' before they get to the end of the first sentence, let alone 'itchy-footed quaffers' which begins the second.

It is clear, then, that this text would pose a number of problems, even for quite advanced learners of English, in that it uses language they do not know, and in some cases cannot even find out about by recourse to a dictionary, even the one which claims to help them with real English. Of course one might argue that readers do not normally process text in this analytic way by fixating on particular words but rather pass lightly over the occasional obscurity. This is true. But language learners, only too aware that they are learning the language, are seldom encouraged to be so cavalier, and anyway it depends of course on how occasional the obscurity is. In the present case it would be densely present for many a student reader, and there would be little that is not obscure for them to take bearings from. The difficulties that I have demonstrated arise from a lack of lexical knowledge, but of words, let us note, that are uncommon or quaintly archaic. Some (for example, 'wassail') would not appear in a dictionary devoted only to the description of current English for precisely that reason, and others that do (for example, 'tippler', 'quaff') would be assigned low priority for learning on the grounds of extreme infrequency. The problem here is that there is no knowing when an archaic word might crop up in a contemporary text, and texts do not consist only of high frequency words. As has already been pointed out in Chapter 6, texts are designed for particular communities of expert users of the language and rely not only on a knowledge of what commonly occurs but also of what rarely occurs, or may indeed not occur in conventional usage at all, but is available in absentia as part of the expert users' knowledge of the language.[2]

It may well be, furthermore, that these abstruse words are crucial to the interpretation of a text. The very fact of frequency makes commonly occurring words less communicatively salient. They play a supporting role. The more significant words are likely to be the *infrequent* ones. So in this text, for example, it is these quaint uncommon words which carry the most pragmatic weight, precisely because they *are* uncommon.[3] Furthermore, in this case, they are weighty because they are loaded with affective meaning. Consider what it is that makes the language real for the readers for whom this text was written. In part, of course, it is that it makes connection with a familiar frame of reference. As with the Chamberlain text that was discussed in Chapter 6, the writer is making assumptions that the reader will already know about certain current affairs, like the French blockade of lorry drivers, but will also be familiar with the fact that it is common practice for certain sectors of the British community to go across the Channel to France to buy cheap alcohol and revel in riotous heavy drinking on the way home. But that, as we noted with the Chamberlain text, is only part of the story. The writer is not only assuming that the readers are in the know about what the words refer to, but that they will also recognize, and respond to, what the words imply. And this, of course, is where affective meaning comes in. Here it is the very infrequency of expressions like 'bibbing tipplers', 'booze-cruise', 'wassail', and 'quaffers' that attracts attention, and carries the weight of affective significance, and it is the realization of this significance that makes the text real for the readers for whom it was designed. They recognize the irony, and that they are being invited to share an attitude of amused contempt. This is *knowing* language, and its use is essentially conspiratorial. You cannot join the conspiracy, of course, unless you are in the know about what the use of these infrequent words implies, what *effect* they are meant to have. So even with the information that 'tipple' (and presumably 'tippler' as well) is an informal word, you cannot infer from this what attitude is expressed in using it. Similarly, if you look up the word 'quaff', you will be told that it is an old-fashioned word for drinking alcohol, so you can infer that a 'quaffer' is a drinker. But this will give you no clue as to why the writer is using such an old-fashioned word, or what effect this would have on the readers for whom this text is written. If you are not in the know, much of the significance of this passage of real English will be lost on you.

People make a text real by realizing it as discourse, that is to say by relating it to specific contexts of communal cultural values and attitudes. And this reality does not travel with the text. So although this is a real example of actually occurring text, learners will be unable to ratify it as an example of discourse if, as outsiders, they are not privy to the contextual conditions upon which the discourse realization depends. Even if they could track down the meanings of all the unknown words in their dictionaries, they are still unlikely to realize the effect of the pragmatic use of these words, which makes the text real for the discourse community for which it was designed.

Of course one can argue that the very problems that learners encounter are an indication of what they have still to learn to function successfully in the language they are learning. In this case, the text can serve as an example of the kind of language use that learners will eventually need to engage with. As such, we might argue, it might indeed be taken as representing the kind of objective we need to specify for the language subject. If this is the kind of language that learners will have to deal with, then this, surely, is the kind of language that a course should set its sights on.

But this line of argument raises a number of problems. It is clear from our discussion of the difficulties of this text that getting students to engage with it as discourse would involve developing in them a familiarity with a forbidding complexity of sociocultural knowledge, all the more complex, and forbidding, because of the very specific way in which texts key into contextual factors. And of course one would need to be confident that one knows in advance what discourse communities particular groups of learners are bidding to join, or at least likely to encounter, when they have completed their course. I will return to such problems later.

But even if we accept, for the sake of the present argument, that a text of this kind can serve as reference for setting the purpose parameter, it does not follow, of course, that it is appropriate to the process of learning. This, presumably, is why one does not simply dump what McCarthy calls 'corpus material' into the classroom. Even accepting that learners will need to gradually approximate to the kind of competence which would enable them to cope with a text of this kind, we still need to address the question of how this process of gradual approximation is to be induced. We need to take pedagogic decisions as to what kind of language data will be most conducive to the activation of learning, and at what stage, and in what manner, 'real' texts (and what kind of 'real' texts) can be most effectively introduced.

So far I have been focusing on the problems that arise in making sense of this particular text. But language data are not presented in class only for students to make sense of, but also, crucially, to learn *from*. The somewhat paradoxical situation arises that the words which the students need to focus on as posing the greatest problem for understanding are those which are likely to constitute the least valuable investment for learning. So the expense of effort in finding out the meaning of such rare and archaic words like 'bibbing', 'tipplers', 'wassail', and 'quaff', can be considered wasteful on two counts. In the first place, it may still leave learners at a loss about the significance of their use in this particular text, and in the second place, it does not provide them with linguistic knowledge that they can put to subsequent use. Even in the unlikely event of their ever needing to use such words, dictionaries give them very little guidance as to when it would be appropriate to do so, and what their effect would be. In short, for many students, the very 'reality' of this text may make it virtually useless as language to learn from.

It can be objected, of course, that teachers are unlikely to introduce students to texts of this kind about booze-cruising, itchy-footed bibbers, and wassail, but would have a care to select more appropriate ones. No doubt this is true. But then we return to the pedagogic question that my discussion of this particular text is meant to raise, namely what is it about a text if not its authenticity that makes it appropriate for learners, or what needs to be done to a text to make it appropriate.

It might also be objected that the text we have been examining is not the kind of real example that Sinclair has in mind. It is unquestionably 'corpus material', to use McCarthy's phrase, in the sense that as an actually occurring instance of contemporary use it would be eligible for inclusion in a corpus. But perhaps what is meant here is not corpus material as such but the findings that emerge from its analysis, as might, for example, be displayed in a concordance. And perhaps that, too, is what Sinclair means by an example. Another of the precepts that he proposes would seem to bear this out. It reads:

Inspect contexts.

We have, of course, been doing just this with the text we have been discussing, trying to reconstitute the contextual conditions which would enable the reader to make pragmatic sense of it as discourse. But this is not what Sinclair means by context. He goes on to say:

> Strictly speaking, I should write 'inspect co-texts', because 'context' often has a wider meaning than the surrounding text . . . I would advocate a much closer inspection of the verbal environment of a word or phrase than is usual in language teaching. A great deal is to be learned from this exercise.
> (Sinclair 1997: 34)

As we have seen, it is context in its wider meaning that is relevant to discourse reality. Co-text is a matter of verbal environment, the way words and phrases combine in the surrounding text. It seems clear that the reality of the examples that Sinclair proposes in his first precept has to do with their co-textual and not their contextual relations. They therefore, as I have argued, exemplify real language in only a limited sense. Nevertheless there is no doubt that the inspection of co-textual relations does indeed, as has already been recognized, reveal facts about recurrent patterns of collocation and colligation in texts beyond the bounds of intuitive awareness. Such recurrent regularities can be discovered precisely because of the capacity of computer programs to inspect verbal environments in vast amounts of text. What humans do is to inspect the inspection, so to speak, by consulting the results of the analysis as displayed in concordances and so on, and this, presumably, is what Sinclair means. Our inspecting co-texts in the primary data for ourselves would reveal little or nothing of regular patterns. Our inspecting the data processed by program *analysis* reveals a great deal.

The examples Sinclair has in mind, then, would be selections from the display of findings that computer analysis provides. The question is what help *they* give to the learner.

The most striking innovation introduced by the *COBUILD Dictionary* was in its provision of examples of this kind, and other dictionaries have been quick to follow suit. Let us now consider what contribution they make to the learning process. We will suppose for the sake of argument that the word 'quaff' in our sample text is one which, for some reason, is worth the effort of students to learn. They turn to a dictionary for information about its meaning. What do they find? Here are some examples:

> **quaff** (*obj*) *v* to drink (something) quickly or in large amounts. °*In Shakespeare's play 'King Henry IV', Falstaff and Bardolph are often seen quaffing in the Boar's Head Tavern. [I]* °*He's always quaffing these strange herbal medicines, which he thinks will make him more healthy.*[T]
> (*Cambridge International Dictionary of English* (*CIDE*) 1995)

> **quaff** (v[Tn]) (*dated or rhet*) drink (sth) by swallowing large amounts at a time, not taking small sips: *quaffing his beer by the pint.*
> (*Oxford Advanced Learner's Dictionary* (*OALD*) 1989)

quaff If you quaff an alcoholic drink, you drink a lot of it in a short space of time; an old-fashioned word. *By the time he had quaffed his third, he was winking playfully at a plump woman who sat across from him.* (*COBUILD Dictionary* 1995)

The entries provide learners with two quite different kinds of information about the word. The first kind has to do with what is semantically encoded as possible in the Hymes scheme and takes the form of a definition. This has traditionally been couched in metalinguistic form, as in the *CIDE* and *OALD* entries. (Another of the *COBUILD* innovations is that the definition here is expressed in natural language form, but it still, of course, serves the same metalinguistic function.) The second kind of information is about the word's co-textual occurrence and this is where the real example comes in. These entries raise again the issue of the relationship between the possible and the performed that we have already discussed in the last chapter in connection with the scope of linguistic descriptions. Our concern now is how these two aspects of language knowledge are to be related in the learning process.

One might suggest that the two parts of the entry are complementary in that the co-textual example in the second part can indicate additional semantic information. Thus in *CIDE* and *OALD* there is no indication in the definition (as there is in the *COBUILD Dictionary*) that the word 'quaff' relates to alcoholic drink, but one might suggest that this can be inferred from the examples given in *OALD*, where we have reference to beer, and in *CIDE*, where a tavern is mentioned. The obvious difficulty here, however, is that the learner cannot know how *representative* these are as co-textual occurrences: that is to say, whether these are examples of collocational regularities of typical use or just random tokens of text, or indeed if they are representative, what they are representative *of*. Thus learners cannot know whether the word's collocation with beer in this particular example is to be extended to cider or wine, or any other alcoholic beverage, or to any other beverage, alcoholic or not, and indeed to anything drinkable in general. The difficulty is compounded in the case of *CIDE* since this provides a second example which directly contradicts the meaning of the word which might have been inferred from the first, and which is quite explicitly specified in the *COBUILD Dictionary*. The only way of avoiding such contradiction is for the learners to infer that this second sample demonstrates an ironic use. But how are they to make such an inference, particularly since in the *CIDE* entry (unlike those in *OALD* and the *COBUILD Dictionary*) there is no indication that the word is old-fashioned, or (*dated or rhet.*)?

So the co-textual part of these entries does not seem to function as a reliable complement to extend the range of semantic meaning in the definition. But it does not actually exemplify this meaning either. In *CIDE*, the occurrence of 'quaff' in the examples does not demonstrate what it means: Falstaff and Bardolph could have been seen doing all manner of things: eating, gambling, arguing, fighting, indulging in riotous or indecent behaviour. All we can tell from the example is that they were (verbing). The same point applies to the second sample in *CIDE*: in quaffing strange herbal medicines, he might be buying them, trying them out, searching high and low for them, praising them, sipping them, injecting them, sniffing them up his nose. Nothing in the co-textual example indicates that quaffing means to drink something, let alone in large amounts. This is also the case with the *COBUILD* example: 'by the time he had quaffed his third'. His third what? Cigarette? Sandwich? Song? Tune? There is no way of knowing by reference to the example alone. Indeed the learner might even think that here we have a kind of formulaic phrase analogous to 'taken his seat', 'plucked up his courage', 'changed his mind', 'seen the light'; 'quaffed his third'.

The problem is that learners are presented with *data* but what these data are *evidence* of is left to them to work out for themselves. The citing of a par-ticular occurrence tells learners how the word has been used on one occasion, but they do not know how representative this occurrence is. The essential point is that such *samples* of real language data do not of themselves serve as *examples* of language to learn from. As token instances of text, they are *in themselves* often of little use to learners. If learners are to *make* use of them they have to be given guidance as to just how they are representative as exam-ples, what types they are tokens of. The inclusion of 'real' language data in their entries no doubt lends dictionaries an obvious face validity (and who after all would want to buy a dictionary that describes unreal language). But its contribution to the actual language learning process is not so obvious.

What I have been discussing so far is the selective use of corpus findings as a source of single samples to include in dictionary entries. There are, how-ever, other and more pedagogically effective ways of exploiting a corpus. Earlier in this chapter I made reference to McCarthy's remark that the use of a corpus is not simply a matter of 'dumping large loads of corpus material wholesale into the classroom' and raised the question of what, then, it *is* a matter of. It seems to me that the sampling of data as fragments of text in dic-tionary entries is effectively a matter of dumping loads of corpus material, small loads though they be. But a corpus can be used in other ways, as McCarthy himself goes on to suggest:

> One can also mediate the corpus, design it from the very outset and build it with applied linguistics questions in mind, ask of it the questions applied linguists want answers to, and filter its output, use it as a guide or tools for what you, the teacher, want to achieve.
> (McCarthy 2001: 129)

The idea of mediating a corpus is, of course, very much in line with the view of applied linguistics (as distinct from linguistics applied) discussed earlier in this book. A corpus actually compiled by reference to pedagogic criteria would be prescriptive by design. But a descriptive corpus can also, of course, be analysed by programs specifically designed for pedagogic use. As has been impressively demonstrated by a number of people, programs can be devised that work with corpus data to engage learners in discovery learning.[4] Here, for example, learners may be presented not with single samples but with an array—a concordance—of token co-textual occurrences with their immediate verbal environments conveniently in focus. With reference data so displayed, learners can discover co-textual regularities for themselves. And they can be aided and motivated by being given tools, even a methodology, that can be applied to corpus material using concordance and other types of program. But in reference to what was said earlier in this chapter, whatever precepts are followed in the design of such programs, they clearly do not 'arise from observations about the nature of language' but are very much concerned with psychological and pedagogical considerations.

Furthermore, it is not simply a matter of presenting real examples, for the very nature of these pedagogic mediations necessarily alters the reality of the data in the interests of making them purposeful for learners and more effective for learning. Thus a concordance display is an analytic contrivance devised expressly to present textual samples in parallel so that their status as examples can be inferred. In this respect they have something of the character of a grammatical paradigm. To the extent that these samples have been extracted from their original texts and arranged as an analytically ordered list, they clearly cannot be said to represent real language as it actually occurs. The concordance program may extend the verbal environment to larger stretches of text, but of course the more text you include, the less apparent do the co-textual regularities become, and the greater the effort of inference called for. It is because the concordance is an analytic contrivance that it can be effectively put to use for discovery learning. But, obviously enough, the closer you get to the reality of actual texts, the further you get from a presentation that is useful for learning. The concordance device clearly can be exploited to pedagogic advantage precisely because it is a device. Unlike the 'real' material in dictionary entries, the samples are presented as examples that learners can learn from.

I have sought to demonstrate in this chapter that the recommendation that teachers of English, or of any other language come to that, should, as a matter of principle, present only 'real' language is misguided, and misleading, on a number of counts. In the first place, it is based on a very limited concept of reality, one which is, in effect, a construct of linguistic analysis. Although recent developments in corpus linguistics have extended the range of description to include attested E-language, it is only one aspect of externalized language behaviour that is described. Secondly, what corpus descriptions reveal are properties of *text*, facts about the frequencies and regularities of co-textual occurrence. This is a very considerable achievement and obviously marks a very important development in linguistic description. But although these facts represent reality of a kind, it is only one kind. For text only has reality for its users when it contracts a relationship with context in the discourse process, in other words (in Hymes' words) when the performed is *related* to the appropriate. So if textual material (whether in small loads or large) drawn from actually occurring usage, is to be presented in class, it can only be made real as discourse to the extent that it can be appropriately related to context.

We should note that, in this respect, examples of the performed are no different from examples of the possible. Consider the following:

1 I have a little book here by a lady called Mystic Meg.
2 I have a little book. The book is here.

The first comes from the *COBUILD Dictionary* and is a sample of actually attested text, and deemed suitable for pedagogic presentation. The second is a pair of sentences I have invented myself and in this respect unreal and so presumably unsuitable. But in both cases what we have are stretches of inert language which need to be activated by some kind of appropriate contextual connection for them to be realized as meaningful. It is of course true that the first, as an instance of the attested language, a text fragment, *did* originally have appropriate contextual connections whereas the second, as an instance of the possible derived directly from the code, never did. But this distinction is pedagogically irrelevant since the original context of the first is unknown, and, unlike its co-textual connections, unrecoverable, and could not be replicated in the classroom anyway. So in both cases the teacher has somehow to contrive an appropriate context of some kind which would make the examples meaningful to learners.

And this, of course, would be infinitely easier to do for the second example than for the first. Indeed, 'unreal' examples like the second are expressly contrived to make them realizable in the contextual conditions of the classroom. In other words, the likelihood is that the 'unreal' example can be more readily *made* real for learners than the 'real' one. Or to use Hymes' words again, as far as the classroom context is concerned (and this is the context we are concerned with) it is easier to make the possible appropriate than the actually performed. And not only easier, but more effective for the process of learning.

In spite of this, there is a persistent prejudice against such contrivance. This is what Willis has to say:

Contrived simplification of language in the preparation of materials will always be faulty, since it is generated without the guide and support of a communicative context. Only by accepting the discipline of using authentic language are we likely to come anywhere near presenting the learner with a sample of language which is typical of real English.
(Willis 1990: 127)

But, as I have tried to show, the 'real' examples of attested text are also simplified, in the sense that they are message forms which are dissociated both from their source in the code potential of the possible and from the complexity of the normal contextual conditions which made them communicatively appropriate in the first place. The original communicative context that constituted their 'guide and support' is no longer in evidence, so it has to be reconstituted in some way. And this way has to be appropriate to classroom conditions which are entirely different from those that attended the production of the text to begin with. It is not the case that contrived language is 'generated without the guide and support of a communicative context'. It is simply that the communicative context is one that has itself to be contrived so as to be real for learners and effective for learning. I would argue that the discipline we have to accept is that of denying ourselves the easy assumption that authenticity is transferable intact in the text from one context to another. What I think we need to recognize is that it makes no sense to present learners with 'real' examples of text unless they can make them real for themselves. Of course, as learners progress they become more capable of reconstituting contexts of use and so engaging with user reality. But this does not invalidate the point. Authentic samples of text are useless, I would argue, unless they can be authenticated as discourse *use*.

And unless the samples can be taken as *examples*. As I have argued, it is not just a matter of making the language real for learners, it has also to activate the learning process. Willis talks about presenting learners with samples that are typical of real English. The point I have tried to make is that typicality does not inhere in samples, but has to be inferred from them. This, as we have seen in our discussion of dictionary entries, means that samples have to be presented in such a way that their typicality as examples can be inferred: *how* a particular sample is typical, and what it is typical *of*.

In these last two chapters, I have been examining the well-established assumption that pedagogic prescriptions are necessarily drawn from linguistic descriptions, that what the linguist describes is what the teachers should teach. Naturally, we should make sure, as Halliday says, that these descriptions are 'as good as possible', that is to say, 'based on sound linguistic principles' (see Chapter 7). One difficulty here, as I have already indicated, is that ideas about what counts as soundness in linguistic principles change over time, and so therefore does the judgement as to whether a description is good or not. Certainly, as we have seen, I-linguists and E-linguists do not see eye to eye on the matter, and indeed one faction of the latter, the corpus analysts, have claimed that their findings require a radical overhaul of the categories and methods of I-linguistics. All descriptions, I have argued, are partial, good at accounting for some aspects of the reality of language, not so good, or no good at all, at accounting for others. The relevant question for our enquiry is what these partial versions are good for in specifying the language of the subject.

It is this pedagogic question that I have been addressing in this chapter, making particular reference to descriptions of language based on corpus analysis. This was singled out because of the claims that have been made for it that it not only captures language reality in ways that other approaches to description do not, but, more significantly for our present discussion, that *because it does so*, its findings should directly and uniquely inform what is included in language courses. In its essentials, the line of argument goes as follows: corpus descriptions account for real language, learners need real language, therefore corpus descriptions provide for the needs of learners. In this chapter I have tried to demonstrate that each of these premises is invalid, and that the conclusion therefore does not hold.[5]

In these last two chapters the focus of attention has been on why linguistic descriptions cannot automatically meet pedagogic requirement, particularly, in this chapter, as far as the process of learning is concerned. What kind of language, then, would measure up to requirement? And what, if it comes to that, *is* the requirement exactly? These questions take us back to the issue that prompted our enquiry in the first place, namely the nature of the language subject, and it is this issue that we return to in the next chapter.

Notes and comments

1 Judging from other remarks that McCarthy makes, whatever such factors might be, they would, in his view, need to be consistent with the presentation of real language.

> The language of the corpus is, above all, real, and what is it that all language learners want, other than 'real' contact with the target language? (McCarthy 2001: 128)

Although there seems to be some ambivalence here in that the second mention of real is actually distinguished from the first by being put in inverted commas, the notion of reality appears to pose no problems for McCarthy. Real language is real language: that is what learners want, and that is what the corpus provides. Nothing could be simpler: common sense. But, as I argued in Chapter 1, it is just such common-sense assumptions that it is the business of applied linguistics to question, particularly when they have an obvious popular appeal. As McCarthy's colleague Ron Carter points out:

> The word 'real' invariably carries positive associations. People believe they want or are told they want or, indeed actually want what is real, authentic and natural in preference to what is unreal, inauthentic and unnatural.
> (Carter 1998: 43)

It is interesting to note how the 'real' is presented here. It is made positive by contrast with terms which are explicitly marked as negative ('unreal', 'inauthentic', 'unnatural') rather than, for example, such terms as 'adapted', 'designed', or even 'custom-made'. If people feel so positive about what is real and natural, one wonders why they take so readily to antibiotics, the internal combustion engine, and all the rest of the artifice and invention upon which their way of life depends. One is led to suspect that an appeal to the real and the natural is a promotional ploy; and this seems to be borne out by the examples that Carter himself gives: 'real ale', 'real country flavour', 'the real thing', 'real English'. And the ploy depends on making an affective impact which distracts attention from matters of truth or factuality. Thus, as Gavioli and Aston 2001 point out, it is simply not the case that 'the term "real" invariably carries positive associations'. Even a cursory glance at a concordance will reveal that it very commonly has negative ones (as in 'a real disaster', 'a real tyrant', 'a real pain in the neck'). It is somewhat paradoxical, to say the least, that the promotion of real English here is in contradiction of the very corpus evidence upon which the case for it depends.

The general point I would want to make is that there should be more concern for *arguing* the case for real English and less on promoting it as a cause, and that this case can only be reasonably argued on pedagogic grounds.

For further discussion on the use of corpus data for language teaching, see the correspondence between Prodromou (1996) and Carter and McCarthy (1996), and the exchange between Cook (1998) and Carter (1998). The whole controversy is reprinted in Seidlhofer (2003).

2 This feature of significant absence is indeed something that corpus analysis reveals very clearly. As Aston points out '... proverbs and clichés are very rarely reproduced verbatim in a newspaper corpus, but the fact that they frequently form the basis of modified citations demonstrates that their prototypical forms are assumed to be available' (Aston 1995: 270).

Thus, when writers use expressions like 'much ado...', 'spare the rod...', 'here today...', and so on, they will assume that readers will be able to supply the missing text ('... about nothing', '... and spoil the child', '... gone tomorrow'). Furthermore, in doing so, readers confirm their insider status as members of the community.

3 Michael Hoey takes a different view, indeed a diametrically opposed one. In his foreword to the recent *Macmillan English Dictionary*, he remarks:

> ... it is often possible to guess the meaning of rare words from their context and ... they have in any case little impact on the overall intelligibility of what one is reading... It is, oddly, more likely to be the most common words that cause the greater problems.
> (Hoey 2002: viii)

Our consideration of the newspaper text in this chapter would suggest otherwise. But, of course, it all depends on what it is one is reading and who 'one' is, and indeed on what 'overall intelligibility' is taken to mean. Thus Gavioli and Aston 2001 point out that readers do not have to be members of the discourse community for which a text is designed to authenticate it as discourse. For they may engage with it as observers rather than participants:

> While the participant interacts with the text as an intended recipient, the observer views this interaction from the outside, adopting a critical, analytic perspective:
> (Gavioli and Aston 2001: 241)

I take their point even if the recipient assumes an observer position, there must presumably be a degree of contextual convergence for the reader to engage with the text at all.

4 These brief remarks do less than justice to the very imaginative and innovative work that has been done on the design of programs which exploit corpora as a learning resource, to develop what Johns refers to as data-driven learning (see Johns 1994; Johns and King 1991). Other work along these lines is described in Aston 2001; Burnard and McEnery 2000; Kettemann and Marko 2002; Tribble and Jones 1997. Of particular relevance to the theme of this book are proposals in Bernardini (2000) which expressly link the learners' use of corpora with the development of the kind of learning capability or capacity I am arguing for here.

5 The argument I have been presenting in this and the preceding chapter is very much in line with earlier thinking in our field about the relevance of descriptive facts to the prescription of language for learning. It needs to be noted that although electronic technology now provides the means for the close investigation of textual data on a vast scale, quantitative analysis of this kind, though not of course to this degree, was conducted long before the computer appeared on the scene. A corpus of German, consisting of 11 million words, laboriously assembled by hand, already existed at the end of the nineteenth century. A great deal of work was done for English along similar lines in the first half of the last century, particularly by the American psychologist E. L. Thorndike, and at the same time, pedagogically motivated people like Harold Palmer and Michael West were collecting data, albeit on a somewhat smaller scale, and considering how far frequency was a factor in the selection of vocabulary for English courses. All three scholars participated in conferences in New York and London, from which emerged, in 1936, the *Interim Report on Vocabulary Selection for English as a Foreign Language* (the so-called *Carnegie Report*) which provided the basis of West's *General Service List of English Words* (West 1953). The relevant point to note here is that frequency based on quantitative analysis was only one criterion in the compilation of this list, and subject to pedagogic evaluation alongside other factors, including those of learnability and teachability. (See Howatt 1984; Mackey 1965; Widdowson 1968.) There was no linguistics applied here, no simplistic equation between description and prescription, but, on the contrary, a

recognition that the relationship was one which needed to be carefully mediated by applied linguistic intervention.

These early efforts at the quantitative analysis of text are crude in the extreme as compared with the scope and sophistication of current corpus descriptions by computer. But the pedagogic issues they sought to address are just as relevant now as they were then. Perhaps it is because we are so lost in admiration of electronic wizardry that we fail to notice them. At all events, it is a matter of some regret that these issues are not followed up in any explicit and systematic way in the current literature on corpora and language teaching (for example, Wichmann *et al.* 1997). Reference to this early pedagogically-oriented work in corpus analysis is, generally speaking, conspicuous by its absence.

This work is, however, mentioned in Coxhead (2000) and Kennedy (1998), though in both cases the focus of attention is on its descriptive shortcomings. In referring to West's *General Service List*, Kennedy makes the ironical observation:

> ...partly for want of anything better, West became an indispensable source of reference in applied linguistics to check unbridled intuitions about language use, and for the design of curricula and teaching materials. (Kennedy 1998: 96)

No mention is made of the pedagogic considerations that were prompted by the work of West and others, nor of the fact that the frequency information recorded in his list was recognized as only one factor in the design of curricula and teaching materials.

9　Pedagogic design

In preceding chapters, I have been arguing that it is misleading to assume that the language which is the object of description for linguists should be equated with the language that is taught as a subject. Different approaches to linguistic description focus attention on different aspects of this object and so yield partial versions of it: each may capture *a* truth, but not *the* truth, the whole truth, and nothing but the truth. The advantage of this focusing is that certain features of language are brought out in detailed relief, and we are provided with facts and insights that would otherwise escape our notice. But at the same time, of course, other features are relegated to the unfocused periphery and left unaccounted for. So no description captures linguistic reality in its entirety, and it would be unreasonable to castigate a particular representation of language for not doing so.

It is interesting to note, however, that linguists apparently think it entirely reasonable to castigate language teachers for the way they represent language on the grounds that it does not measure up to their descriptions. Both pedagogic and linguistic representations are of their nature partial, limited by particular perceptions of relative significance, but the assumption generally appears to be that linguistic partiality necessarily carries greater authority and must always be preferred to any pedagogic alternative. Linguists have few inhibitions about pointing out the limitations of pedagogic versions of language, but bridle at any suggestion that their own versions might be limited from a pedagogic point of view, putting such suggestion down to ignorance and complacency. While it is apparently quite in order for a linguist to propose pedagogic precepts based on linguistic analysis, the idea that a language teacher might propose descriptive precepts based on pedagogic considerations is strenuously resisted.

It is, in other words, descriptive partiality that rules, and pedagogic partiality is required to conform. If it does not, it will, in the words of Willis, 'always be faulty'. And a good deal of effort has been expended over recent years in demonstrating just how faulty pedagogic prescriptions of English can be. The usual procedure is to show how the representation of certain grammatical or lexical features in textbooks fail to match up with the findings of corpus analysis. The following are typical of the kind of statements that are routinely made:

> For all areas of grammar which we have studied so far it has become clear that the English which is taught in German textbooks is at variance with

the language used by native speakers ... The same is true of statements in a number of widely used handbooks of English grammar on which these textbooks are based.
(Mindt 1997: 42–3)

The examples make it clear that corpus-based studies of grammar which are geared to foreign language teaching can do much to bring the teaching of English into better accordance with actual language use.
(Ibid.: 50)

I have no doubt it is the case that the English in the textbooks that Mindt studied is not in accordance with that used by native speakers as revealed by corpus analysis. The facts are indeed clear, and not in question. What *is* in question is the implication, also quite clear in these statements, namely that they *should* be. On this account, the subject English as a foreign language is necessarily concerned with the performed rather than the possible, in Hymes' terms, and furthermore with what is attested as the performance of native speakers and not other users of the language.

But a moment's reflection makes it clear that what is taught in classrooms in certain crucial respects *cannot* be in accordance with actual language use. Actual language use occurs naturally within the continuities of social life, appropriately activated by context, and motivated by the needs of communication and the expression of communal and individual identity. The language subject does not occur naturally at all: it appears, like other subjects, discontinuously on the timetable, fitted into a schedule as suited to administrative convenience. Usually, there is no natural communal or individual impetus to use the language: contexts have to be contrived and motivation created. And this is done within restricted units of time called periods and units of activity called lessons, which are organized into such things as exercises, tasks, tests, group work, and so on. Furthermore, these events are, for the most part, controlled and orchestrated by teacher authority, and directed at an eventual measurable outcome. On the face of it, it is hard to see any resemblance to the natural conditions of actual language use at all.

As I have said before, the idea of introducing actual, or real, or authentic language use into the classroom is an appealing one, and seems to offer an escape from what is often seen as the confinement and routine drudgery that seem to typify orthodox language pedagogy.[1] But the appeal is also an illusion. The classroom contexts within which language has usually to be learnt are totally different from those within which the language is used. You cannot simply replicate the sociocultural conditions which made the language actual for its users in the first place. Of course, you can to some degree modify classroom contexts, but that is simply to say that you contrive conditions to make them approximate more closely to the reality of use. As I pointed out in the previous chapter, this is a difficult thing to do. Paradoxically enough, the closer you try to get to user authenticity, the more contrivance you will need to resort to, for you have to somehow reconstruct the original contexts and make them accessible, while at the same time making them appropriate to the learning process.

There is a curious contradiction in all this. While it is taken as axiomatic that reality is a function of appropriacy to context, the axiom is denied when the context concerned is that of the classroom. The reason for this would seem to be that the classroom is considered to be inherently unreal and therefore does not count as a valid context at all. But what, one might ask, is so unreal about the classroom? It is real enough for students: whether they like it or not, they spend most of their waking hours in it. True, it is specially constructed for a purpose and can be said to constrain natural behaviour to that end, but exactly the same can be said of the contexts of ordinary everyday life. People at work are also constrained to conform to conventions devised to further certain purposes in the most efficient way. We do not generally think of offices or building sites, as we do of classrooms, as being remote from the real world.

It seems to me that we need to recognize that the classroom is a social construct and as such, like any other, has its contexts and purposes, its own legitimate reality. Naturally, like any other social construct, it is dynamic, subject to variation and change. As I suggested in Chapter 1, it can be misleading to talk about *the* classroom in generic terms, as if all classrooms were alike, just as it could be misleading to talk of *the* office or *the* workplace as if they were all the same. Nevertheless, locally different though classrooms are bound to be, they share the common feature that *makes* them all classrooms, namely that they are the site for contrived contexts designed to achieve a pedagogic purpose. So instead of thinking of the classroom as an artificial and arid place that can only be brought to life by injections of reality from the 'real' world outside, we need to think of it as a setting capable of creating a reality of its own. As far as the teaching of English is concerned, or the teaching of any language, we need to consider what language is appropriate for the classroom on its own contextual terms and for its own purposes.

What, then, are the purposes for which classroom contexts have to be contrived? As we have seen, the general assumption is that they are to get students to model themselves on the competence of native speakers and their norms of linguistic behaviour. The belief seems to be that language courses should be a kind of rehearsal which prepares learners for real life performance in native-speaker roles. In previous chapters I have questioned this belief on the grounds that for many, perhaps most, learners it is not their purpose to bid for membership of native-speaking communities, or for their approval, but to provide themselves with a means for international communication. But the rehearsal objective is not only of doubtful validity, it is of doubtful viability as well. All the evidence indicates that it is rarely if ever achieved. However one defines native-speaker competence, and as was indicated in earlier chapters, it is very elusive of definition. Most learners at the end of their course fall well short of its attainment, even if we think of competence as having to do only with knowledge of the possible in a narrow sense. If one then extends the concept to include a knowledge of textual patterns actually performed by natives with all their idiomatic complexity, and the contextual conditions attendant on their appropriate use, the learning problems become insurmountable, particularly since these patterns are, of course, continually in flux. It is no wonder that a common feeling among English learners is a sense of inadequacy in failing to measure up to native-speaker norms. As an objective for learning, real English is unrealistic English.

These difficulties all arise, I would argue, from the basic, and mistaken, assumption discussed earlier: the object language that linguists seek to describe is to be equated with the language subject that teachers have to teach. I have already pointed out that in certain obvious respects the language as subject, organized in periods and lessons, is bound to be quite different from the language that occurs naturally in social contexts of use. But there are other differences too, and these can be brought to light by a little elementary linguistic analysis.

Subjects are what teachers teach. Grammatically speaking, 'teach' is a transitive verb and therefore takes an object. But the objects can be of two different kinds. Consider the following examples:

She teaches English.
She teaches adults.

When combined, the second of these becomes an indirect object, as in:

She teaches adults English.
She teaches English to adults.

To specify native-speaker use as the content to be taught in effect defines objectives in reference only to the direct object, English, and in disregard of the indirect object, the students. What is to be taught is defined without reference to who it is being taught to. But what teachers teach is a *subject*, and the subject can only be defined by taking both direct *and* indirect objects into account, and crucially, how they relate to each other. Thus if we consider the acronym TESOL, one cannot separate the E from the SOL. The subject is not English *to* speakers of other languages (E→SOL) but English *for* speakers of other languages (ESOL). This formulation implies that what is to be taught is not English as it is already spoken, but English as expressly designed for those who do not yet speak it but are learning to do so. Or, to take another abbreviation, EFL, the subject is not just the E in isolation. What is taught is not English as such, but English *as a foreign language*, and this, by definition, cannot be the English of native speakers.

Again, we see that we have two quite different realities here. What makes the language real for its native users is its familiarity, but what is real for learners is the fact that it is unfamiliar, foreign to them. And it is this foreignness that the subject has to be designed to cope with. And, of course, English will be foreign in all kinds of different ways depending on who the learners are and which other languages they are speakers of. Clearly, you can only define the foreignness of a language by reference to a language, or languages, which are familiar. It follows that in defining ESOL or EFL at least one other language is implicated. If you separate the E from the SOL or the FL, then you can maintain the illusion that the subject is a monolingual one, only concerned with English. But if you integrate the E with the SOL or the FL, then it becomes clear that the subject is in certain respects bound to be a bilingual (or multilingual) one. I shall take up the implications of this in Chapter 11.

What kind of language, then, is appropriate for courses in English as a foreign language? As already argued (in Chapter 2) it has to be specified along two parameters: in terms of the objectives to be eventually achieved, and in terms of the process that has to be activated to get there. In respect to objectives, I think we need to reject as irrelevant and unrealistic the idea that these should be defined in terms of authentic native-speaker use. What students need to have acquired at the end of their course, it seems to me, is a knowledge of the language which will provide them with a capability for further learning. This has essentially to be a knowledge of the possible, a knowledge of how meaning is semantically encoded in English, and how it can be drawn on as a resource for pragmatic use. This need not be, indeed cannot be comprehensive: the pedagogic task is to identify what features of the possible have the most potential for subsequent realization. In other words specifying objectives is a matter of investment in what seems likely to yield the best returns.

To think of objectives in terms of investment, rather than rehearsal, is to recognize that the end of a course of teaching does not by any means constitute the end of learning, but is only a stage in its development. The purpose of the course is to give momentum and direction, to establish vectors, so to speak, for subsequent learning, and thus to provide bearings whereby learners can make sense and learn from their own linguistic experience. It recognizes too that there are aspects of language that can be taught, and others that can only be learnt by exposure to, and involvement in, contexts of use that cannot be replicated in class. The communicative fine-tuning into what is particularly appropriate and actually attested is something that learners can only do for themselves as and when the occasion arises.

So what kind of language needs to be presented in class, and how does it need to be presented, to activate the process of learning towards this objective? It seems clear that it needs to meet two essential conditions. The first is that it has to engage the learners' attention and interest: it has to be made real in some way or other, it has to have point for them. This is not, let me emphasize again, a matter of simply presenting authentic user language, but of presenting language that learners can authenticate for themselves. We might say that in the context of the classroom, appropriate language is language that learners can appropriate. The second condition is that it has to be language that can be learnt from, it needs not only to be purposeful for the learner, but it must also serve the purpose of learning. Given our objective, this means that it must be presented in such a way that makes apparent how it exemplifies the semantic encodings of the possible. Taken together, these conditions ensure that students both acquire a knowledge of how meanings are encoded in English, and how these encodings constitute a communicative resource that can be put to purposeful use. It is this that constitutes what I have referred to as the capability that can be drawn on and extended in further learning.

As we saw in the last chapter, samples of language drawn from attested use do not as such and of themselves meet either condition: the contexts which make them real as communication are generally unknown, and indeed alien to learners, and the sample does not of itself show what it is an example *of*, so it gives the learner little to learn *from*. If the conditions are to be met, then the language, and the activities associated with it, have to be designed to meet them. In other words, since what naturally occurs seldom serves our pedagogic purpose, we need to contrive something that does.

But all this talk of setting the code as a learning objective, and this commendation of contrived language in the classroom sounds retrograde and reactionary, and seems to take us back to the dark ages of English teaching before the advent of the communicative approach and authentic language, back to what N. S. Prabhu (Prabhu 1987) has dubbed SOS—the structural-oral-situational approach to English teaching, with its focus on form and its practice of sentence patterns.

It has long been fashionable to be uncritically dismissive of SOS, and to suppose that its tenets in their entirety are rendered invalid by the new enlightenment of communicative language teaching (CLT): the language subject redefined, the old pedagogic paradigm discredited and superseded by the new. But it is worth giving critical consideration to just what it was about SOS that was so open to objection, and why CLT was taken to be so obviously an improvement.

The most commonly cited difference between the two, repeated over and over again in the literature like a mantra, is that with SOS there is focus on form (which is bad), whereas with CLT there is focus on meaning (which is good). But even the most fleeting acquaintance with SOS shows that this is simply not the case. It did very definitely focus on meaning, and its typical techniques were designed expressly for that purpose:

TEACHER (holding a book in hand): Book. This is a book.
TEACHER (pointing to a book elsewhere): That is a book.
  (i.e. The word 'book' means this object. 'This is a book' contrasts with 'That is a book'. 'This' is a word which means here, close to me, proximal. 'That' is a word which means there, away from me, distal.)
TEACHER (pointing): The door is there.
  (i.e. The word 'the' means something we all know about.)

TEACHER (matching the action to the word): I am walking to the door.
TEACHER (getting a student to do likewise): She is walking to the door.
  (i.e. This form of the verb means continuous and concurrent action.)

And so on. Clearly there *is* focus on meaning here, and indeed it is the very purpose of the demonstration to provide it. But the meaning focused on is, of course, semantic or encoded meaning, meaning in form—informed meaning, we might say. It is not the pragmatic meaning that is achieved when this semantic resource is put to appropriate contextual use. So it is that if set against the norm of what naturally occurs, this representation of language is unnatural and unreal, and so *pragmatically* pointless. This is bound to be the case, for what makes this contrived context appropriate for the demonstration of semantic meaning is precisely what makes it inappropriate as a context for pragmatic use. The appropriacy conditions are based on diametrically opposing principles. Consider the expression:

I am walking to the door.

To demonstrate the semantic meaning of this I have to match action to word exactly, and walk to the door as I say the sentence. If I get my timing wrong and I arrive at the door in mid-sentence, then the demonstration fails. The context has to *duplicate* the language. In the normal circumstances of use, however, context and language are in a *complementary* relationship. We only say what is *not* apparent from the context. So it would be distinctly odd for somebody to come up with this expression when performing the action it refers to. We do not normally provide such a running (or walking) commentary on our actions. So, if, for example, I were to be entertaining guests at home, and I were to get up from the table and head for the door, I would not duplicate the information that is contextually provided by saying 'I am walking to the door'. I would complement the context by saying something that is not obvious from my actions.

I think that was the doorbell. I'll just check to see if the chicken is cooked.
I think we need another bottle of wine.

But these utterances, of course, give no inkling as to what the sentence means semantically. If I were to utter the obvious 'I am walking to the door' my guests would assume that what I meant by it is something other than what the language means, disregard what is actually encoded, and look for some significance beyond what the language itself signifies by exploring the context for clues.

I am walking to the door.
(He means that he is going to call the police. He means he is not as drunk as we think he is. He means that he has completely recovered from his knee operation.)

So the principle of duplication, so crucial to the focus on semantic meaning, runs directly counter to the principle of complementation which is in force in natural pragmatic uses of language. And if one judges SOS demonstrations by applying the complementation principle they are obviously artificial and entirely unrealistic. But the fact that they do not represent language use does not make them useless. There is no doubt that, whatever their shortcomings, they do meet the second of the necessary pedagogic conditions that were proposed earlier in the chapter: they direct attention to the encodings of the possible. With reference to the distinction made in the previous chapter, these demonstrations deal in examples, not samples of language and make it perfectly plain just what these examples are examples of.

Of course, directing attention to semantic encodings does not guarantee that students will pay attention to them so as to take them in to become part of their knowledge. It is for this reason that SOS typically follows up demonstration with practice, providing students with the opportunity to repeat the encodings in exercises of various kinds so as to consolidate their knowledge. Critics make the point that this second procedure has the effect of making the language even more unreal since the kind of repetition involved does not correspond with what goes on in normal uses of language. Against this objection, one might point out that in actual fact repetition is a quite normal feature of some kinds of language, and is very much in evidence in the linguistic experience of children learning their own language. Nevertheless, one can agree that this is unlike the kind of serried repetition that SOS goes in for, and that this is indeed pragmatically anomalous. But as with the demonstration procedures considered earlier, lack of correspondence with user reality is not necessarily a disadvantage, pedagogically speaking.

The real problem with practice, I think, lies elsewhere. It is that the very repetition of the encodings has the effect of draining them of their meaning so that their forms alone come into focus. Alfred Tennyson, so it is said, would sometimes induce a trance-like condition, conducive, as he thought, for poetic composition, by repeating his own name again and again until it became a mysterious and meaningless pattern of sound (readers might wish to try this out for themselves). Repetition does indeed seem to have this effect, as is evident from some kinds of ritual or liturgical uses of language. The problem with repetitive practice, then, is that it tends to shift the focus from meaning to form, so that whatever is internalized as a result are encodings which are semantically reduced. What we need to look for is a kind of repetition that does not have this reductive effect.

So far we have been looking at how far SOS satisfies the second pedagogic condition that was proposed, namely that the language presented has to be such that learners can learn from it. But the first condition has to be satisfied as well, namely that the language has to be made real for learners, put to some use recognized by them as purposeful. This condition is clearly crucial for motivation, for if the interest of students is not engaged, the learning process is unlikely to get off the ground at all. But it is also crucial because it is in the purposeful use of encodings that students realize their communicative value, the pragmatic potential of their semantic meaning. It is this condition that the typical SOS techniques of presentation and practice manifestly fail to satisfy.

But it is not satisfied either by the simple expedient of presenting real samples of actually occurring text. As I have argued they do not, of themselves, meet our conditions either, for as far as the learners are concerned their reality is difficult to engage with, and as far as the learning process is concerned, they are not examples, so they cannot be readily learnt from.

So how, then, can these conditions be satisfied? The solution must lie in some kind of pedagogic artifice whereby language is contrived to be both engaged with and learnt from. With this in mind, let us return to SOS and its shortcomings. The problem with it, it seems to me, is not that it did not focus on meaning, which it obviously did in its presentation of language by demonstration, but that this was not effectively exploited by subsequent practice activities which tended to nullify semantic meaning by repetition that brought form into focus. There is, however, a third stage in the SOS approach which we need to take note of. After presentation and practice comes production, to complete the familiar PPP cycle. In this production phase, activities are provided which are indeed intended to get learners to put their knowledge of the code to purposeful pragmatic use. The problem is, however, that their ability to do this depends on their having already learnt the code as a meaning potential that can indeed be pragmatically realized in this way. Whatever capability for communication and further learning is to be exploited and extended in the third phase, it has to be developed to some degree in the first two. If, as I have suggested, the presentation and practice stages in SOS typically fail to meet our conditions for effective learner engagement, then this failure will be carried over into the production stage. This is why this stage tends typically to reduce to the further manifestation of encoded usage rather than realization as purposeful use. (See Widdowson 1978.) As Willis puts it:

It is no longer a stage in which learners seek to achieve some communicative purpose as best they can—a process which might incidentally involve the use of the target form. Instead it becomes a stage at which they are at pains to display the target form and incidentally to go through the appearance of using language to achieve a communicative outcome.
(Willis 1996: 47)

The SOS approach, then, has serious shortcomings on this account, and one might be inclined to simply dismiss it as an outmoded aberration. It seems more reasonable, though, and more constructive, to examine these shortcomings more closely and consider how they might be remedied.[2]

With this in mind, let us look again at the kind of language that we find in SOS textbooks. The following might be taken as typical. We are presented with a picture of a sitting room: a picture on the wall, a mat on the floor, perhaps even a cat on the mat. There are people in the room: a man is sitting in a chair and a woman is standing by a table. Alongside the picture is a text. It reads something like this:

> This is a man. He is John Brown; he is Mr Brown. He is sitting in a chair. This is a woman. She is Mary Brown; she is Mrs Brown. She is standing by a table. Mr Brown has a book. The book is in his hand; he has a book in his hand. Mrs Brown has a bag...

By reference to the criterion of pragmatic normality, this is obviously absurd. The text, with its sequence of simple and repetitive structures, bears little or no resemblance to any that actually occur in real life. The relationship between the structures is not so much one of combination as equivalence, so the text looks like the forced textualization of a paradigm:

> This is a man.   He is...ing   He has...
> This is a woman.   She is...ing   She has...

But not only does this not have the *form* of a normal text, it does not *function* like one either. The duplication of visual and verbal is such that the text has no pragmatic point. What we have here, then, is only the appearance of text, since it has no discourse implications whatever. It is simply a display of encodings, a device for demonstration. As such, it offers nothing for learners to engage with, and this brings us to what is most seriously at fault with this text: it is *boring*. Given all these shortcomings, what then are we to do about them?

One answer, of course, and the one currently in vogue, is to abandon such an approach altogether, have no truck with such contrivance, and replace these absurd travesties with authentic language: present real examples only. But, as we have seen, such a solution simply creates other problems. An alternative might be to modify the text in some way to give it a pragmatic point and make it less boring. And this turns out to be easy enough to do. Even the slightest of adjustments will change the character of the text quite radically. For example:

> This is a man. He is John Brown; he is Mr Brown. He is sitting in a chair. This is a woman. She is not Mrs Brown. She is standing by a table. She has a look in her eye. Mr Brown has an idea in his head. He has a book in his hand...

All I have done by the simple addition of a negative particle here, the change of lexical item there, is to reduce duplication and introduce complementation by verbalizing information not recoverable from the context in the picture, thereby creating a fictional state of affairs that might engage the reader's interest. Expectations are aroused. What happens next? The book in Mr Brown's hand is not now just there to display a structure: there must be some point in its being mentioned. 'Mr Brown has a look in his eye' and 'He has a book in his hand' are no longer equivalent paradigmatic structures in parallel: they are parts of a developing narrative. The language itself remains just as artificial as before, but these simple adjustments, I would suggest, prompt learners to make a reality out of it. We should note too that the repetitions remain in place. But, again, they are not there for their own structural sake, but have a point.

Of course, there is no guarantee that this particular text would engage the interest of all learners so as to realize its pragmatic potential. There will always be the problem of deciding which texts, however adjusted, will have the desired effect on particular learners. But this does not invalidate the general point that it is possible to present language which is, on user criteria, unreal in the extreme in ways which learners can make real for themselves. By the same token, of course, there is no reason why language which *is* real on user criteria cannot be subjected to the same process, adjusted too to accommodate to classroom conditions. But the point at issue is that wherever the language comes from, it has to be adjusted to pedagogic requirement.

One might say that in making these simple adjustments to this textbook extract, I realized its fictional possibilities, and, in a very modest way, made literature out of it. I would not want to make any great claims for it as verbal art. It is interesting to note, however, that this kind of artificial language has figured in a text that is unquestionably of literary status. Consider the following:

Here is the house. It is green and white. It has a red door. It is very pretty. Here is the family. Mother, Father, Dick and Jane live in the green-and-white house. They are very happy. See Jane. She has a red dress. She wants to play. Who will play with Jane? See the cat. It goes meow meow. Come and play. Come play with Jane. The kitten will not play. See Mother. Mother is very nice. Mother, will you play with Jane? Mother laughs. Laugh, Mother, laugh. See Father. He is big and strong. Father, will you play with Jane? Father is smiling. Smile, Father, smile. See the dog. Bow wow goes the dog. Do you want to play with Jane? See the dog run. Look, look. Here comes a friend. The friend will play with Jane. They play a good game. Play, Jane, play.

This is the opening paragraph of a Pulitzer Prize winning novel by Toni Morrison called *The Bluest Eye*. Here too we have language which is artificial and unreal in reference to what is attested in the contexts of actually occurring use. But it is far from meaningless. On the contrary, its very artificial nature is turned to artistic advantage. The fact that it derives directly from the pedagogically contrived language of textbooks designed for teaching basic literacy lends it a particular significance. What, we are prompted to ask, is the purpose of using such artificial language? We are drawn into realizing it as meaningful in this context. Here is Jane, her conceptions confined by the simple language of her reading books, trying to make sense of the world in reference to them, a childlike world of repetitive events and deprivation, where she is lonely and longing for company, and so on. There are many ways in which this text can be interpreted as a discourse, but the crucial point is that it *is* so interpreted. It induces us to create contextual conditions whereby we make sense of it.

The essential point, with regard to both my own trivial literary effort and this passage from Morrison's novel, is that unreal though the language is in reference to normal contextual use, it can inspire engagement and be *made* real by the play of the imagination which projects a contextual significance *from* the text. They are, in both cases, ludicrous as representations of how English is usually realized. But the term ludicrous is derived from the latin *ludere*, to play. This is ludic language, language to play with, and language play, as Cook has argued so convincingly (Cook 1997, 2000), is also a part of our reality. And it is one that can be readily exploited in the classroom context.[3]

And it is easy enough to see how the kind of contrived language we have been discussing can be played with, and indeed *is* played with by Toni Morrison. And in playing with the language, students will at the same time be practising it, thereby satisfying the second of our pedagogic conditions. Thus, given the kind of ludicrous passage about Mr Brown we have been considering, students might, for example, be asked to continue the narrative, or devise their own, drawing on a list of words and structures provided. Here the repetition would be motivated by a meaningful purpose, and so would resolve the problem of diminishing significance that arises with the pointless repetitive practice in SOS exercises.

Or consider another stock SOS practice device, the substitution table. Here we have a display of words in rows and columns as follows:

The	doctor	loves	the	nurse
A	nurse	hates	a	doctor
My	patient	sees	my	patient

This is a mechanism for the automatic repetition of equivalent sentences as formal patterns. The student selects a row of words randomly, one from each column, and produces a correctly formed sentence each time, time after time: 'The nurse loves a doctor', 'The nurse hates my patient', 'My nurse sees my patient', etc. etc. The idea is that the mechanical repetition will have the effect of so impressing the structure in the mind that it becomes habitual. Be that as it may, the effect, of course, is to focus on form in dissociation from meaning. It does not matter which combinations the student chooses as far as lexical items are concerned, for they are only there to fill in structural slots. The different combinations bear no relationship with any context: the definite article 'the', for example, has the pragmatic function of signalling shared knowledge, but students are not supposed to enquire as to who this particular doctor or nurse might be. Nor is there any co-textual relationship between the combinations: the third choice is not required to follow on from the second or the second from the first. The device is designed for the generation of sentences, not for the composition of text. All in all, the substitution table, as a mechanism for mindless conformity, seems to have little to commend it.

But there is no reason, in principle, why, this device could not be made into a game for students to play with for a purpose. With a small effort of imagination, one might think of more promising lexical items, and set a condition that different combinations *do* have to be co-textually related. Repetition is not now at the expense of meaning: the substitution table now becomes a device for the generation of different narratives—rudimentary, no doubt, but real in the sense of having a point. In a simple way, the students are realizing the semantic potential as pragmatic use, remote though this might be from native-speaker normality.

The substitution table displays structures vertically in parallel. Using it to make a prose narrative puts the structures end to end on a horizontal plane, co-textually connected. There is a use of language, however, where co-textual connections are brought about by vertical arrangement, namely verse. Thus combinations read off from a substitution table can be taken as lines of poetry. And there is indeed a poem, attested as actually written, whose first line takes exactly the form of one such combination:

THE BED
The doctor loves the patient,
The patient loves his bed,
A fine place to be born in,
The best place to be dead.

The doctor loves the patient,
Because he means to die,
The patient loves the patient bed,
That shares his agony.

The bed adores the doctor,
His cool and skilful touch,
Soon brings another patient,
Who loves her just as much.
(A. D. Hope *The Wandering Islands* 1955)

The poem consists of repeated linguistic forms, recurring words and structures which are equivalent not only grammatically, but metrically too. But the repetitions are co-textually connected into a pattern, confirmed by the rhyme scheme. This is no longer a list of sentences but a text, and as a text it prompts the reader to derive some meaningful discourse from it. What is the point of these repetitions, this permutation of words? The sentences taken separately are semantically simple, but, as with the Morrison example, it is their pragmatic significance that is elusive. Pondering on what this significance might be prompts a re-reading of the text, so the patterns get naturally and purposefully repeated: the focus on form is motivated by the quest for meaning.

Of course, this is not to say that this poem in particular will always prompt this quest. For many students, no doubt, it will inspire no interest whatever, and so they will not engage with it. It will always be necessary, as I have argued, to select language and design activities which are locally appropriate to particular groups of learners. What I have said about this poem is meant to illustrate the general point that purposeful repetition is a typical feature of poetic texts, and of our response to them. That being so, and if we accept that purposeful repetition is what (in part at least) is needed for learning, then poetry would seem to have an obvious potential to be pedagogically exploited, either by getting learners to process existing poetic texts, or, with suitable guidance, composing their own. [4]

This playing with language in literary mode is problem-solving of a kind, and problem-solving activities have, of course, long been a familiar feature of the English subject. Traditionally these tended to be tactical support activities, and the problems typically focused on were those concerned with correct encoding. Subsequently, and especially as proposed by Prabhu, problem-solving was adopted as a strategic pedagogic principle, and conceived of as an essentially pragmatic activity, defined not as an exercise in linguistic manipulation, but as a task which required the contingent use of language for its solution. (See Prabhu 1987; Widdowson 1990.) Prabhu's tasks were designed in response to a local situation. Over recent years, task-based instruction has been promoted to the status of a globally valid approach to language teaching (see Nunan 1989; J. Willis 1996), and provided with impressive backing in psycholinguistic research (see Crookes and Gass 1993; Skehan 1998a, 1998b). This is clearly an important and influential development in language pedagogy, and one that calls for careful consideration. I have argued in this chapter that activities in the language classroom have to satisfy two crucial pedagogic conditions. One is that the problem that is set has to be such as to engage learners in what they will take as purposeful activity; in other words it has to be appropriate to their reality. The second is that it has to be effective in activating their learning, which means that it has to develop their knowledge of the possible as a semantic resource for making meaning. It will be of interest to consider how far the current definition of the nature of the task corresponds to these conditions. Skehan has provided the most comprehensively theoretical rationale for task-based learning, so it seems reasonable to take his definition of the task as having some authority. This is what he says:

> ...a task is regarded as an activity which satisfies the following criteria:
> * Meaning is primary.
> * There is a goal which needs to be worked towards.
> * The activity is outcome-evaluated.
> * There is a real-world relationship.
> (Skehan 1998b: 268)

With regard to the first of these criteria, the indeterminate use of the term 'meaning' brings up the issue already discussed at length in this chapter concerning the distinction between semantics and pragmatics. Earlier in the paper from which this quotation is taken Skehan refers to a previous era

> ... in which form was primary and a concern for meaning only followed the establishment of control over specific forms.

It would appear from this that he subscribes to the familiar view that meaning as encoded semantically in form does not count. What is primary for him is pragmatic meaning.

The second and third criteria are clear enough on a general level, but they do not specify what *kind* of goal or outcome a task to be designed for. And again the semantic/pragmatic distinction is crucial. If the goal is to achieve an immediate communicative objective, there is no guarantee that this will make any effective contribution to the process of learning, for, of course, it is possible for learners to get their message across without the means of doing so being internalized as a semantic resource available to be acted upon on future occasions. As was pointed out earlier in this chapter, this depends on the learners' ability to infer what a particular instance of language is an example of. Much the same observation can be made of the evaluation of the outcome. The outcome may be evaluated as entirely satisfactory as far as getting the task done is concerned, even if minimal language is used, or none at all. Evaluating the outcome in terms of what language has been learnt from the task is a very different matter. Furthermore, the effects on learning may be long-term and not at all evident from the immediate outcome. It cannot be assumed that investment will always yield immediate returns. Indeed, the evidence of the 'silent period' phenomenon would seem to suggest otherwise. In short, these criteria do not distinguish between the aims and outcomes relating to the performance of the task, and those which relate to the competence which it is the pedagogic purpose of the task to develop. However, Skehan's later comments seem to indicate that it is immediate task performance that he has in mind:

> What counts in task-based approaches, is the way meaning is brought into prominence by the emphasis on goals and activities (*sic* – ? outcomes?)

As formulated here, the criteria so far are defined in such broad terms that they can be said to apply equally well to the PPP activities of SOS teaching that task-based instruction claims to have superseded. This is not the case, of course, with the last criterion with its reference to the real world. What *kind* of relationship a task must have with the real world is not spelt out. But again subsequent comments are revealing:

> ... the real-world relationship implies that an activity focused on language itself cannot be a task. A transformation drill, for example, is an activity

which fills class time, but does not happen in the real world and so fails to meet this criterion.

A point that might be made here is that it is by no means unknown, of course, for focusing on language itself to happen in the real world, as is well documented in the sociolinguistics literature.[5] But leaving that aside, we should note that the assumption Skehan makes here is that, as with Willis's communicative contexts discussed earlier in the chapter, there is only one real world: that of the language user, and this must be somehow replicated if the learning activity is to be valid. As has been argued earlier, what this ignores is that what happens in the real world of language users may be utterly unreal for learners, for they inhabit quite different worlds. In another formulation of this criterion, Skehan modifies this requirement:

> ... there is some sort of relationship to comparable real-world activities. (Skehan 1998a: 95)

But of course, formulated thus, this is a criterion that would apply to almost anything that goes on in the classroom. Even what goes on in the most reactionary of SOS lessons can be said to be *sort of* related to the real world, comparable up to a point. How close to replication does an activity have to be to count as comparable? If any purposeful use of language counts, then whatever the learners do with the language to make it meaningful to them would meet the criterion. And, as we have noted, learners are quite capable of creating fanciful worlds of their own, of appropriating the language to their own purposes and making it real for themselves on their own terms. Even such activities as a transformation drill can be converted by learners into something real and meaningful, whereby they exploit the very foreignness of the language. (See Kramsch and Sullivan 1996; Sullivan 2000.) Learners can engage with language, and learn from it, without reference to the kind of transactional goals and outcomes that obtain in language use in the ordinary way. They may indeed subvert them by language play, which, as previously noted, has a powerful reality of its own, and is an effective device for learning for children and adults alike (Cook 2000).[6]

Task-based learning is widely represented as a new and improved way of conceiving of what the subject English is, or should be, all about. The criteria that are proposed as defining features of tasks are, however, so loosely formulated, it seems to me, that they do not distinguish tasks from other and more traditional classroom activities. True, the real world criterion would, on the face of it, appear to be distinctive, and of course it is consistent with the current advocacy of authenticity. But even this is so hedged in its wording that it seems to allow for almost any interpretation that is convenient. And when one looks at actual examples of tasks, this becomes quite apparent. The following are identified as task-based activities:

- completing one another's family trees;
- agreeing on advice to give to the writer of a letter to an agony aunt;

- discovering whether one's paths will cross (out of school) in the next week;
- solving a riddle;
- leaving a message on someone's answer machine.
(Skehan 1998a: 95–6)

The first of these is hardly an activity which normally occurs in the routine of everyday life: its relationship with the real world is surely tenuous, to say the least. Solving a riddle is even more so. The essential point about a riddle is precisely that it prevents a normal contextual connection with the real world. It is a device which usually plays on words and the problem that it poses is not a pragmatic but a semantic one. Solving a riddle crucially depends on focusing on language itself, so on Skehan's own account fails to qualify as a task. The second of these activities is no doubt one that figures in the real life of some people, but is surely not of regular occurrence, and the third would only happen if there were some purpose in doing it (arranging to meet for lunch, for example): one does not just discover where paths cross as a matter of inconsequential fact. Of all these activities, it is only the last which can be said to correspond with the normal uses of language in everyday life.

It is hard to see how these activities could have been identified by applying the proposed criteria. What they most obviously have in common is that they are all devices for contriving a context in the classroom which will give some purpose to a repetitive use of language. Although lip service may be paid to the criteria which supposedly define task-based learning, in practice they appear to be more honoured in the breach than the observance. This becomes clear, I think, if we examine the activities here specified with reference to a list of features that are said to define what tasks are *not*. Skehan again:

A complementary approach (*i.e. to specifying defining criteria*) is to show what tasks are not, since it is often just as clarifying to specify what an alternative position represents. In this respect, and following Willis (1996), tasks:
- do not give learners other people's meanings to regurgitate;
- are not concerned with language display;
- are not conformity-oriented;
- are not practice-oriented;
- do not embed language into materials so that specific structures can be focused upon.
(Skehan 1998a: 95)

It seems to me that the activities that Skehan proposes (completing a family tree, for example, or solving a riddle) actually *do* have these features which are supposed to disqualify them as tasks. Consider the first and third of these features.

Learning a language, whether your own or somebody else's, must always be in some degree a matter of learning other people's meanings and conforming to the conventions for their encoding and communicative use. As corpus descriptions reveal so clearly, the reality of ordinary everyday uses of language is that they are marked by patterns of co-occurrence in varying degrees of formulaic fixity. It is this which constitutes its distinctive idiom. Much of our normal language behaviour is a regurgitation of the patterns we have picked up from others. If students are to approximate to normal language behaviour in completing their family trees, or writing their letters to agony aunts, or leaving their messages on an answer machine, they will have to regurgitate and conform. Otherwise, they will produce English which is unreal, being, in Hymes' terms, neither possible, nor appropriate, nor actually attested. The other non-task features mentioned here have essentially to do with the avoidance of a focus on form.

Tasks are supposedly not designed as devices for language practice, but on the evidence of the examples we are given they clearly are, and if they did not embed specific structures and focus on them to some degree, it is hard to see how they can induce the language learning process. As to language display, if tasks have no concern with this at all, then how, one wonders, are outcomes to be evaluated? The learners themselves know well enough that the tasks require them to put on display what they know of the language and how to use it.

Of course there may be good reasons for disguising these features and even pretending that they are not there, but there seems little point in denying them. It might be objected that they are not actually being denied: it is not that conformity, practice, structure focus are excluded, but only that tasks are not 'oriented' to them. But if this is to be a specification of task features, we need to know precisely just how orientation is to be defined, and if these non-oriented features are also to have a role to play, just what that role might be.

It seems clear that there *is* a concern for formal encoding in task-based instruction (TBI), but that it is considered as a secondary and contingent matter. It is assumed that, given pre-task and post-task prompting, it will be learnt as a corollary to the communicative activity the task itself is designed to bring about.

The essential difference between SOS and TBI is not, as seems generally to be supposed, that the former involves pedagogic contrivance and the latter does not. Both of them set up contexts in the classroom which are designed to induce learning. Tasks do not naturally occur any more than do the situational demonstrations that we discussed earlier. The difference is that in SOS, contexts are devised to get learners to internalize semantic meaning, on the assumption that its pragmatic use could be left for the learners to work out for themselves, whereas with TBI contexts are devised to get learners involved in pragmatic use, on the assumption that this will activate the acquisition of semantic encoding. Generally speaking, the belief underlying the SOS approach is that competence is primary, and performance will emerge as a by-product. The TBI belief is the reverse: get performance right and competence will, with some prompting, take care of itself.

The great advantage of tasks is that they allow for learner engagement in realizing the communicative potential of the encoded semantic resource in ways that SOS neglects to do. But then the encoded potential has to be accounted for in their design. The problem with the definition of tasks in TBI, at least in the formulation we have been considering, seems to be that, in setting itself up in opposition to SOS, it has given undue prominence to the pragmatic side of things to the relative neglect of the semantic. Furthermore, the pragmatic side of things is defined in reference to 'authentic use', what normally happens in the real world, so that the classroom should replicate the conditions of 'real' communication as closely as possible. This, as I have argued, is not just an unnecessary criterion for task design, but is also one which it is impossible to meet. What is more, attempting to satisfy it is likely only to compromise the very effectiveness of the task, which must depend on devising contexts of use in the classroom which are both purposeful for the learners and provide them with language to learn from.

One gets the impression that for proponents of TBI it is this authenticity criterion that is of primary importance, and that all the other criteria have to defer to it. Hence the ambivalence about the so-called 'focus on form'. This, on the one hand, makes for unreal language and so it must be avoided at all costs. But on the other hand, it seems that learners need to focus on form to learn the language, and so it is brought in through the back door, so to speak, before the task proper, or after it. The fact that in consequence you inevitably reduce the authenticity of the task is not, it would seem, a relevant consideration.

The way in which SOS defined what language the subject should deal with, and how, had its shortcomings. In essence it concentrated too fixedly on getting learners to internalize the possible, how semantic meaning is encoded in form, and neglected to make it real by engaging learners in realizing this meaning as a resource for communication. The problem with SOS is not that it dealt with contrived language, but that its contrivance, in the three phases of presentation, practice, and production, lacked pragmatic point for the learners. One reaction to this is to reject this approach altogether as an outdated remnant of an earlier era and replace it with a new one: out with SOS and in with TBI. Another, and to my mind preferable, procedure is to give critical attention to the basic tenets of SOS and TBI to establish where they correspond and where they might complement each other.

And this is what I have sought to do in this chapter in the context of our discussion on what kind of English, and what activities using it, are appropriate to the purposes of the subject, how one might define English *as a foreign language*, or English *for* (not *to*) speakers of other languages. In talking about the language to be presented in the class and the activities with language that are to be engaged with, we have, of course, made reference to the agents involved in these processes, the teachers and learners of English. We now need to consider what implications arise from our previous discussion about the roles these classroom participants might play. We have so far concentrated on how the E of ESOL is to be defined. In the next chapter, we focus our attention on the learners—on the SOL, the speakers of other languages themselves—and on the teachers—those concerned with the T of TESOL.

Notes and comments

1   Some advocates of authentic language go so far as to suggest that contrived language is not only pedagogically unsound but unethical into the bargain. Consider these comments:

> We know from our own knowledge of our first language that in most textbook discourse we are getting something which is *concocted* for us, and may therefore rightly resent being *disempowered* by teachers and materials writers, who, on *apparently laudable ideological grounds*, appear to know better.
> (Carter and McCarthy 1996, emphasis added)

In this view, the decisions that teachers and materials writers make under the pretence of knowing better are motivated not by any pedagogic considerations but by a misconceived, even devious ideology that in effect disempowers learners and denies them the right to learn. I do not know which teachers and textbook writers Carter and McCarthy have in mind, but those of my acquaintance do not fit this description, and would 'rightly resent' this interpretation of what they are trying to achieve.

2   The PPP cycle that typifies the SOS approach has become the target of heavy attack in recent years, particularly in Willis 1996. In that volume, for example, Lewis, in promoting his 'lexical approach', declares that

> ...any paradigm based on, *or remotely resembling*, Present-Practise-Produce (PPP) is wholly unsatisfactory, *failing as it does to reflect either the nature of language or the nature of learning*. It is not sufficient to suggest that such a paradigm represents one of a number of ways in which language is learned; *the fact is that the PPP paradigm is, and always was, nonsense*.
> (Lewis 1996: 11, emphasis added)

I do not know how Lewis can be so certain about the nature of language and learning as to make such a confident assertion of fact, but it seems a touch extravagant, to say the least, to condemn a well-tried approach, and anything remotely resembling it, in such dismissive terms.

Other condemnations of PPP are rather less extreme and more reasoned. Thus Skehan, in the chapter that follows Lewis, concedes that the approach has its advantages before going on to give reasons why none of the advantages is actually pedagogically valid and proposing that it should be abandoned in favour of a radically different task-based approach. I put forward reasons myself later in this present chapter why this may not be as radically different an alternative as Skehan suggests.

But there is another point to be made about Skehan's criticism of PPP, and this bears on the very principles of applied linguistic enquiry which I discuss in the first chapter of this book. Inadequate, discredited, wrong-headed though the PPP approach is said to be, it has nevertheless persisted. Why should this be so? This is what Skehan has to say:

> Given that there is little *evidence* in its favour, or *theory*, it is surprising that it has been so enduring in its influence. To account for this, we must return to points that were made regarding its convenience for the teaching profession. It has served to perpetuate a comfortable position for teachers and teacher trainers.
> (Skehan 1996: 18, emphasis in the original)

The suggestion here seems to be that the approach has endured because it is a soft option which teachers have gone for because it suits them, without bothering about its effect on learners, deliberately ignoring the evidence that it is useless. What teachers are charged with here is tantamount to unprofessional conduct, the wilful dereliction of pedagogic duty. Against this, one might suggest that the approach has endured because teachers genuinely believed in it, and found some basis of their belief in their classroom experience. Now there may be reasons for questioning this belief, but this surely does not justify just airily dismissing it as wrong. This, for generations of teachers is their pedagogic culture, their reality, and it needs to be taken into account in the mediation process. Whatever evidence or theory can be invoked by academic enquiry as grounds for calling the approach into question, these cannot simply be unilaterally applied.

It is worth noting that this is not just a matter of applied linguistic principle, but of practical feasibility. Even if there were grounds for a complete rejection of everything that PPP (or anything remotely resembling it) stands for in favour of a radically different approach, this approach has to be such as to be *teachable*. And this surely calls for teacher conversion on a massive scale. If teachers continue incorrigibly to consult their own comfort rather than the interests of their students, then the demands imposed on them by the very radical nature of the new approach will be such that it is unlikely ever to get off the ground as a practicable alternative.

3   Children appear to be particularly adept at constructing imagined realities out of the most seemingly arid of didactically designed language, and learning from it in consequence. Consider this extract from Nabokov's autobiography *Speak, Memory*:

> I learned to read English before I could read Russian. My first English friends were four simple souls in my grammar—Ben, Dan, Sam and Ned.

> There used to be a great deal of fuss about their identities and where-abouts—'Who is Ben?', 'He is Dan', 'Sam is in bed', and so on. Although it all remained rather stiff and patchy (the compiler was handicapped by having to employ—for the initial lessons, at least—words of not more than three letters), *my imagination somehow managed to obtain the necessary data.* Wanfaced, big-limbed, silent nitwits, proud in their possession of certain tools ('Ben has an axe'), they now drift with a slow-motioned slouch across the remotest backdrop of memory...
> (quoted in Brumfit 1991: 29, emphasis added)

In the case of Nabokov's grammar, the imagined reality that Nabokov as learner derived from it was, presumably, incidental to its intended design. But compilers of traditional language teaching textbooks have very often turned their handicap to creative advantage and composed stories and dialogues out of limited language designed to engage the interest and imagination of learners. The kind of deliberate exploitation of simple language to create a literary effect that I have illustrated in this chapter is a common feature of language textbooks. Such materials are effective to the extent not that they are true to life, but that they represent a fictional world that carries conviction. In this respect, the writing of language textbooks can turn into an exercise in literary creativity.

4 I have discussed the use of literary texts as a resource for language teaching elsewhere (for example, Widdowson 1984, 1990), and various activities which involve learners in their own literary composition by textual manipulation are proposed in Widdowson 1992b. Such manipulation, it is argued, is motivated by a pragmatic purpose: it necessarily focuses the learners' attention on linguistic features in the process of realizing their meaning and their possible literary effect. The case for the use of literary texts is also argued in Kramsch 1993, and demonstrated in Carter and Long 1987; Duff and Maley 1990, and is, of course, consistent with ideas about the significance of language play expounded in Cook 2000. For a dissenting view, see Edmondson 1997, and for a reaction to it, Widdowson 2000c.

5 See, for example, Holmes 1992: Chapter 13; Bauer and Trudgill 1998. Although, as we have seen, it has become received wisdom that focusing on form is a kind of linguistic abnormality that only happens in language classrooms, it is in actual fact a widespread and entirely normal feature of language in its social context. As is clear from the work by Cameron and Preston referred to in Chapter 7, Note 2 (Cameron 1995; Preston 1991, 1998), 'ordinary' folk think and talk explicitly about language a good deal, and pay considerable attention to what they consider to be the proper norms of correct usage.

6 In a recent article, Cook has argued for the use of 'ludicrous invented sentences in language teaching' on the grounds that they are both imagina-
tively appealing and noticeable (Cook 2001). In his view, therefore, they
have the potential to meet both of the pedagogic conditions that I have
been discussing in this chapter: they both engage the learner's reality, and
activate the learning process. His article provoked a rejoinder from his
namesake V. Cook, who takes a starkly different view. He comments:

> …input for language acquisition mostly provides data for the mind to
> work on, just as the digestive system works on the vitamins in one's
> food. The message of the input sentences could be anything at all, pro-
> vided they contain the necessary language elements on which the mind
> can build; it doesn't much matter what your food tastes like or whether
> you eat liver or spinach provided you get iron in your diet.
> (V. Cook 2002: 265)

In this view, the condition of learner engagement is irrelevant. You do not
have to whet the appetite for the language or develop a taste for it. The
learner, it would seem, is conceived of not as a human being but as a diges-
tive system.

10 Metalanguage and interlanguage

Earlier in this book (in Chapter 6), I made the point that uses of language are associated with purposes of some kind; when we talk about English for specific purposes, we refer to the kind of encodings and conventions of use that have been developed by particular discourse communities to serve their needs for communication and a sense of identity. The language of classroom teaching has its specific purposes, too, designed to meet the needs of particular communities of learners, and in the discussion in the last two chapters I have been considering how that language might be defined. I have argued that the kind of encodings that are selected, and the kind of activities devised to present them and put them to use have to be pedagogically appropriate and cannot be simply imported directly from the actually attested texts and contextually appropriate discourses of native-speaker users of the language. In the terms used in Chapter 6, we can talk about language pedagogy with reference to its registers (the encoded forms) and the genres (the exercises, tasks, or other activities) that are suited to the needs of particular groups of learners.

There is, of course, one crucial difference between classroom language and that which occurs in discourse communities of users. It is unilaterally determined and controlled. Whereas in other domains, the language develops by the natural process of multilateral interaction and communal accord, in the classroom the teacher takes charge of its development: directs it, corrects it, and sets the conditions of appropriate use. Although, as we shall see later in this chapter, learners will always find room for manoeuvre, it is the teacher who sets limits on their initiative. Inevitably, what we have in the classroom is an unequal encounter, and one, of course, which is further marked by a sharp disparity of linguistic knowledge: one party, the teacher, is competent in English (or whatever the language subject is), and the other, the learners, are not. The process that goes on in the language lesson involves the bringing together of two versions of English: that which is provided by teacher and textbook as input to the process, and that which learners have made of this input, the current state of their proficiency. Typically, of course, the two do not correspond. And typically, neither of them corresponds with what passes as normal language in its communities of users.

The teacher/textbook language, as I have indicated in the previous chapters, is designed for instruction, no matter how 'authentic' its original source. Its purpose is to engage learners in the process of learning, to explain, and to exemplify. It is, in short, language designed to teach language. In this chapter I will use the term teacher *metalanguage* (stretching it a little, perhaps) to refer to all cases when language is put to this didactic purpose. One of the obvious features of metalanguage in this sense is that, in principle at least, it always conforms to the possible (in Hymes' terms), to what is accepted as correct encoding.

The learners' version of English is quite different. Its most obvious characteristic is its failure to conform. It seems to have a life of its own, and this has, of course, been extensively documented in second language acquisition research. The learners' idiosyncratic nonconformities, can, from the teacher's point of view, be seen as deviations, errors of encoding to be corrected. But they can be regarded, and these days generally *are* regarded, positively, as evidence of learning beyond teacher/textbook input, states of *interlanguage* which learners must necessarily go through on their way to native-speaker competence. These interim versions of English are, in fact, exploitations of the virtual language. (See Chapter 5.)

The obvious problem for language pedagogy is to establish how teacher metalanguage (ML) designed to induce learning, and learner interlanguage (IL), the learning that actually takes place, can be most effectively related. Traditional thinking holds that IL should be brought in line with ML. More recent thinking reverses the dependency and argues that it is ML that should be brought in line with IL. In this chapter I will consider these positions in some detail, but first, we need to consider what form the teacher's ML takes.

When considering dictionary entries in Chapter 8, it was pointed out that two kinds of information are typically provided. First comes the definition of the semantic meaning of the word. Here ML takes the form of *explanation*:

quaff (*obj*) *v* to drink (something) quickly or in large amounts. (*CIDE*)

The metalinguistic function here is marked by a kind of analytic shorthand. Although the defining phrase is in English, it is not meant to represent normal pragmatic utterance. The same point would apply to the definition of other word classes. Thus the word 'cat' might be defined as 'small domesticated furry feline animal'. This again is an analytic expression, a verbalization of semantic features that are lexicalized as the word 'cat'. As was observed in Chapter 3, the use of such an expression in the course of an ordinary conversation would strike us as distinctly odd, contextually out of place. But this is because we know what is pragmatically normal and what is not. For learners, problems might arise if they do not recognize these defining expressions as metalinguistic devices and so not freely transferable to contexts of use. The problem does not perhaps arise with the domesticated furry feline animal, but it could well arise with other cases where the defining terms are less obviously marked as such. Consider, for example, the words 'crab', 'lobster', 'prawn'. These might be defined by using the more general term 'crustacean', but in respect to actual use this has a more restricted range of use and (as the findings of corpus analysis would reveal) collocates very differently from any of the words it defines. 'Shellfish' might be preferable, but even here, the appropriateness conditions will be different. Furthermore, both of these terms might be rejected on the grounds that they are not sufficiently transparent to function as part of an explanation. One of the principles of pedagogic dictionaries is that the terms used to define a word should be simpler than the word defined. Following this principle, dictionaries will often specify a defining vocabulary. But this does not resolve the problem; on the contrary, in some ways, it exacerbates it. For a defining vocabulary is generally drawn from the most frequently occurring words, that is to say those which have the widest pragmatic currency, and this must encourage the assumption of general contextual appropriateness. So in the present case, in the definition of the words 'crab', 'lobster', and 'prawn' we might find the term 'sea animal' or 'sea creature'. But these are not expressions which anybody would normally use. If you are at a fishmonger, the contextually appropriate word is 'shellfish'; if you are at a restaurant, 'seafood', but neither is sufficiently explicit as explanation, and neither is likely to figure in a defining vocabulary.

The metalinguistic function of the first part of a dictionary entry, then, is to *explain* denotation, or what is semantically encoded in the language, and the learners need to understand that the defining terms that are used do not, in spite of any appearance to the contrary, have the character of the normal use of words. The function of the second part of the dictionary entry is to *exemplify* how the word is used, and here, obviously, the expressions provided are meant to be taken as conforming to normal usage.[1] Traditionally these expressions are plausible inventions based on the dictionary maker's own intuitive knowledge of the language, prompted by reference to other dictionaries. More recently, as we have seen, they are samples from a corpus of attested usage. But in either case, whether this is done by invention or selection, the expressions need to give some indication to the learner of just what they typify as examples. Inventions tend to relate to the definitions more closely and so to exemplify how the semantic meaning of the words finds expression in possible sentences. As we have seen in Chapter 8, exemplifying the typical patterns of textual use is a much more difficult thing to do, and in practice will often involve not only the careful selection but also the editing and adaptation of language samples. Again we see how metalinguistic requirement calls for contrivance of some kind and to some degree.

However well exemplifications are invented, selected, or adapted, they will always depend on explanation, and their order of appearance in dictionary entries represents this dependency. No dictionary to my knowledge ever reverses this sequence, allowing learners to infer a definition inductively from examples, although, we might note in passing, such a discovery procedure can be activated by computer programs of the kind pioneered by Johns and his colleagues referred to in Chapter 8 (Johns 1994; Johns and King 1991).

No matter how well invented, selected, and adapted, exemplifications will always be partial and pose some problem for the learner as to what exactly they exemplify. But explanations are also necessarily partial, and this too is something that learners need to understand. Dictionary entries cannot obviously provide an exhaustive account of every semantic feature of a word, but only those which are assumed to be central or salient in some way. Thus we noted in the last chapter that in the definition of the word 'quaff', one dictionary includes the information that the verb denotes drinking alcohol, and another does not. The assumption in the second case, presumably, is that the learners can infer the missing information for themselves, perhaps with the aid of the examples subsequently provided. The same point applies to the way dictionaries vary in the number of distinctive meanings they identify for a particular word.

The variation reflects pedagogic assumptions about what learners need to have made explicit and what they can be left to infer themselves by subsequent learning. Take the case of the word 'drink', for example. A dictionary might specify that as a count noun this denotes an amount of liquid taken into the body through the mouth, but make no further specification about what kind of liquid this might be. Another might distinguish two senses: 'drink 1)', where the liquid is alcoholic, and 'drink 2)', where it is not. Another might also provide the information that when the noun is used alone without postmodification it is generally the first sense that applies, and not the second (so if someone says that they need a drink, it is alcoholic liquid they have in mind). All this, of course, brings up the issue of how much information about collocational and colligational normality, as mentioned in Chapter 7, should be incorporated into semantic definition, that is to say, how far the possible is to be defined by reference to the regularities attested in the actually performed. From the pedagogic point of view, the question has to do with what was referred to earlier (in Chapter 8) as effective investment: what needs to be included in explanation to provide for the subsequent process of further learning.[2]

The metalinguistic use of language for learning in dictionaries, then, takes the form of explanation and exemplification of word meanings, and we would expect both to be regulated in reference to pedagogic judgement as to what will most effectively activate the learning process. The same is true of pedagogic descriptions of grammar. Here, too, we find language used to describe language in the formulation of grammatical rules and regularities, statements about generalities of form and meaning. Consider these examples:

> **The simple past tense**... describes events, actions or situations which occurred in the past and are now finished. A time reference is usually given or strongly implied.
> **Sam phoned a moment ago.**
> (Alexander 1993: 288)

We use the **simple past** for **complete finished actions**. We often use it in **stories**. *I **wrote ten letters*** yesterday. A man ***walked*** into a police station and *asked*...
(Swan and Walter 2001)

As with the dictionary entries, we have explanation coupled with exemplification. And again, what have been singled out are features of this tense form which are thought to be salient. The exemplifying expressions would appear in both cases to be inventions rather than attested samples of use, metalinguistically designed indeed to be examples of the meaning of the tense form that has been explained (hence the appearance of the adverbial time indicator). They resemble kernel sentences rather than actually occurring utterances (see Chapter 7). As with the dictionary entries, the explanations are partial precisely because of their pedagogic focus on what is thought to be essential. It is easy enough to point to their shortcomings as comprehensive descriptive statements. Thus, the simple past is not the only verb form that signals completed actions in the past. The present perfect does as well ('Sam has phoned for a taxi', 'I have written to my accountant'). Nor does the past tense only signal past time. It can indicate actions which are hypothetical ('If you consulted your accountant more often, your finances would be in better shape') and can signify modality in the present ('I wondered if you could phone for a taxi'). Indeed, it can be argued that the past tense, in spite of its name, is only incidentally associated with past time, and that its essential semantic is that it denotes *distancing* of the speaker from the proposition expressed. Time is one dimension of distance, but only one.

But to say this is to apply descriptive linguistic criteria and these, as we have argued in previous chapters, are not necessarily relevant to pedagogic prescriptions of this kind, which are designed not to account for all aspects of meaning but those which can be accessed and acted upon most readily by learners. The quality which these prescriptions need to have is what we might refer to as learning valency. This is a term which linguists borrowed from chemistry to refer to the capacity of a sentence constituent to contract relationships with others. According to the *OED*, the term 'valency' denotes:

The combining power of an atom measured by the number of hydrogen atoms it can displace or combine with.

In respect to pedagogic prescription, we might define valency as the power certain encoded features have to combine with other features to activate the learning process. Valency, therefore, is a measure of investment value as discussed in Chapter 8, and has to do with language which is useful for learning more language. This is distinct from what is sometimes known as surrender value, which is a different measure of usefulness, being concerned with the extent to which the language learnt so far can be put to communicative use in situations outside the classroom, and which is therefore more consistent with the rehearsal rather than the investment principle as defined in the last chapter. The two kinds of usefulness are not necessarily at odds with each other, but in recent years, in certain versions of communicative language teaching, the tendency has been to prefer surrender value to valency and to concentrate on rehearsing learners in patterns of communicative performance at the expense of a longer-term investment in competence.

The point is, then, that metalanguage does not directly reflect the actual facts of language as it occurs, but is a device to explain and exemplify linguistic features of high learning valency. Indeed, if it *did* reflect the actual facts, it would *de*flect attention from what is seen as essential for learning.

There are however objections that can be raised against this line of argument, and these we must now address. The first is that whatever the pedagogic justification for the use of metalanguage, there is no escaping from the fact that it is, nevertheless, a misrepresentation of the facts of natural language which learners will eventually have to acquire. That being so, they will be misled into learning things that they will subsequently have to unlearn. Thus these partial explanations and invented examples would seem to compromise the very purpose they are meant to serve. This is the kind of argument that is put forward in favour of presenting real language and the actual facts of usage in the classroom. This is what John Sinclair has to say on the matter:

> The relation between the conscious impressions we have of language and subliminal usage is also vital information for the language professional. As a corollary to this it should not ever be necessary for students to 'unlearn' anything they have been taught. They cannot be taught everything at once, and because our knowledge of the textual detail of language has been so vague, they have been taught half-truths, generalities which apply only in some circumstances. However, we now have the information on which accurate selection can be made.
> (Sinclair 1991: 499–500)

There are two points that need to be made here, both, I believe, of fundamental pedagogic significance. This first is that it is not just that learners cannot be taught everything *at once*, but that they cannot be taught everything *at all*. As I have argued in previous chapters, there are some things, perhaps even most things, about the language and its use, including idiomatic nuance and the specifics of contextual appropriacy, that have to be left to be learnt. Hence the need to get learners to invest in those things which have the most valency and so generate further learning. The second, and related, point concerns the nature of learning itself. Although there are differences of view about the language learning process, there is a general acceptance that whatever else it might be, it is not simply additive. The acquisition of competence is not accumulative but adaptive: learners proceed not by adding items of knowledge or ability, but by a process of continual revision and reconstruction. In other words, learning is necessarily a process of recurrent unlearning and relearning, whereby encoding rules and conventions for their use are modified, extended, realigned, or abandoned altogether to accommodate new language data. The whole learning process is a matter of continual conceptual adaptation whereby the learner gradually approximates to the second language norm, however that is defined. In other words, the process involves passing through different transitional stages of interlanguage, each of which is an adapted version of the one preceding. Learning can only proceed by unlearning.

But this, one can argue, does not address the point that Sinclair is making. For what he says is not that it should never be necessary for students to unlearn what they have *learnt*, but what they have been *taught*. And a little later in the paper from which I quoted earlier he makes the distinction quite explicit:

> Students may have to unlearn some of their own projections and hypotheses, but that is a different matter from unlearning what has been authoritatively put forward as an accurate observation about the language. (Sinclair 1991: 500)

But these projections and hypotheses presumably derive in some way from the language that is taught, and represent what students make of the input data they receive. As every teacher knows, what is put forward to be taught, whether it claims to be an accurate observation about the language or not, cannot be equated with what will be learnt. If this is so, then the concern that students might have to unlearn what they have been taught seems to be unfounded since the chances are they will not have learnt it in the first place. Rather, in the natural process of learning, they will have used it to make their own projections and hypotheses. In effect, therefore, students do quite naturally unlearn what they have been taught. You have to assume, contrary to all the evidence, that learning maps directly on to teaching to believe otherwise. And is it really the case that what teachers and textbook writers put forward is represented as accurate observations about the language, and that the students take it as such? Students are surely fully aware that they are being taught a subject which, like any other subject, is a genre which sets its own conventions, so that what they are getting is language designed for a specific instructional purpose. So when they encounter the Brown family at breakfast in their textbooks exchanging well formed sentences with each other, it seems unlikely they will be deceived into thinking that this is how native speakers actually use English, and suffer culture shock later when they discover otherwise. It does not seem to me that teachers and textbook writers who deal in contrived language are pretending that it is anything else. They do not claim that their examples are 'real' or their observations 'accurate' but that they serve to activate the learning process, and therefore allow for subsequent unlearning.

In sum, it seems very doubtful that what is prescribed as language for learning is generally put forward as an accurate observation about the language, that is to say about the language as used normally in native-speaker contexts. It is put forward as a pedagogic version of that language with a meta-linguistic function, appropriate for instruction because it is designed to activate just the projections and hypotheses which Sinclair refers to. And I do not think that students are deceived into thinking otherwise. They know full well that they are indeed students, and as such are required to study the language as a subject, and this, like any other subject, has been designed to take them through different stages of learning and so from simpler to more complex versions of factuality or reality.

The first objection to metalinguistically motivated contrivance, that it is a deceptive misrepresentation of real language, does not, then, seem to be peda-gogically tenable. There is a second objection, however, which is less easy to counter. Metalanguage, I have claimed, is justified on the grounds that it facili-tates learning. But learners, it would appear, have their own agenda, continu-ally adjusting their projections and hypotheses as they move through different stages of their interlanguage. So how do we know that metalanguage keys into this process? In certain crucial respects, after all, the two phenomena are quite distinct. Metalanguage is deliberately regulated by the teacher as *input*. Interlanguage is unintentionally regulated in the learner's mind and a matter of *intake*. So how are the two to be brought into correspondence? For if the way language is prescribed, exemplified, and explained does not correspond with the way learners actually learn, then it surely becomes an imposition which, far from facilitating the learning process, actually makes it more difficult.

This issue has figured prominently in discussions about the design of the foreign language syllabus. As we have noted in previous chapters, the syl-labus defines the content of the subject in terms of what is to be achieved as eventual objective and in terms of the process that is to be followed to achieve it. The objective sets conditions on the selection of language to be taught; but how it is then to be sequentially ordered, or graded, depends on how the *process* is conceived. And here is the crux of the matter. The familiar conven-tional procedure is to grade language items along a continuum of increasing linguistic complexity on the assumption that simpler items will be easier to learn and will also have what I have called a greater valency on the grounds that they can be extended and combined to make more complex structures and meanings. This seems reasonable enough, but what if the natural process of learning does not follow this kind of rational progression? What if the learners' interlanguage, quite literally, takes a different course, perhaps fol-lowing a valency principle not directly derivable from notions of linguistic complexity, or determined by other factors either of a universal cognitive kind, or specific to particular groups of learners? The fact of the matter is that the design of language instruction, including the metalinguistic devices of exemplification and explanation that we have been discussing in this chapter, has generally not been based on any empirically secure theory of second language learning.

There has, of course, been no shortage of research on the question. On the contrary, second language acquisition (SLA) studies have produced a massive amount of it in journals and books, enough to fill a library. This extensive work carried out over the past several decades has explored many a hypothesis and provoked much thought about the different factors affecting second language acquisition. Stimulating and suggestive though such work has been, however, it has not yielded anything in the way of conclusive findings upon which a relationship between metalanguage and interlanguage can be definitively established.

Nor, in my view, is any likely to be forthcoming in the future. And for reasons which would seem to be fairly obvious. Research on second language acquisition, focusing predominantly on grammar, enquires into the complexity of factors which affect language learning in general, and may extrapolate from particular cases to do so. But even when those cases are of actual classroom events rather than of controlled experimental design, the validity of the findings is bound to be limited to the particular conditions from which they are drawn. They give some of the essential bearings by which a teacher can steer a course, but they cannot determine the direction of the course itself.[3]

Here again we come up against the issue of partiality. I have already discussed, at some length, the necessary partiality of linguistic descriptions, no matter how comprehensive they claim to be. (See Chapter 8.) The same point applies to descriptions of language learning. Just as no linguistic description can account for the specific complexities of contextual conditions of use, so no research in second language acquisition can account for the varying complex of factors that come into play in the contexts of particular classrooms. In both cases there may be, and indeed have been, claims that reality has been captured: this is how language is really used on the one hand, and this is how language is really learnt on the other, but the reality is, and can only be, a partial one, a function in some degree of the mode of enquiry itself, and its relevance to classrooms is not self-evident but needs to be pedagogically established.

To establish this relevance, we need to consider a further point about second language acquisition research, and this has to do with the relationship between teacher and learner roles, as mentioned in Chapter 2, and more specifically with the direction of the dependency relationship between ML and IL that was mentioned earlier in this chapter. The traditional assumption in language teaching, or in the teaching of anything else if it comes to that, is that learning is essentially a matter of conformity, with teachers directing affairs and students deferring to their authority. When students showed signs of deviation, voluntarily or not, they were brought back into line, and made to see the error of their ways. This assumption has now, at least in many quarters, been rejected in favour of one diametrically opposed to it, namely that teaching should not proactively direct the learning process but should reactively respond to it. In this view, it is not now teacher authority but learner autonomy that is the essential determining factor in deciding what should go on in classrooms. In this case the teacher's task is to set up conditions which allow learning to take its natural course, and whatever ML is devised, it has to correspond with IL.

Here again we have the belief that in defining the subject we have to approximate as closely to reality as possible. Whereas with the authenticity principle, it is a matter of replicating the conditions of language use, with the autonomy principle, it is a matter of replicating the conditions of natural language learning. In neither case is the possibility recognized that the classroom might be a place where conditions can be *created* by contrivance to make language real and learning more effective. I made the point earlier (in Chapter 9) that the most obvious reality about the language subject is its intrinsic artificiality: it consists of a few periods a week appearing at random intervals and arbitrarily juxtaposed with other subjects as parts of the patchwork of the school timetable. Such circumstances do not lend themselves readily to the replication of authentic use. Nor for that of natural learning. It is an appealing idea that learners should be allowed to follow their own natural learning instincts, just as the idea that they should be forced into unnatural learning is an appalling one. But as with real English, the notion of natural learning is, I believe, pedagogically suspect.

Although there may be universal cognitive constraints that are a property of the human language faculty in general, the natural learning of a particular language depends on a whole host of fortuitous factors which have to do with the circumstances learners find themselves in, what kind of language they are exposed to, their attitude to its speakers, and so on; what they learn will be controlled, and confined, by these factors. We can infer from this what people learn in these naturally occurring circumstances, but not what they are *capable* of learning if the circumstances were different. The whole point of education is that it provides opportunities for developing this capability by fashioning circumstances which do not naturally occur. Its essential purpose, whatever the subject concerned, is to induce kinds of learning and ways of learning that would not otherwise happen. So what subjects do, and English or any other language subject is no exception, is in this sense to short-circuit the natural learning process, or direct it into different circuits altogether. And this has to be done within the very few artificially delimited periods allotted to the subject dotted about on the school timetable. Quite apart from the doubtful efficacy of natural learning, there is very little time for it to take its course.

So even if research were to provide us with reliable evidence about natural learning, it would be *circumstantial* evidence, and would not tell us what kinds or ways of learning might be induced by ML interventions. So it will not do to simply reverse the ML/IL dependency. This is not to say that in teaching we should deliberately set out to oppose learner initiative and insist on conformity, but only that such initiative needs to be given guidance. As was argued earlier, teaching cannot determine the learning process, but it can give it direction along lines learners would not easily discover for themselves, or would not discover at all. It is this, of course, which justifies the ML of explanation, as discussed earlier in this chapter. It may well be that some learners will sometimes, and after some time, induce conventions of encoding, or idiomatic patterns of usage, by using language 'naturally' in tasks or other kinds of communicative activity. But others might not. And some indeed might find that they can learn the language effectively by explanation and exemplification without doing tasks at all.

These points about the relationship between IL/ML can be referred back to what was said in the last chapter about the acronym TESOL. The advocacy of real English, I suggested, in effect treated the E as quite separate from the SOL so that the subject was defined as English which was incidentally being taught to learners who happened to speak other languages. I argued then that we need to define our subject in terms of the relationship between the E and the SOL, and therefore as essentially the teaching of the language as designed *for* speakers of other languages. The advocacy of natural learning, I would argue, is also based on isolating one part of the acronym and disregarding its relationship with others. In this case, the SOL is separated from the T. The SOL in TESOL relates as much to the T as to the E. As learners they are not just speakers of other languages but *students*, their role defined in relation to the other party in the pedagogic process, namely the teacher. Defining the subject, then, is not a matter of picking on one feature of TESOL and giving it preference over the others, but of working out how all of the features interrelate and affect each other.

By virtue of its relationship with T, then, the S of SOL refers to students, and it is this relationship between the two activities of these classroom participants that has been focused on in this chapter. But the point was also made in the last chapter that by virtue of its relationship with SOL the E of the subject is *English as a foreign language*. Since foreignness can only be identified in reference to another language which is not foreign, the subject, I suggested, must always be bilingual by implication. But the specific nature of this foreignness must be a matter of what the other languages are that its learners speak. All of this raises the question of how, if at all, the other language should figure in defining the subject English, and this is a matter I shall consider in the next chapter.

Notes and comments

1 Traditionally, the semantic explanation of denotation is couched in an analytic shorthand which makes its metalinguistic function quite distinctive. One of the innovations introduced by the *COBUILD Dictionary* was to change the style of the definition to give it the appearance of natural language. (See Chapter 8.) Compare the following entries for the verb 'drink':

drink. Take (liquid) into the mouth and swallow
(*OALD*)

drink. When you **drink** a liquid, you take it into your mouth and swallow it. (*COBUILD Dictionary*)

As the introduction to the *COBUILD Dictionary* has it, this is 'setting out the meaning in the way one ordinary person might explain it to another' (Sinclair 1995: xi). But the occasions when an ordinary person might be called upon to provide such a definition to another ordinary person must be rather few and far between. So we need to note, I think, that although the COBUILD entry takes the *form* of natural utterance, it is pragmatically abnormal in that it is unlikely to occur in normal circumstances of use. It is indeed an invented expression, not taken from a corpus of actually occurring language, and so unnatural by the criteria of the dictionary itself. The natural language form has the effect of blurring the distinction between semantic explanation and pragmatic exemplification. There may be a pedagogic rationale for this, of course, but in the absence of explanation, it remains unclear why this semblance of what ordinary persons might do is of help in explaining meaning to the language learner.

2 Another pedagogic issue arises here, namely how much of the detail of usage provided by the corpus analysis by computer it is helpful to display in dictionary entries. The computer is an extremely powerful device for description and can reveal collocational patterns which can serve as the basis for assigning different meanings to a word, and ranking these meanings according to frequency. It does not follow, however, that this information is necessarily helpful for learners. To present several meanings serially under different numbers might suggest that they are semantically distinct, whereas in many cases there is a core meaning from which others can be inferred. In this case, one can argue that understanding the core meaning is the best learning investment. And this core meaning, of course, is by no means always the most frequently occurring, so the learning process might not be best served by giving prominence to the most frequent meaning by presenting it first. Again we see how descriptive and pedagogic criteria might be at odds. (For further discussion on this, see Widdowson 1990.)

This primacy accorded to frequency finds expression in another feature that was introduced by COBUILD (and copied subsequently by other English dictionaries for learners). I refer to the information given in the frequency bands, which, according to Sinclair, 'means that when you look up a word you can immediately see how important it is' (Sinclair 1995: xiii). Thus the most frequent (and important) words in English are given five black diamonds, whereas the most infrequent (and unimportant) get none. I have already argued against the assumption that what is descriptively frequent is necessarily pedagogically important, and arguments against this assumption go back a long way. (See Mackey 1965, Chapter 6 and Chapter 8, Note 5.) These frequency bands, however, pose an additional problem even in their own descriptive terms. For they are attached only at the beginning of an entry and apply to the occurrence of the *form* of the word, not to any distinctive meanings it might have, nor even, it would seem, to its different grammatical functions. Thus our word 'drink', for example, is given a four diamond rating, but no indication is given as to how relatively frequent it is as a noun or verb, nor indeed in any of eleven different meanings that are assigned to it. Having carefully distinguished different meanings by reference to concordance evidence, it seems somewhat perverse to conflate them in one frequency band. And as Michael West noted half a century ago, if frequency is to be pedagogically relevant, then it is the meanings not just the forms of words that count, and need to be counted (West 1953).

3 It should also be added that the account that SLA gives of the process of learning is based on an idealized notion of native-speaker competence. The concept of interlanguage presupposes transitional stages from one well defined competence in the L1 to another in the L2. But as we have seen in earlier chapters, what actually constitutes native-speaker competence is extremely elusive of definition. Researchers in SLA have a way of talking about degrees of success and failure in achieving this competence without providing any specification as to what it actually consists of (see Cook 1999). Even if such a specification were to be provided, there is no reason why achieving such native-speaker competence should be taken as the only acceptable objective. On the contrary, as has been argued earlier, there are good reasons for rejecting such a goal as both irrelevant and unattainable. From the SLA point of view, any sign of nonconformity to native-speaker norms, non-defined though they are, is taken as evidence of fossilized learning. Clearly, there is a problem in reconciling the concept of interlanguage with the development of English as an international language.

For a comprehensive survey of research in SLA, see Ellis 1994. For a more succinct introduction see Ellis 1997; and Sridhar and Sridhar 1986.

11   Bilingualization and localized learning

The objective of a language subject is to develop in students a capability in a language (L2) other than their own (L1). Just how this capability is to be defined in respect to English was explored in the early chapters, and I shall return to it later in the concluding chapter. But however it is defined as an appropriate setting on the objective parameter, in achieving it students become bilingual in English and at least one other language. And, as I have already suggested in the previous chapter, the very foreignness of English means that the other language is implicated in some way in the process of achieving this capability as well. In short, English as a foreign language is bound to be a bilingual subject, and the purpose of this chapter is to enquire into what implications arise from this for the way the language is taught and learnt.

We begin with the general question of what it means to be bilingual. A distinction is routinely made in sociolinguistics between societal and individual bilingualism. Two languages may coexist in a particular society but they may be coordinate in the sense that they serve separate institutional and communal purposes, and so not all members of that society will necessarily have them both in their own heads. But it is only when the two languages *are* in individual heads that there is any contact between them. We may talk loosely about languages in contact, but there can only be contact through bilingual language *users*. As Spolsky has observed:

> However explained neurophysiologically, the phenomenon of bilingualism is the prime example of language contact, for the two languages are in contact in the bilingual.
> (Spolsky 1998: 49)

Now, as we have already noted, in teaching English as a foreign language our business is bilingualism. Our students come to class with one language (at least) and our task is to get them to acquire another one. So if bilingualism is the prime example of language contact in the individual, presumably we should be busy getting the first language (L1) and the foreign language (L2) into contact in our learners. But in many ways what we seem to be busy doing is exactly the opposite.

Language contact is traditionally thought of as a relationship between languages, and traces of transference of encodings (borrowed words, for example) are taken as evidence of its having taken place. There may be contact without any transference, of course, but the only evidence of contact is the change that is brought about as a result. It would seem to follow that if the contact occurs in individuals there must be some compounding of the two languages in their minds.

Spolsky, as do other sociolinguists, speaks of bilingualism as an achieved *state* (although acknowledging that the definition of that state is problematic); but what of the *process* of acquiring an additional language such as is induced in second language pedagogy? Bilingualism, in varying degrees, is the object-ive, but there has to be a learning process of *bilingualization* whereby this is achieved. There is plenty of evidence of contact here, of course. This is often described negatively as interference, and it is a common assumption that its effects need to be minimized, and eliminated completely if at all possible. Indeed the widely accepted idea that the first language should be avoided at all costs in the second language classroom, and translation resolutely discour-aged, is based on the belief that contact between the two languages is the last thing you want. So it would appear, paradoxically enough, that if bilingualism is to be defined as two languages in contact in the individual, conventional lan-guage teaching procedures are designed to stifle rather than promote it.

But *is* bilingualism satisfactorily defined in this way as a matter of language contact in the individual? I mentioned earlier that, if there is such contact, the languages concerned must be compounded in some way. Another distinction that is routinely made in the sociolinguistics literature is that between *com-pound bilingualism*, where the two languages fuse into a single signifying sys-tem, and *coordinate bilingualism*, where the two languages are kept apart as separate systems. It would appear that in seeking to prevent contact, and there-fore compounding, second language pedagogy sets out to keep the L1 and L2 quite separate, and so to promote coordinate bilingualism in learners directly.

But, as was discussed in the last chapter, all the evidence is that although the teacher may strive to induce coordinate bilingualism, what learners do is to go through a process of compound bilingualization through interlanguage stages. Now it may be that coordinate bilingualism occurs naturally in the *simultan-eous* acquisition of two (or more) languages in parallel in the primary social-ization process of upbringing. But in the case of the *consecutive* acquisition of an additional language as induced by instruction, this has to pass through a compounding period of interim interlanguage stages before coordinate compe-tence can be achieved. We might represent this learning process as follows:

L1 → L1/2 → L1 + L2

The teaching process, on the other hand, would appear to be more like:

L1 → L2 → L1 + L2

It would appear, then, that we have a disparity here between teaching pro-cedures, which are directed at keeping the languages coordinately separate by seeking to suppress L1, and learning that can only proceed by compounding them. This would seem to be rather a curious state of affairs, and one that warrants a little further enquiry.

The conventional wisdom that holds that monolingual teaching is the best way of getting bilingual results dates back a century at least, and is a legacy of the Direct Method (see Howatt 1984). As the accepted orthodoxy in language pedagogy, it was sustained by the behaviourist notion that learning was essentially a matter of regulating responses by controlled exposure to the target language. This was supposed to have the effect of establishing habits which would override interference from the learner's mother tongue, and so counteract bilingual compounding. Such interference was anticipated by the contrastive analysis of the L1 and L2 to establish the differences between the two languages in respect to their lexical, grammatical, and phonological encodings.

But contrastive analysis was used as a preventive measure: its purpose was to provide a basis for the specification in advance of course content which would counteract the effects of the L1. The findings remained in the background and were not meant to be overtly exploited in classroom activities as an aspect of methodology. The presence of the L1 in the *process* of learning the L2 was given no pedagogic warrant. As Stern points out:

> Contrastive analysis was not intended to offer a new method of teaching; but it was a form of language description across two languages which was particularly applicable to curriculum development, the preparation and evaluation of teaching materials, to the diagnosis of learning problems, and to testing.
> (Stern 1983: 159)

Contrastive analysis was designed for diagnosis and prevention: it was to provide the prophylactic means whereby the learning of the L2 might, as far as possible, be protected against L1 contagion. Its findings were not meant to inform methodology: there was no question of exploiting the learners' existing linguistic experience and expertise in their own language to facilitate the learning of the L2. On the contrary, the assumption was that all influence from the L1 was necessarily negative, and that the L2 could, and should, be directly internalized by the metalinguistic (ML) devices of demonstration and practice in accordance with behaviourist ideas. So contrastive analysis was directed at making monolingual *teaching* more effective, the essential purpose of which was to induce a separate modular development which, at the end of the day, yielded another language to be added as a coordinate to the one that learners already had.

What is curious, however, is that assumptions of the validity of monolingual pedagogy should have survived the discrediting of contrastive analysis as a diagnostic device, and the demise of behaviourist ideas. For with more cognitive views of learning comes the realization that learners cannot be immunized against the influence of their own language, that there is bound to be contact, and that language learning is indeed of its nature, in some degree, a compound bilingual experience. Just what kind of contact this is, and the extent of its effect on the learners' IL have, as was pointed out in the last chapter, been the concern of SLA research, and still remain matters of controversy and conjecture. But there seems to be no question that this effect, now more neutrally referred to as *transfer*, is a crucial phenomenon to be reckoned with, and one, furthermore, which is not to be avoided but positively welcomed. As Ellis puts it:

> ...there is now clear evidence that the L1 acts as a major factor in L2 acquisition. One clear advance in transfer research has been the reconceptualization of the influence of the L1, whereas in behaviourist accounts it was seen as an impediment (a cause of errors), in cognitive accounts it is viewed as resource which the learner actively draws on in interlanguage development.
> (Ellis 1994: 343)

There is a good deal of scepticism about the relevance of SLA research to practical pedagogy. Its findings are partial and unstable, at times methodologically suspect, and, as I have already argued in the last chapter, one needs to be circumspect about the extent to which they should determine the design of classroom instruction. But one thing comes across loud and clear: though we may not know just how and why, there is no doubt that the L1 is in some way implicated in L2 acquisition. Here is something we can be sure about: a finding we can accept with confidence. But, perversely enough, it is just this one certain thing that language pedagogy seems resolutely to ignore.

If the L1 is no longer to be viewed negatively as an impediment, which teachers would naturally wish to avoid or remove, but positively as a *resource*, then why, it seems reasonable to ask, do teachers not use it as such as well? If learners actively draw on this resource why, one wonders, do teachers not take advantage of this fortunate circumstance and devise ML procedures which do take into account a major factor in the learners' IL by encouraging them in the exploitation of this resource? The influence of the L1 may have been reconceptualized in SLA research, but this seems to have brought about no corresponding reconceptualization in second language teaching. In the proposals for task-based learning that were considered in Chapter 9, for example, though supposedly underwritten by SLA research, the influence of the L1, far from being seen as a major factor, seems to be given no explicit recognition whatever. The assumption is still that the only reality that is to be admitted to the classroom is that which is associated with the L2. Reconceptualization is conspicuous by its absence. The dominant pedagogy remains determinedly monolingual.

One might, of course, take the view that the beneficial effects of the LI depend on its *not* being overtly recognized as a resource, that to be effective the learners' active drawing upon it has to be an undercover operation, a process of resistant autonomy: if the resource were to be officially sanctioned, and incorporated into pedagogy, it would lose its appeal. From this arises the interesting thought that some learning at least may result from a reaction *against* what is taught, so that teaching (some teaching at least) might be deliberately designed to provoke a resistant response. So if it is the case that the development of learning depends on the learners naturally drawing on their L1 as a resource, one way of ensuring that they keep on doing this is to insist that they should not do so. It has been common knowledge in human affairs since the Garden of Eden that nothing is more enticing than what is forbidden by authority.

Monolingual teaching would be justified (indeed positively required) in a provocative pedagogy of this kind, based on a 'forbidden fruit' principle. However, the deliberate provocation of resistance is not a principle which would be easy to practise, and to my knowledge it has never been seriously proposed. What *has* been seriously proposed is what we might call a permissive pedagogy: one which allows for, even encourages, the learners' engagement of the L1, but again makes no acknowledgement of its existence in the design of instruction itself. Monolingual teaching is justified in this case on the grounds that input in the L2, so long as it is comprehensible, will automatically activate learning (see Krashen 1985 and passim). Since this learning proceeds through interlanguage stages which are themselves, as Ellis points out, subject to substantial L1 influence ('a major factor'), then in effect this permissive approach to teaching is based on the assumption that learners will draw on the resources of their own language anyway, and that language contact will happen in the learning process without any need for it to be explicitly promoted by actual teaching. The monolingual ML input will be naturally converted into an IL intake which is modified by L1 influence.

Let us suppose that we subscribe to this belief in natural learning (even though, as we have seen in the last chapter, there are good reasons for scepticism). If it is to happen, the input; it is said, has to be comprehensible. The question arises as to how the learner makes the input comprehensible: in part, no doubt, by reference to context, but in part also, one must suppose, by invoking L1 equivalents. It would seem unlikely, to say the least, that the learner takes in items of the L2 *per se* and only subsequently, in the process of interlanguage development, relates them to the L1. The L1 is surely in on the act from the start in processing the input, and in a sense can be said to act as a kind of filter: not an affective one, but a cognitive one. If this is the case then, again, one might plausibly argue that explicit reference to the L1 would assist the learner in making the input comprehensible. Furthermore, such explicit reference would have the additional advantage of making formal features of the second language meaningful and noticeable at the same time, thereby meeting the second of the conditions for learning that were discussed earlier in Chapter 8. It is interesting to note that the importance of this 'noticing' condition is one which *is* now recognized as 'a major factor' in acquisition (see Schmidt 1990; Skehan 1998a), but there appears to be no recognition of the one factor which would guarantee that features of the L2 would be noticed, namely an appeal to the L1.

Thus, in discussions as to how pedagogy might be designed to facilitate the comprehensibility of the input, or, less unilaterally, how students might be given the latitude to negotiate input for themselves, the possibility of translation never seems to be considered. Among the factors that are thought to inhibit the natural acquisition process, the unnatural suppression of the L1 does not figure. The one that does is the so-called affective filter, which concerns the temporary disposition of the learner, but no consideration is given to the possibility that this disposition may well depend on how learners react to the alienating effect of having to cope with something foreign without being allowed to refer it to what is familiar. Although teachers may think what they are teaching is a *second* language, an additional language separate from the first, for the learners it is essentially a *foreign* language which quite naturally disposes them to relate it to their own. The notion, well established in other areas of education, that new knowledge (for example, of L2) is only acquired, and recognized as new at all, by reference to what is familiar (for example, in L1) has no place, it seems, in this scheme of things.

So, one of the most striking features of monolingual second language *teaching* is that it would appear to take no principled account whatever of a major factor in second language *learning*. The L1 resource that learners draw on so extensively is almost entirely ignored. As a result, L2 teaching practises a kind of sustained pedagogic pretence that it is dealing with only one language, whereas it is obvious that as far as L2 *learning* is concerned there are (at least) two languages involved. While teachers are busy trying to focus attention on the L2 as distinct from the L1, thereby striving to replicate conditions of coordinate bilingualism, the learners are busy on their own agenda of bringing the two languages together in the process of compound bilingualization. That the processes of teaching and learning should be so at odds is surely, to say the least, odd.

In reference to our earlier discussion (in Chapter 9), it seems clear that this disparity comes about because of a failure to define the second language as foreign language subject. It is the foreignness of the language which is most obviously apparent and problematic for learners, and the foreignness, therefore, which must be accounted for in the definition of the subject to be taught. The notion of a second language implies the existence of a first, and you cannot recognize what is foreign in a language without relating to another which is familiar, and, of course, for different groups of learners the second language will be foreign in different ways. So as soon as we accept that the subject we are teaching is a foreign language, then at least one familiar language (typically the L1) is necessarily implicated. In other words, the very subject we teach is, by definition, bilingual. How then can you teach a bilingual subject by means of a monolingual pedagogy?

Only, one might suggest, with some difficulty. And one might hazard the suggestion that it may well be that many of the problems that monolingual language pedagogy has sought to grapple with over the years are self-inflicted, and therefore, of course, also inflicted on learners; that much of its energy has been devoted to resolving difficulties of its own making rather than those that learners themselves encounter in the learning process. The question naturally arises as to why, in the face of this contradiction, monolingual language teaching, particularly in the case of English, has persisted as an orthodoxy for so long, and has never been seriously challenged.

One reason springs immediately to mind: namely that those who have most cause to challenge it, are in no position to assert themselves. The learners' own bilingual compounding in IL is a kind of challenge to teacher authority, but learners are nevertheless obliged to go along with the pedagogic pretence imposed upon them. For their part, non-native teachers are generally persuaded by those in native-speaker authority that to acknowledge the bilingual nature of the subject is to diminish it, that any concession to the L1 in the classroom is unprofessional and amounts to a betrayal of pedagogic principle. And over recent years, as we have seen in previous chapters, with the development of discourse linguistics and the availability of corpus-based descriptions, these teachers have been enjoined not only to restrict themselves to the L2 in respect to its internal encoded features, its grammar, and lexis, but also, and indeed more importantly, to the L2 as it is really experienced, that is to say as it is pragmatically realized in actual contexts of native-speaker use. Since many of these teachers, perhaps most of them, will have had only limited experience of such use, such an injunction makes difficult demands upon them. They are, in fact, doubly disadvantaged. On the one hand, whatever the learners may do under their own steam, their teachers cannot actually *teach* them by drawing on the shared resources of the L1 they both know. On the other hand, the teachers are told that the features of the L2 that they should focus on are those that bear the hallmark of authentic use, which in many cases they may be in no position to recognize, let alone teach. So it is that they are denied the exploitation of a bilingual competence they have and at the same time exhorted to exploit a communicative competence they do not.

Against this one might argue that now that the findings of corpus linguistics are becoming available, non-native teachers *do* have direct access to the facts of actual usage, and so can now learn to recognize authenticity when they see it. They are no longer dependent on the imperfect intuition of the native speaker: they need only consult the corpus or the concordance. The difficulty here, to recapitulate our earlier discussion, is that the concordance will only reveal usage as recurring patterns in the text that people produce. It will not reveal the actuality of use, the discourse process whereby meanings are pragmatically achieved under various contextual conditions. It will not tell you in what particular circumstances it is appropriate to use the patterns of occurrence on display. Information about usage on a screen will not provide you with a vicarious experience of use: it will not magically transform into an ability to negotiate meaning or find your way through the socio-cultural subtleties of communication. You will know more about the language but this will not necessarily make it any less foreign. Indeed it may well be that it will indicate more clearly just what is foreign about it. And since the usage that is revealed presupposes complex conditions of use that remain unrevealed, the effect could be the discouraging one of bringing home to you how little you actually know of the language you are supposed to be teaching. Consider these remarks by Medgyes:

> ...we suffer from an inferiority complex caused by glaring defects in our knowledge of English. We are in constant distress as we realize how little we know about the language we are supposed to teach.
> (Medgyes 1994: 40)

Such distress derives directly from a misconception of the subject. The English that teachers have to teach is not that which is monolingually realized in contexts of native-speaker use, but that of the bilingual subject English as a foreign language. The feelings that Medgyes refers to are bred in students from the beginning by setting monolingual requirements they cannot meet and denying them recourse to their own language. And if Medgyes, an extremely competent user of English, feels such constant distress at his inadequacy, what kind of signal does this send to aspiring learners? Whatever their efforts, their only prospect, it would seem, is one of continuing failure. But the real failure lies in the pedagogic misconception of the subject, defining the E of TESOL without regard to the SOL, without recognizing, and acting upon, its essential foreignness. Looked at in this way, Medgyes knows more about the language he is supposed to teach than any native speaker, who, by definition, has had no experience of English as a foreign language at all.[1]

It is, of course, in the interests of native-speaking institutions to disregard this foreignness, promote monolingual pedagogy, and define the subject in terms of the achievement of user norms rather than the process of bilingualization that must be engaged in order to achieve bilingual capability. The ideas about how a foreign language should be taught, or what constitutes adequate achievement, do not generally come from an experience of its foreignness. Their most common source is the experience of native-speaker teachers who typically do not even know the language of their students, at least not to the extent that they can draw confidently upon it as a resource, so they have no choice but to focus exclusively on the language they do know. And where the teaching takes place in the L2 country itself, as in English language schools in Britain, for example, students come from a variety of linguistic backgrounds, and so it is not feasible to teach in any other way. Thus, monolingual teaching makes a virtue of necessity. It is necessary as an expedient solution to the problems of the bilingual incompetence of teachers and the multilingual competences of students. To make it a virtue one claims that the subject is essentially the real language as experienced by native-speaker users, and this is a reality, of course, to which native speakers have privileged access.

But as has been pointed out in Chapter 4, this is not the only reality, nor indeed the most relevant one, with respect to the objective to be set for the subject. Native speakers may claim to own English, and to have special, if not exclusive, rights to it as a resource, to be exploited and marketed like any other commodity. But in reality it is no longer their property. Since English is an international language, it cannot be patented by people in Britain or any other native-speaker community. And yet the assumption persists that it can, and that native-speaking teachers, therefore, are uniquely qualified to retail it as a product. So it is that in the section on 'Satisfying the demand for English' in the 1998 British Council Annual Report the opening statement reads: 'English language teaching is a major British export'. And inside that section we find highlighted an endorsement by the British Foreign Secretary:

> I have been round many countries where I have visited the British Council and for every pound spent on the British Council it often produces much more business for Britain, particularly in English language teaching.
> (The British Council 1998: 10)

In the same spirit of commercial enterprise, the report on the future of English in the world (Graddol 1997) talks of the importance of establishing a British brand in the global market for the language:

> A debate would be timely on how Britain's ELT providers can cooperatively prepare for the need to build and maintain the British brand and how the promotion of English language goods and services relates to the wider image of Britain as the leading-edge provider of cultural and knowledge-based products.
> (Graddol 1997: 63)

One can, of course, see, that such an attitude to English has much to commend it from the commercial point of view, and one understands why the British brand of English should be so vigorously promoted as the quality product. And, as in so much commercial promotion, the appeal is seductive, particularly when the image of British English as the genuine article is enhanced by royal endorsement. There is a preface to Graddol 1997, written by no less than the Prince of Wales. Its first sentence reads:

> English has become the world's global language.

And its last:

> I commend this work to all who see a strong and vigorous future for our language.

There is an assumed equation in this commendation between English 'our language', 'a major British export' and English 'the world's global language'.

And herein lies the deception. For, as we have noted earlier in the book, the two are not the same at all. English has become a global language precisely because it has extended beyond its original parochial confines and is no longer exclusively British. The language that the Prince of Wales speaks of as his own is L1 English as a national and domestic language. This may be the Queen's English, or the Prince of Wales' English, but it is decidedly not English as an international and global language, and you do not provide for the latter by exporting the former. Obviously enough, once the language goes global, it necessarily loses its domestic L1 status. And whereas speakers of English as a domestic language are typically monolingual, global English, for a large and increasing number of its users, coexists bilingually with other languages. English can only have a strong and vigorous future to the extent that it is *not* promoted as the monolingual property of its native speakers. And you cannot export what you have not got.

So what is being branded as British and globally promoted cannot be the global language, by the very fact that it *is* branded as British. Furthermore, since the brand is of the usage of a particular community of users, it cannot serve as the definition of English as a subject, for reasons we have already extensively discussed in Chapter 9. The British cannot brand the subject because they cannot know what it is, for, as I have argued, the foreignness is a function of the particular relationship that English contracts *locally* with other languages, and so it will be foreign in all kinds of different ways for all kinds of different learners. And it is crucially *their* reality which pedagogy must account for. The teaching of English as a *subject*, as a *foreign* language, crucially involves localizing the language in accordance with particular conditions of learning.[2]

The English that the British can claim to own, then, is limited as an exportable product for two reasons: firstly it does not represent the language of international use, and secondly it cannot represent the language as subject. It follows from this that what British teachers, the retailers of this product, have to offer is equally limited. As informant users, they can only speak with authority about their own variety of English, and as subject teachers they can have no experience of its local foreignness. It is widely believed, and the belief widely promoted, that native-speaking teachers are necessarily better equipped to teach the language, so that Britain can be relied upon not only to provide high quality English, but consequently high quality English teachers as well. But the very advantages that are claimed for them are in reality, in pedagogic reality, disadvantages. This is not to say that such natural disadvantages cannot be overcome, but then we first need to recognize them for what they are. To return to the point I made in Chapter 1 about theoretical claims being made in the guise of practical advice, it seems to me that those who claim authority on the basis of their experience as native-speaking teachers can, because of their apparent plausibility, have a particularly pernicious effect on local language teaching. If we make the underlying argument explicit it seems to run something like this: 'I am an English teacher and so are you, so we are doing the same thing, but I am also a native speaker of English, so obviously I am doing it better, and so I can show you how to do it better too'. The point I would make is that they are not doing the same thing, and that it is no more valid to claim pedagogic authority on the basis of your user experience in the language than on the basis of your expertise as a language analyst.

Graddol talks about Britain's ELT providers cooperatively meeting the demand for English. That may be true of English: the branded commodity made in Britain. But these providers cannot meet the needs of the *subject* English by cooperating internally with themselves: they have to cooperate externally with people for whom the language is foreign, and for whom it must be pedagogically localized. Such external cooperation has not figured very prominently in the past. Instead, as Phillipson argues, the providers of expertise have tended to consult their own internal interests (Phillipson 1992). But this, it seems, is precisely what Graddol proposes for the future too. Promoting a British brand of the English product can only sustain the very proprietorial and hegemonic attitude to the language that Phillipson deplores. It is all the more curious to note (in passing) that Phillipson finds that Graddol's book is one he 'can warmly recommend' as 'a very astute, sober and scientifically informed book on global English' (Phillipson 1999).

This view of English as a British branded product is then, it seems to me, mistaken. It fails to recognize that the English we are concerned with is not that which is experienced by (a certain select section of) its native speakers in Britain (or in the United States or any other Inner Circle setting). The English we are concerned with is that which, on the one hand, serves as an international means of communication, and, on the other hand, has to be learnt in classrooms. In other words, our concern is with English which is global in its use, and local in its learning. The established or official position, the orthodox view, is diametrically the opposite to this, for it sees English as local in its use and global in its learning: the language to be taught is that which native speakers locally produce, and its monolingual teaching is assumed to be exportable as a global commodity, universally applicable, whatever the local circumstances of the learners. Of course, this makes sense from a commercial point of view. But commerce is in the business not only, indeed perhaps not mainly, of providing people with what they need but with what they will be persuaded to buy, whether they need it or not. Market forces, one might argue, are essentially engendered by producers and directed primarily at creating needs rather than meeting them.

I have argued that this monolingual teaching is at odds with the bilingualization process which learners necessarily engage in when they draw on the language they know as a resource for learning the language they do not. One obvious way of dealing with this disparity is to devise a bilingual pedagogy which exploits this process and seeks to direct it. Such a pedagogy would involve bringing contrastive analysis into classroom methodology in the form of translation and other activities which engage the learners in the exploration of the relationship between the two languages as alternative encodings of meaning. If transfer is such a major factor in interlanguage development, as according to Ellis the SLA literature makes plain, then it is hard to resist the conclusion that activities of this kind should be a major factor in the teaching which seeks to induce it.

This is not, of course, to say that there will be no resistance to the conclusion. Translation has a bad name in language teaching circles, particularly in those which have generally called the tune of pedagogic fashion where it is not an option anyway. It is commonly associated with the universally condemned grammar-translation method. But over recent years there has been a rehabilitation of grammar, brought about in large part by the recognition of its role as a necessary resource in the achievement of pragmatic meaning (see Chapter 9). There is no reason why translation should not be rehabilitated as a resource in like manner. As the concept of grammar has changed to take on a more communicative character, so the concept of translation needs to be changed accordingly. Translation has been too long in exile, for all kinds of reasons which, as I have tried to indicate, have little to do with any considered pedagogic principle. It is time it was given a fair and informed appraisal.

In this chapter I have argued for a bilingual approach to teaching essentially on the practical pedagogic grounds that it goes with the grain of the learners' experience whereas monolingual teaching goes against it. But there is another kind of argument that supports it: not so much a pedagogic as an educational one. And here we return to the more general issues about objectives that were brought up in Chapter 2.

In proposing general parameters with reference to which the English subject might be defined, it was suggested in that chapter that the setting of objectives would involve consideration of two different perspectives on the purpose of education. One of these sees schooling, broadly speaking, as an initiation into existing values, a continuation of cultural heritage. The other sees it as being not retrospective but prospective, as providing for future social and other needs. Now of its nature, the learning of English as a foreign and further language is directed at providing for opportunities beyond those which would be served by the students' L2. These opportunities, as argued in Chapters 5 and 6, have predominantly to do with the membership of global discourse communities and their institutional uses of English as an international language. It was the recognition of this purpose which led us to question the relevance of objectives determined by exclusive reference to the language of native-speaker communities in the Inner Circle.

But such a purpose might also result in the rejection, or at least the reduction, of the relevance of the students' own L1. For the economic and sociocultural values associated with English might be so highly prized that they come to replace those associated with the students' L1. English might then begin to infiltrate other languages and seem to threaten their cultural integrity, or gradually take over their functions and deprive them of their vitality. The increasing spread of English as an international language can then be seen as a malevolent growth that destroys linguistic diversity and the sociocultural values that go with it. (See Chapter 5, Note 1.) What happens, one might say, is that the global opportunities for material gain are bought at the expense of local spiritual deprivation. And teachers of English are willy-nilly complicit in bringing about these negative effects. Whether they realize it or not, and whether they like it or not, what they do is bound to have ideological implications.

Over recent years much concern has been expressed that the promotion of English as 'the world's global language' has the effect of diminishing the status, and the use, of other less prestigious languages. Thus, it is argued, English only flourishes at their expense. (See, for example, Pennycook 1994; Phillipson 1992.) This issue of the debilitating effect of English is not new. It is taken up by I. A. Richards in the first chapter of a little book about Basic English published over 50 years ago. The chapter is entitled 'On the choice of a second or world language', and in it he presses the claim of English as the natural choice. But he is alive to the difficulty that others might object to it being foisted upon them:

> Is it conceivable that the very natural objections of individuals and nations to having the language of one section of the earth's population put into such a privileged position can be overcome.
> (Richards 1943: 13)

Will there not be a cry, he asks (anticipating Phillipson), that 'This is linguistic and cultural imperialism'? Not, says Richards, from those who would have to learn English:

> Neither those who learn English nor those who teach it as a foreign language have in general any feeling that they are submitting to or furthering a process of intellectual subjugation. On the contrary, they are more likely to feel that they are helping themselves or others to resist such influences. The Chinese, for example, are not in the least afraid of English. What they do often feel is that an excessive amount of time given up to learning English may be damaging to the study of their own language. And that they rightly believe would be disastrous.
> (Richards 1943: 14)

I do not know how Richards can speak with such apparent authority about the feelings of the Chinese, nor, in general, on what empirical grounds he makes such confident assertions. But at all events, times have changed, and it is certain that, whatever the situation was in 1943, there is at present a well-attested concern among 'those who teach English as a foreign language' about 'intellectual subjugation' and the debilitating effect of English on other, less powerful languages.

This concern is impressively confronted in a recent article written by two teachers of English, originally from India, but now working in South Africa.

The article does not simply lament the hegemony of English but makes practical proposals, based on the experience of the authors themselves, about 'what ELT professionals can do to promote indigenous languages in multilingual societies like India and South Africa' (Joseph and Ramani 1998). For them, unlike Richards, it is not just a matter of making an adequate *separate provision* for the teaching of English and the other language(s), but of the *simultaneous promotion* of both by the kind of bilingual/multilingual methodology that I have argued for in this chapter. What they propose recognizes the need to make explicit reference to the other language(s) that the learners already know, and they lend empirical weight to the proposal by giving an account of translation activities in class. In the terms of our present discussion, what Joseph and Ramani do is essentially to redefine English to make it a foreign and therefore bilingual/multilingual subject. So defined, the other languages are no longer suppressed, or at best reluctantly tolerated, but overtly recognized and made prominent as necessarily part of what second language learning is all about.

If we acknowledge that TESOL—the teaching of English to speakers of other languages—cannot effectively be done without reference to the other languages, that guiding the development of bilinguals has to be attuned to the bilingualization process, and not by the imposition of an exclusive monolingual pedagogy, then there is some hope at least that English can be learnt without denying the legitimate rights of less privileged minority languages.

Joseph and Ramani conclude their discussion as follows:

> We strongly believe that ELT specialists need to radically reconceptualize their role in language education. As a profession we should openly support multilingualism in education, and problematize our current role as English language teachers. In addition, we need to identify and create opportunities within our own institutions for the fullest development of multilingualism. (Joseph and Ramani 1998: 222)

Joseph and Ramani talk of the need for ELT people to 'reconceptualize their role in language education'. Ellis, in remarks quoted earlier in this chapter, talks about the 'reconceptualization of the role of the L1'. What he says, as I have argued, has implications for the *pedagogy* of L2 teaching. What Joseph and Ramani say has to do with the role of the L1 in association with the L2 in the *education* process. So there are two different perspectives here.[3] But they converge on the same conclusion: the need to reconceptualize the subject as essentially concerned with the process of bilingualization.

Notes and comments

1 This observation caused offence when it was first made (in a talk which later appeared in print as Widdowson 1994). Martin Parrott, for example, read into it the charge that native-speaker teachers of English are

ignorant about the linguistic features of English as a foreign language. He remarks:

> native speakers can't make themselves into non-native speakers but, in my experience, native speaking teachers are avid language learners and analysts and researchers of their learners' languages and linguistic strengths and difficulties in learning English.
> (Parrott 1998: 20)

How far one can generalize from Parrott's experience of native-speaking teachers I do not know. But even if one accepts what he says, it does not bear on the point at issue. Of course native-speaking teachers can, and one would hope do, enquire into features which make English foreign to their students, but they cannot *experience* the language as foreign. There may be advantages in such detachment, but my point would be that in that case they have to be argued for, not simply, as if often the case, assumed as self-evident. For further comment, see Jenkins 2000: 216–20.

2 Localizing language teaching to accommodate to local conditions involves more than reference to the learners' own language(s), of course. It also has to do with sociopolitical and economic factors, and the culturally informed attitudes, values, and traditions that have to be taken into account if the pedagogy is to be appropriate to the situation. (See Holliday 1994.) It has to do, too, as Michael West pointed out more than forty years ago (West 1960) with mundane practical matters concerning the availability of basic facilities and resources.

3 These two perspectives have to do with the setting of the purpose parameter as discussed in Chapter 2. One might wish, for example, to set this parameter to encompass the broader educational perspective of making learners aware of the sociocultural values of the community that speaks the language they are learning. This would be not only to make them more effective users of the language, but also to promote an understanding and tolerance of this other community. It would at the same time develop a critical perception of their own taken-for-granted sociocultural assumptions. (See Kramsch 1993.) One might indeed conceive of a language subject which gave primacy not to the pedagogic objective of developing capability in a particular language, but to the educational objective of developing a general understanding and acceptance of linguistic and cultural diversity. If one wanted to design a course to meet such a general educational purpose, the obvious thing to do would be to deal with two or more languages alongside the learners' own, draw attention to the differences in semantic encoding and pragmatic use, and explore their cultural implications. The investment in capability in any of the foreign languages would be correspondingly decreased, but then such capability would not be the object (or objective) of the exercise. (For further discussion, see Widdowson 1992a.)

I have argued in this book that it is, however, the objective of the learning of English as an international language, which is necessarily dissociated from the particular cultures of Inner Circle native-speaking communities. But clearly, if such an objective can be reconciled with a broader educational purpose of making learners aware of linguistic and cultural differences, so much the better. The point I make here, about making the teaching of English as a foreign language an explicitly bilingual subject, in common with Joseph and Ramani, is that it has a possible educational dimension: it allows for the development of an awareness of such differences, whereas monolingual teaching does not.

12   Taking account of the subject

Throughout this book I have been talking about the subject English as a pedagogic construct designed to develop a capability in the learners as an investment, and I have argued against a concern for immediate surrender value, the teaching for returns in the short term. This is all very well, it can be objected, but the fact of the matter is that learners are required to provide a measurable return on their investment in the form of assessment. I pointed out earlier (in Chapter 9) that what distinguishes English as a subject from its naturally occurring namesake is that, like other subjects at school, it is divided into lessons that appear as periods on a timetable. And in common with other subjects, another of its distinctive features is that it is tested. This is obviously something that needs to be taken into consideration, particularly when one bears in mind the current obsession in the educational domain, and elsewhere, with accountability, productivity, immediate payoff, and the short-term measurement of attainment. The idea of investment for eventual benefits in the longer term is unlikely to find favour unless it is reflected in how many marks you get in an exam at the end of the year.

I want to suggest that the investment proposal I am putting forward is feasible in respect to this feature of the language subject, that capability, in other words, is, to a degree at least, measurable, and certainly to a greater degree than the alternative proposal which seeks to develop communicative competence through the use of authentic language.

The concept of communicative competence has been explored in some detail earlier in this book (in Chapter 7) in the context of our discussion of the scope of linguistic description. It is also routinely prescribed as the pedagogic objective of English teaching programmes. It is not always clear, however, just what communicative competence is taken to consist of. Hymes is regularly cited as the main, if not the only, begetter of the concept, but how it is understood is not always based on a first-hand consideration of what he actually said about it. So it would be as well to look again at his original formulation.

As we have seen in Chapter 7 (page 78), Hymes proposed four constituent features of communicative competence as kinds of judgement that one could be capable of making about a particular instance of use: whether (and to what degree) it is *possible, feasible, appropriate*, and actually *performed*. Since the possible was meant to be taken over from Chomsky's notion of linguistic competence, which was exclusively a matter of grammatical knowledge, it would follow that, in this formulation, part of communicative competence is the capability of distinguishing a grammatical from an ungrammatical sentence in isolation from context. So it would also follow that the much maligned structuralist approach to language teaching, and testing, focused as it was on the possible in this sense, was indeed dealing with communicative competence in part. But only in part, and that, one might say, was precisely the problem. But by the same token, teaching and testing what is appropriate is only dealing with communicative competence in part as well. The essential point is that if these are *components* of a competence, but they are only components to the extent that they *relate*, the whole is a function, and not a sum, of its parts.

What Hymes does is to isolate four features. What he does not do is to indicate what their relationship is. But this is a crucial omission. For what is possible in isolation may be equated with Chomsky's concept of generative grammar, but what is possible *in relation* to what is appropriate (or feasible, or performed) cannot be. For one thing, appropriateness to context applies as much to lexical as to grammatical choice, and, as corpus linguistics illustrates so abundantly (and as we have seen in Chapter 7), what is grammatically possible does not correspond at all with what is 'in fact done, actually performed' in terms of lexico-grammatical co-occurrence. So you cannot talk about the formally possible in relation to the appropriate and the performed without extending its scope into lexis. The other features that Hymes distinguishes are similarly interrelated. Expressions which would be judged unfeasible or impossible in isolation as manifestations of the language code (elliptical phrases, fragments of talk, and so on) are judged differently when they occur appropriately in context. There is, interestingly enough, a hint of the relational implications in Hymes' own text. In his specification of the fourth feature, the performed, he adds the phrase: 'and what its doing entails'. What a linguistic doing actually entails in terms of communicative result must depend on context, and therefore must relate to the appropriate. But this relationship is left inexplicit. And of the others there is no hint at all. So in this formulation Hymes conceives of communicative competence as essentially a matter of making absolute judgements about each of the four features as separate components. But to do this is itself an analytic and non-communicative thing to do, for communication, as we have seen in Chapters 6 and 7, is an essentially pragmatic activity which involves not the identification of separate features, but the realization of relationships between them.

After Hymes, there have been other attempts to define communicative competence. Canale (1983) in his modification of Canale and Swain (1980) also proposes four features, namely the grammatical, the sociolinguistic, the discourse, and the strategic. The correspondence with Hymes' scheme is difficult to discern. The grammatical may be said to be a terminological variant of the possible, and the sociolinguistic component to correspond with the appropriate. But the feasible and the performed seem to have disappeared.

And again the interdependencies are not apparent. Although grammatical competence is now said to incorporate lexical knowledge, we are not told how sociolinguistic knowledge acts upon it in the contextually appropriate choice of particular grammatical or lexical forms. Discourse is distinct from sociolinguistic competence and is said to account for how linguistic elements are combined to form larger communicative units (in speech or writing). But it would seem that this competence must involve reference to grammatical competence, if it is concerned with textual cohesion, and to sociolinguistic competence, if it is to be concerned with discourse coherence. But cohesion without coherence makes no sense, since in actual communication it is not processed as a separate textual feature but only as an indicator of pragmatic meaning. (See the earlier discussion about the analytic isolation of text in Chapter 7.) The point then is that discourse competence, isolated in the Canale scheme as a separate component of communicative competence, only exists as a function of the relationship between the grammatical and the sociolinguistic; without this relationship it has no communicative status whatever.

But what of strategic competence? This is said to consist of

> verbal and non-verbal communication strategies that may be called into action to compensate for breakdowns in communication due to performance variables or to insufficient competence.
> (Canale and Swain 1980: 30)

And, more generally, to 'enhance the effectiveness of communication' (Canale 1983: 11). What is referred to does not seem to be a separate component of competence, but rather a tactical process whereby the other components are related and brought into pragmatic play as required for a particular communicative occasion. As such it is hard to see how it can be specified. It seems reasonable enough to talk about a knowledge of grammatical rules or socio-cultural conventions, but knowing how to compensate for relative incompetence will surely often, if not usually, be a matter of expedient tactical manoeuvre. We should note, too, that such compensatory behaviour is not confined to language learners; you can be competent in your language but not very capable (for one reason or another) of using it. Compensatory behaviour can indeed be said to be normal pragmatic practice. How people will draw on what they know, how they will exercise their ingenuity in exploiting what knowledge resources they have at their disposal would seem to be almost entirely unpredictable.[1]

It seems to me that the 'competencies' which Canale and Swain identify are really rather a mixed bag. As we have seen, if we compare them with what Hymes proposes, the grammatical can be said to correspond with the possible, the sociolinguistic with the appropriate. Here one might reasonably talk about what people know (of the rules of their language and the conventions of its use). But discourse and strategic 'competencies' have to do with how people *act* upon what they know in the immediate achievement of pragmatic meaning, and this involves a consideration of all kinds of contextual conditions. Indeed, all of the performance variables that Canale and Swain refer to as causing breakdowns in communication must be potentially implicated in successful communication as well.

The general difficulty about all this is that as soon as one begins to extend the concept of competence to include communication, it begins to unravel. As I have indicated elsewhere (Widdowson 1989), fault lines appear in Hymes' formulation when you submit it to scrutiny, and they become even more apparent in the Canale and Swain version. And their version, we should note, is an applied linguistic one which is designed to be operational. Whereas Hymes' scheme is a general programmatic one, a piece of suggestive speculation about the scope of language description, the Canale and Swain scheme has a pedagogic purpose: it is expressly designed to provide a prescriptive framework for language teaching and testing. It is meant to be applied to the specification of what should be taught and tested in language courses. But in the case of two of these 'competencies', it is hard to see how, in principle, they can be so specified. On the other hand, if they are not brought pragmatically into operation to realize the other two in reaction to particular contextual requirements, no communication actually takes place. So if you teach and test grammatical and sociolinguistic competences on their own, there is no way of knowing whether you are getting at the learners' ability to communicate at all. Skehan makes the following comment on the Canale and Swain scheme:

> There is no direct way of relating underlying abilities to performance and processing conditions, nor is there any systematic basis for examining the language demands of a range of different contexts. As a result, it is not clear how different patterns of underlying abilities may be more effective in some circumstances than others, nor how these underlying abilities are mobilized into actual performance.
> (Skehan 1998a: 159)

The main motivation for proposing communicative competence was to bring linguistic description into touch with reality, and to extend its scope to account for what people actually do with their abstract linguistic knowledge. But if there is no way, direct or otherwise, of relating this underlying competence to actual performance, it cannot represent the reality of what people do with their knowledge when they communicate. To use a Firthian phrase, there is no 'renewal of connection'. But without such a connection, the model cannot be made operational: it remains an ideal analytical construct.

There have been more recent formulations of the concept of competence (Bachman 1990; Bachman and Palmer 1996) but they do not resolve this difficulty. On the contrary, they tend to compound it. For now the components of competence proliferate, and as they do the relations among them become more problematic. Bachman separates strategic competence from language competence. Within the latter, sociolinguistic competence has been

demoted to a sub-component of pragmatic competence along with illocutionary competence, and grammatical competence is subsumed under
organizational competence alongside textual competence, and these are further distinguished until we eventually arrive at no less than fourteen distinct
components (Figure 12.1).

But of course the more distinctions you make, the greater the problem of
accounting for the possible relationships between them. In fact, this kind of
constituent analysis necessarily cuts the components off from relational
connections. So in the Bachman diagram, for example, the only way that any
terminal component can relate to any other is through some superordinate
node. So knowledge of vocabulary on the extreme left, for example, is totally
distinct and separate from, say, knowledge of rhetorical organization, which
belongs to another node, and is even more remote from sensitivity to register.
This would seem to suggest that this model of competence cannot account for
how certain words might be used as markers of a particular rhetorical organization, or as appropriate to a particular register. As before, it would appear that,
as Skehan puts it, 'there is no direct way of relating underlying abilities to performance'. Of course, it can be argued that it is strategic competence that does
all that and makes the necessary contextual connection to achieve actual communication. But then we are back with the problem of defining what this competence actually is, and how it operates to bring about the expedient reaction
to immediate contextual conditions that communication involves.

The essential problem with these different models of communicative competence is that they analyse a complex process into a static set of components,
and as such cannot account for the dynamic interrelationships which are

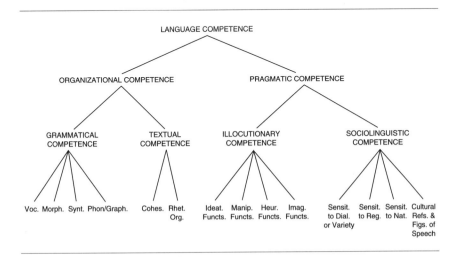

Figure 12.1 Components of language competence (Bachman 1990)

engaged in communication itself. As a consequence, in trying to make such models operational in language teaching and testing, one finds that one can only deal with the separate parts as discrete features, since the essential inter-relationships that make the whole are missing.

But to do this is not to depart radically from the SOS approach (as discussed in Chapter 9), but rather to follow its example. The main criticism of this approach was that it dealt with linguistic knowledge as something separate, and unrelated to the normal contextual circumstances of its use. Since linguistic knowledge is a component of communicative competence, this is tantamount to saying that this approach concentrated on only one component, and failed to show how it related to the others. But you do not remedy this deficiency by adding more components (textual, illocutionary, sociolinguistic, or whatever), for they are no more communicative, as separate components, than is linguistic competence.

As one deconstructs these models, one begins to have doubts as to whether *any* model of communicative competence can be made pedagogically operational as a framework for language testing. The assumption behind their development from Hymes to Bachman and Palmer seems to be that the more differentiations the analysis can yield, the greater its operational value. But this surely presupposes the very discrete item view of language testing that these models are designed to discredit. If you want to assess the ability to cope with the relational nature of communication, quite the opposite would seem to be true: the greater the differentiation of your analysis, the *less* operational it is likely to be. This is because it becomes more difficult to contrive reconstituted contexts which will systematically, and measurably, bring all the components into play. We are, it would appear, confronted with a paradox: as frameworks for communicative testing develop to be more refined, the more remote they get from the phenomenon they are developed to test.

But then if these frameworks are rejected, what is the alternative? How else is communicative competence to be assessed? One might propose that the deliberate design of tests as contrived reconstituted contexts should be abandoned altogether in favour of some simulation of an 'authentic' situation requiring a communicative outcome. There are, however, obvious objections to such an ad hoc procedure. One is that there is no way of knowing how representative the particular situation is of more general communicative demands that might subsequently be made on the learner. There is no way either of knowing how representative the learner's performance is of a more general ability to communicate. The learner might be successful by the ingenious use of avoidance strategies, and these may not be distinguishable from an adherence to the 'least-effort' principle that characterizes normal pragmatic uses of language. In this case, in effect, all you get is evidence of the so-called 'strategic competence' without knowing whether it is compensatory or not, or if it is, what it is compensating for.

So, it would seem that on the one hand we have a means of measurement which cannot of its nature measure communication, and on the other hand we have a means for eliciting communicative behaviour which cannot be measured. What we have to do with here is the troublesome relationship between validity and reliability. As Davies puts it:

> ... no test can ever be wholly valid or wholly reliable. Indeed, a completely reliable test would measure nothing; and a completely valid test would not measure.
> (Davies 1990: 50)

'In all cases', he says, 'compromise is required'. But it is difficult to see how such a requirement is to be met without compromising the whole enterprise of communicative language testing as this is represented by these models of competence.

My own view of the matter is that communicative competence will always be elusive and cannot be measured by the means proposed in these models. I would suggest that communicative tests are impossible in principle, which is why it is not surprising that they have proved so difficult to design, that you just cannot test the ability to communicate, and so it is pointless to try. And you cannot teach it either, if it comes to that. All you can teach, and test, is some aspect of it. So the question to consider is not how many different components or features do we have to specify to provide as comprehensive an account as possible of what constitutes communicative competence to be taught and tested, but which component can be taken as the most salient, and as primary in the sense that it can serve as the nexus to which the others can be related. That is to say, instead of trying to juggle with a number of different competencies, you fix on one and consider how the others impinge upon it. In doing this, one would, in line with the general argument of this book, shift the emphasis from the linguistic description of communicative competence to the pedagogic prescription of what might provide the best investment for the learning of communicative capability.

One might propose that the component to be given this primary focus is linguistic competence, what Hymes refers to as the possible, and what we have referred to in previous chapters as a knowledge of the semantic encodings of the language. The immediate objection to this might be that to focus attention on that is to go back to square one, and reinstate the discredited procedures of the discrete point testing of linguistic forms. But this is not so. As I pointed out earlier, if linguistic competence is to be a *component* of a more comprehensive competence, it cannot retain its Chomskyan character as a knowledge of the formal property of sentences in isolation, for it has to play its part, and it can only do that in relation with the other components. So the question we need to consider is how linguistic competence can be defined so that it *does* play its relational part: in other words, how can it be conceived as being a part of a more general capability for communication. And this is a cue for Halliday to make an appearance in the argument.

In Brumfit and Johnson (1979), Halliday is featured alongside Hymes as a seminal influence on the development of a communicative approach to language teaching. But whereas Hymes' influence is apparent in that, as we have seen, different models of communicative competence can be said to derive in some way from his original programmatic scheme, evidence for the influence of Halliday is not easy to find. The term 'communicative competence' is not even part of his vocabulary. The term 'meaning potential', however, very definitely is. And this indicates, I think, a crucial conceptual difference between him and Hymes. In Hymes' scheme of things, language seems to retain its Chomskyan independence as a code or formal system (the possible), and communication occurs when it comes into (appropriate) contact with context. So meaning is an external pragmatic function. This, as we have seen, leaves us with the problem of how this actually comes about, of what it is in the code that makes it *relatable* to context. There must be some potential in the code itself that is contextually realized.

And this, of course, is where Halliday comes in. His conception is of a code that is functionally motivated: it is indeed the evolved encoding of features of its contextual use, a formal abstraction of contextual features (Halliday 1973, 1994). So what happens when code comes into contact with actual context is that certain internally encoded contextual features get activated and become externalized: the potential gets realized. To put it another way, communication is a matter of the conditional projection of code meanings, and it is the context which provides the conditions whereby some meanings are actualized and others not. Clearly, in this conception linguistic competence is indeed, and of its very nature, a part of the ability to communicate, and indeed the central part.

What, then, for Hymes is the possible, for Halliday is the potential. Linguistic knowledge is not something separately defined in formal terms with an unspecified relationship with other components, but is naturally integral in that it incorporates these components in condensed abstract form. Thus its combination with these other components is a realization of its own potential. In this view, communication is immanent in the code.[2]

If we can restore language to its essential centrality in this way, then this provides us with something specifiable to deal with, and language tests become, again, tests of language. Instead of analysing communicative competence into more and more disparate features, which not only misrepresent the very nature of communication, but become well-nigh impossible to incorporate into effective test design, it makes more sense, I would suggest, to focus attention on the communicative potential in the language itself, and the extent to which learners are capable of realizing it.

But, in line with the argument I have been developing in this book, I would propose extending this concept of the potential beyond what Halliday intends by it. In his conception, meaning potential is incorporated within the actual encodings of the established lexico-grammar of the language. What I would also want to include is the unrealized resource for meaning which the code provides. In the discussion of the spread of English in Chapter 5, I introduced the notion of virtual language, by which I meant the potential inherent in the language for innovation *beyond* what has become established as well formed or 'correct' encodings. In Chapter 10, I suggested that the nonconformities of learner language can be understood as realizations of this virtual language, and that such exploitations of linguistic potential are comparable to those which result in dialectal variation in language spread. The difference is that they do not stabilize: learners are induced into a conformity with actual encodings. But they are evidence of a developing capability for exploiting the virtual resources of the code, and it is just such a capability, I have argued, that teaching should be designed to develop. Although learners will obviously adjust to the conventions of actual encodings as a course progresses, we should recognize that this process can only be partial and will have to continue after the course is over, as learners learn for themselves how to adjust appropriately to the encoding conventions they encounter. Capability on this account combines two things: the ability to exploit the virtual language, and the readiness to adjust to the conventions of actual encoding as and when required.

The first of these is given some recognition in the current attitude to 'error', which is now widely accepted as positive evidence of learning. Even so, it is the second aspect of capability which is given prominence in teaching, and the assumption generally is that these learner nonconformities will need to be ironed out as the course progresses. And they will certainly need to be ironed out before the time comes for testing. For here there is no tolerance of this aspect of capability at all. Tests measure how far learners have learnt actual encoding conventions, and any nonconformist realization of virtual potential is penalized as failure.

If language testing is to be consistent with language teaching which is essentially concerned with the development of capability, as I have defined it, then its focus of attention needs to be on meaning potential in this extended sense. What this implies is that instead of only measuring the degree to which learners are capable of producing encodings in conformity with convention, tests would need to give credit to nonconformist language which showed an ability to exploit the virtual resource, and which therefore provided evidence of investment in capability for further learning.[3]

I would argue, then, that in language teaching and testing our focus of attention should be on the language as a resource for making meaning, on what Halliday calls meaning potential, but taken to include what is virtual in the language as well as what is actual in its encodings. This view has something in common with that expressed by Davies:

> What remains a convincing argument in favour of linguistic competence tests ... is that grammar is at the core of language learning. Grammar is far

more powerful in terms of generalizability than any other language feature. Therefore grammar may still be the most salient feature to teach, and to test. (Davies 1990: 64)

But there is more to linguistic competence than a knowledge of grammar, and more to language capability than linguistic competence. And it is capability, I have suggested, which is 'at the core of language learning'. The discussion in this book leads to the conclusion that it is the meaning potential of English that is 'the most salient feature to teach, and to test'. This is the E of subject TESOL. Contriving ways of getting learners to engage with it and to appropriate it is, I would argue, what the subject is all about.

Notes and comments

1 The problem of predictability is compounded by the further problem that, as was pointed out in Chapter 8, the norms of competence against which learner achievement is to be measured have never been clearly defined. So not only is it difficult to know how to interpret performance data as evidence of competence, but we do not even know just what the competence is that the data are supposed to be evidence of. The assumption seems to have been carried over from Chomsky that competence is some kind of complete uniform knowledge that all native speakers have in common as a shared possession. Such an assumption may have some justification if competence is defined narrowly in terms of the grammatical knowledge of the possible, but if it is more broadly defined to take in the ability to communicate, then it surely becomes untenable. For this ability depends very much on disposition and opportunity, and is not evenly distributed at all. Some people are clearly better at communicating than others, for individual and social reasons that may have very little to do with their knowledge of language or its conventions of use. It would be unreasonable to require learners to aspire to the eloquence of public oratory, but we would not want them to model themselves on inarticulate or reticent native speakers either. So what norms of communicative behaviour would it be appropriate and practicable to set as an objective for teaching, and a target for testing?

2 In this view what is encoded in the language is not the grammatically possible in the restricted Chomsky sense but a complex system of lexico-grammatical relations which derive from the communicative functioning of language. Such a model allows for the incorporation of regularities in textual patterning of the kind that corpus analysis reveals, and to the extent that these co-textual patterns correspond with particular contextual uses (see Note 6, Chapter 7), one can say that the possibility of relating the different aspects of communicative competence is inherent in the notion of meaning potential.

3 But this, I recognize, is easier said than done. Capability as a concept has still to be operationalized as a testable construct. It needs to be borne in mind too, that tests are not just designed to reveal what has been achieved in the process of learning, but as the means for providing documentary evidence of success and failure in measuring up to course requirements so that learners can be graded and categorized. Clearly, therefore, whatever is to be tested has also to be measurable and gradable, otherwise how would they serve this institutional purpose of discrimination and control? It is easy to see how this selective gatekeeping function can be in conflict with a more sensitive and less categorical evaluation of learner progress, and can give rise to all kinds of complex social, educational, and ethical issues, which I have not touched on here. (See Shohamy 2000; Spolsky 1995, 1997.) The literature on language testing is vast. For a succinct and current account of its principles and practices, see McNamara 2000.

Conclusion

In this book I have been giving critical attention to a range of issues that arise when considering how the subject English is to be defined. I have argued that setting objectives for learners to achieve must take account of the way the language has been appropriated internationally as a means of communication, and that this should lead us to think again about defining such objectives in reference to native-speaker norms. I have suggested that rather than seeking to specify goals in terms of projected needs, which for the most part are highly unpredictable, it would be preferable, and more practicable, to focus on the development of a more general capability which would serve as an investment for subsequent learning.

This capability is essentially a knowledge of how meaning potential encoded in English can be realized as a communicative resource. A consideration of the language that expert users, typically native speakers, actually produce makes it quite clear that this potential is only very partially realized on different occasions of use. The reason for this is obvious: people use their language pragmatically as a complement to context. The more informative the context, the less explicit the language needs to be. Effective communication depends on the subtle online regulation of the relationship between the two, and this will involve recognizing when it is contextually appropriate *not* to draw on the semantic resource at your disposal. But the crucial point to be made is that the resource is available when you need it. So although, for example, the analysis of actual conversation will reveal that people interact by means of elliptical utterance, with phrasal fragments of talk, these can be extended, if need be, by more explicit linguistic means. It is, of course, true that actual language behaviour does not consist of well formed syntactic expressions, quite simply because they are surplus to requirement, but speakers nevertheless know what they are, and can draw on this knowledge as a resource in cases where it turns out that they are not surplus to requirement after all. The language that people actually produce as observable behaviour presupposes a vast knowledge of language as unexploited potential. If learners of a language are to become capable in a language, they cannot clearly just learn the patterns of what actually occurs as behaviour, but must also have a knowledge of the back-up linguistic resource that this behaviour presupposes.

Actual communication calls for contextual fine-tuning which is bound to be specific to local circumstances. It is not, therefore, something that learners can be rehearsed to do, except in cases where the specifics are known in advance. It would therefore make better pedagogic sense, I have argued, to get learners to invest in a more strategic ability, or capability, which involves the realization, in both senses of that term, of the communicative potential of meaning encoded in the language itself. As far as setting the objective for the subject is concerned, this would seem to constitute a realistic goal. As far as the process of learning is concerned, I have argued that we need to reject simplistic notions of authenticity, and explore how the language can key into the learners' reality so that they can be induced to engage with the language on their own terms, and learn from it. Looked at in this way, the development of capability as an objective is a function of the very process of learning both during the course and beyond it.

If English as a subject is to be designed with this objective in mind, it cannot, I have argued, be directly derived from linguistic descriptions of native-speaker usage. Clearly, such descriptions need to be referred to, but their relevance has to be determined in the light of pedagogic criteria and cannot simply be taken as self-evident. Teachers need to *refer* to linguistic descriptions, but not to *defer* to them. Linguistic models of description are themselves necessarily partial and cannot fully account for all aspects of a language as experienced by its users. The key question is how far these versions of linguistic reality match up with versions that are prescribed as appropriate for learning. We have, then, two relationships here: one between English as experienced by its users and models of description devised by the discipline of linguistics, and the other between these models and the language that is prescribed on pedagogic criteria as suited to the subject. We can show these diagrammatically as follows:

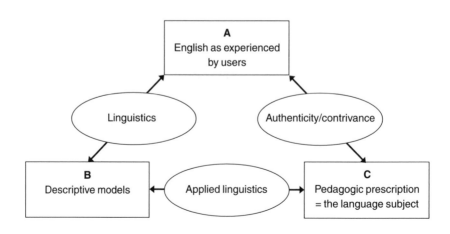

The relationship between A and B has to do with the principles and scope of linguistics as a discipline, with questions of idealization and relative validity. These I have touched on in passing (in Chapter 7) but they are not central to the concerns of this book. The relationship between B and C, on the other hand, very definitely is. For it is this that calls for mediation, the applied linguistic process I discussed in Chapter 1, whereby issues in the domain of practical pedagogy are identified and reformulated in the light of insights from linguistic analysis, and the findings of research in general. The mediation works both ways: language teaching makes reference to linguistic analysis; linguistic analysis is made relevant to language teaching.

The relationship between A and C is also one that needs to be mediated. Here we come to the advocacy of authenticity. Against this, I have argued the case for contrivance. In so doing, I have rejected the idea that what goes on in the classroom should seek to replicate 'authentic' contexts of reality and rehearse learners in native-speaker performance. I conceive of the classroom quite differently: as a place where contexts can be contrived to create local realities conducive to learning. Of course, it may be that these conditions can be met by the judicious deployment of actually attested samples of 'authentic' language, but then the conditions require that they be authenticated by the learner. I am not suggesting that the data of actual language occurrence should be rejected out of hand as a matter of perverse principle. But it is what learners *make* of the data that counts.

In my view, then, in language teaching the language has, in one way or another, to be designed for learning, and so contrivance, or artifice (to use a rather less negative term) is not something reprehensible to be avoided. It is, on the contrary, the very essence of language pedagogy. The English of the subject can never be directly equated with the language as experienced by its users, or with the partial version of its description by linguists, quite simply because the subject is English *as a foreign* or *other language* and has to be fashioned as such. And as I have indicated (and as is indeed obvious) it is 'foreign' in very different ways for different groups of learners. It follows that the English to be taught and learnt as a subject, the E of TESOL, can only be locally prescribed in relation to the learners (the SOL) and the teachers (T). We can propose general parameters, as I have done in Chapter 2, but their specific settings must be a matter for local decision.

This decision making can be informed, I would suggest, by a consideration of the kinds of issue that I have examined in the preceding pages. It is not the purpose of this book to pre-empt local decisions by the persuasive advocacy of any particular course of pedagogic action. On the contrary, I have argued that we need to look with a critical eye at the different approaches and precepts that have been proposed, explore their assumptions and implications, and raise questions about their claims for global validity. To do this is not to deny the value of such proposals, but to recognize that their value lies not so much in the solutions they provide as in the problems they raise.

They challenge us to think again about our own settled beliefs and assumptions. Ideas about SOS, the lexical approach, task-based learning, communicative language teaching, authenticity, real English, and so on are valuable, I would argue, to the extent that they are *not* readily accepted, but serve to stimulate critical thinking about their validity and relevance.

And the same applies to the ideas that I have myself proposed in this book. I have, of course, put them as persuasively as I could, but they are not meant to be accepted without question. They, too, are only of value to the extent that they provoke critical, and creative, thinking about the issues that are implicated in coming to decisions about the locally appropriate way of defining English language teaching. In the preface to this book I referred to language teaching as a kind of pathfinding. In the first chapter I argued that applied linguistics was not in the business of recommending, but of pointing things out. What I have tried to do throughout these pages is to point out certain things, from my own perspective, in the hope that teachers of English might find them of some use in finding their own way.

Bibliography

Achebe, C. 1975. *The African Writer and the English Language. In Morning yet on Creation Day*. London: Heinemann.

Aitchison, J. 1994. *Words in the Mind. An Introduction to the Mental Lexicon*. Second edition. Oxford: Blackwell.

Alexander, L. G. 1993. *Longman Advanced Grammar*. London: Longman.

Aston, G. 1995. 'Corpora and language pedagogy: matching theory and practice' in B. Seidlhofer and G. Cook (eds.). *Principle and Practice in Applied Linguistics*. Oxford: Oxford University Press.

Aston, G. (ed.). 2001. *Learning with Corpora*. Bologna: Clueb.

Austin, J. L. 1962. *How to do Things with Words*. London: Oxford University Press.

Bachman, L. 1990. *Fundamental Considerations in Language Testing*. Oxford: Oxford University Press.

Bachman, L. and A. Palmer. 1996. *Language Testing in Practice*. Oxford: Oxford University Press.

Bauer, L. and P. Trudgill. (eds.). 1998. *Language Myths*. Harmondsworth: Penguin.

de Beaugrande, R. 2001. 'Interpreting the discourse of H. G. Widdowson: a corpus-based critical discourse analysis'. *Applied Linguistics* 22/1.

Bernardini, S. 2000. *Competence, Capacity, Corpora*. Bologna: Cooperativa Libraria Universitaria Editrice.

Bernstein, B. 1990. *Class, Codes and Control 4*. London: Routledge.

Bex, T. and R. L. Watts (eds.) 1999. *Standard English: The Widening Debate*. London: Routledge.

Bhatia, V. J. 1993. *Analysing Genre. Language Use in Professional Settings*. London: Longman.

Biber, D., S. Johansson, G. Leech, S. Conrad, and E. Finegan. (eds.). 1999. *Longman Grammar of Spoken and Written English*. London: Longman.

Breen, M. P., B. Hird, M. Milton, R. Oliver, and A. Thwaite. 2001. 'Making sense of language teaching: teachers' principles and classroom practices'. *Applied Linguistics* 22/4.

Breyer, K. 2002. 'Review of Pennycook 2001'. *International Journal of Applied Linguistics* 12/1.

The British Council. 1998. *Annual Report*. London: The British Council.

Brumfit, C. J. (ed.). 1991. *Literature on Language: An Anthology*. London: Macmillan.

Brumfit, C. J. 1997. 'Applied linguistics as pure and practical science'. *AILA Review* 12. *Applied Linguistics across Disciplines*.

Brumfit, C. J. and K. Johnson. (eds.). 1979. *The Communicative Approach to Language Teaching*. Oxford: Oxford University Press.

Brutt-Griffler, J. 1998. 'Conceptual questions in English as a world language: taking up an issue'. *World Englishes* 17/3.

Brutt-Griffler, J. 2002. *World English: A Study of its Development*. Clevedon: Multilingual Matters.

Burnard, I. and T. McEnery. (eds.). 2000. *Rethinking Language Pedagogy from a Corpus-Based Perspective*. Bern: Peter Lang.

Cameron, D. 1995. *Verbal Hygiene*. London: Routledge.

Cameron, D. 2000. *Good to Talk? Living and Working in a Communication Culture*. London: Sage.

Canale, M. 1983. 'On some dimensions of language proficiency' in J. W. Oller (ed.). *Issues in Language Testing Research*. Rowley, Mass.: Newbury House.

Canale, M. and M. Swain. 1980. 'Theoretical bases of communicative approaches to second language teaching and testing'. *Applied Linguistics* 1/1.

Carter, R. 1987. *Vocabulary: Applied Linguistic Perspectives*. London: Allen & Unwin.

Carter, R. 1998. 'Reply to Guy Cook'. *ELT Journal* 52/1.

Carter, R. and M. Long. 1987. *The Web of Words. Exploring Literature through Language*. Cambridge: Cambridge University Press.

Carter, R. and M. McCarthy. 1996. 'Correspondence'. *ELT Journal* 50/4.

Chomsky, N. 1965. *Aspects of the Theory of Syntax*. Cambridge, Mass.: MIT Press.

Chomsky, N. 1966. 'Linguistic theory' in R. G. Mead (ed.). *Language Teaching: Broader Contexts. Northeast Conference on the Teaching of Modern Languages: Reports of the Working Committees*. New York: MLA Materials Center. Reprinted in J. P. B. Allen and P. van Buren (eds.) 1971. *Chomsky: Selected Readings*. Oxford: Oxford University Press.

Chomsky, N. 1980. *Rules and Representations*. New York: Columbia University Press.

Chomsky, N. 1986. *Knowledge of Language: Its Nature, Origin and Use*. New York: Praeger.

Chomsky, N. 1988. *Language and Problems of Knowledge*. Cambridge, Mass.: MIT Press.

Cook, G. 1997. 'Language play, language learning'. *ELT Journal* 51/3.

Cook, G. 1998. 'The uses of reality: a reply to Ronald Carter'. *ELT Journal* 52/1.

Cook, G. 2000. *Language Play and Language Learning*. Oxford: Oxford University Press.

Cook, G. 2001. ' "The philosopher pulled the lower jaw of the hen." Ludicrous invented sentences in language teaching'. *Applied Linguistics* 22/3.

Cook, G. 2003. *Applied Linguistics*. (In the series *Oxford Introductions to Language Study*.) Oxford: Oxford University Press.

Cook, V. 1999. 'Going beyond the native speaker in language teaching'. *TESOL Quarterly* 33/2.

Cook, V. 2002. 'The functions of invented sentences: a reply to Guy Cook'. *Applied Linguistics* 23/2.

Cook, V. and M. Newson. 1996. *Chomsky's Universal Grammar: An Introduction*. Second edition. Oxford: Blackwell.

Coxhead, A. 2000. 'A new academic word list'. *TESOL Quarterly* 34/2.

Crookes, G. and S. Gass. (eds.). 1993. *Tasks in Pedagogical Context. Integrating Theory and Practice*. Clevedon, Avon: Multilingual Matters.

Crystal, D. 1997. *English as a Global Language*. Cambridge: Cambridge University Press.

Davies, A. 1990. *Principles of Language Testing*. Oxford: Blackwell.

Davies, A. 1999. *Introduction to Applied Linguistics: From Practice to Theory*. Edinburgh: Edinburgh University Press.

Duff, A. and A. Maley. 1990. *Literature*. (In the series *Resource Books for Teachers*.) Oxford: Oxford University Press.

Edmondson, W. 1997. 'The role of literature in foreign language learning and teaching: some valid assumptions and invalid arguments'. *AILA Review* 12.

Ellis, R. 1994. *The Study of Second Language Acquisition*. Oxford: Oxford University Press.

Ellis, R. 1997. *Second Language Acquisition*. (In the series *Oxford Introductions to Language Study*.) Oxford: Oxford University Press.

Fairclough, N. 1995. *Critical Discourse Analysis*. London: Longman.

Firth, J. R. 1957. *Papers in Linguistics 1934–51*. London: Oxford University Press.

Flowerdew, J. (ed.). 2002. *Academic Discourse*. London: Longman.

Freeman, D. and J. C. Richards. 1996. *Teaching Learning in Language Teaching*. Cambridge: Cambridge University Press.

Fromkin, V. and R. Rodman. 1998. *An Introduction to Language*. Sixth edition. Fort Worth: Harcourt Brace.

Gavioli, L. and G. Aston. 2001. 'Enriching reality: language corpora in language pedagogy'. *ELT Journal* 55/3.

Gougenheim, G., R. Michéa, P. Rivenc, and A. Sauvageot. 1956. *L'élaboration du français élémentaire*. Paris: Didier.

Graddol, D. 1997. *The Future of English?* London: The British Council.

Greenbaum, S. 1988. *Good English and the Grammarian*. London: Longman.

Halliday, M. A. K. 1973. *Explorations in the Functions of Language*. London: Edward Arnold.

Halliday, M. A. K. 1994. *An Introduction to Functional Grammar*. Second edition. London: Edward Arnold.

Halliday, M. A. K., A. McIntosh, and P. Strevens. 1964. *The Linguistic Sciences and Language Teaching*. London: Longman.

Hoey, M. 2001. *Textual Interaction. An Introduction to Written Discourse Analysis*. London: Routledge.

Hoey, M. 2002. 'Foreword' in M. Rundell (ed.). *Macmillan English Dictionary for Advanced Learners*. Oxford: Macmillan Education.

Holliday, A. 1994. *Appropriate Methodology and Social Context*. Cambridge: Cambridge University Press.

Holmes, J. 1992. *An Introduction to Sociolinguistics*. London: Longman.

House, J. 2002. 'Developing pragmatic competence in English as a lingua franca' in K. Knapp and C. Meierkord (eds.). *Lingua Franca Communication*. Frankfurt/Main: Lang.

Howatt, A. P. R. 1984. *A History of English Language Teaching*. Oxford: Oxford University Press.

Howatt, A. P. R. 1987. 'From structural to communicative'. *Annual Review of Applied Linguistics* 8.

Hymes, D. H. 1972. 'On communicative competence' in J. Pride and J. Holmes (eds.). *Sociolinguistics: Selected Readings*. Harmondsworth: Penguin Books.

Jenkins, J. 2000. *The Phonology of English as an International Language*. Oxford: Oxford University Press.

Jenkins, J. 2002. 'A sociologically based, empirically researched pronunciation syllabus for English as an international language'. *Applied Linguistics* 23/1.

Johns, T. 1994. 'From printout to handout: grammar and vocabulary teaching in the context of data-driven learning' in T. Odlin (ed.). *Perspectives on Pedagogical Grammar*. Cambridge: Cambridge University Press.

Johns, T. and P. King. (eds.). 1991. *Classroom Concordancing (English Language Research Journal 4)*. Birmingham: English Language Research.

Joseph, M. and E. Ramani. 1998. 'The ELT specialist and linguistic hegemony: a response to Tully and Mathew'. *ELT Journal* 52/3.

Kachru, B. 1983. *The Indianisation of English: The English Language in India*. Oxford: Oxford University Press.

Kachru, B. 1985. 'Standards, codification, and sociolinguistic realism: the English language in the Outer Circle' in R. Quirk, and H. G. Widdowson (eds.). *English in the World*. Cambridge: Cambridge University Press.

Kaplan, R. and R. Baldauf. 1997. *Language Planning from Practice to Theory*. Clevedon: Multilingual Matters.

Kennedy, G. 1998. *An Introduction to Corpus Linguistics*. London: Longman.

Kettemann, B. and G. Marko. (eds.). 2002. *Teaching and Learning by Doing Corpus Analysis*. Amsterdam: Rodopi.

Kramsch, C. 1993. *Context and Culture in Language Teaching*. Oxford: Oxford University Press.

Kramsch, C. and P. Sullivan. 1996. 'Appropriate pedagogy'. *ELT Journal* 50/3.

Krashen, S. 1985. *The Input Hypothesis*. London: Longman.

Labov, W. 1969. *The Logic of Non-standard English (Georgetown Monographs 22)*. Washington, D.C.: Georgetown University Press.

Labov, W. 1988. 'The judicial testing of linguistic theory' in D. Tannen (ed.). *Linguistics in Context: Connecting Observation and Understanding*. Norwood, N.J.: Ablex.

Larsen-Freeman, D. 2000. *Techniques and Principles in Language Teaching*. Second edition. Oxford: Oxford University Press.

Lewis, M. 1996. 'Implications of a lexical view of language' in J. Willis, and D. Willis (eds.). *Challenge and Change in Language Teaching*. London: Heinemann.

Lindstromberg, S. and M. Rinvolucri. 1990. *Introduction to Pilgrims Longman Resource Books*. London: Longman.

McCarthy, M. 2001. *Issues in Applied Linguistics*. Cambridge: Cambridge University Press.

Mackey, W. F. 1965. *Language Teaching Analysis*. London: Longman.

McKay, S. 2002. *Teaching English as an International Language: Rethinking Goals and Approaches*. Oxford: Oxford University Press.

McNamara, T. 2000. *Language Testing*. (In the series *Oxford Introductions to Language Study*.) Oxford: Oxford University Press.

Maguire, L. 1996. *Shakespearean Suspect Texts*. Cambridge: Cambridge University Press.

Medgyes, P. 1997. *The Non-Native Teacher*. London: Macmillan.

Mindt, D. 1997. 'Corpora and the teaching of English in Germany' in A. Wichmann, S. Fligelstone, T. McEnery, and G. Knowles (eds.). *Teaching and Language Corpora*. London: Longman.

Nihilani, P., R. Tongue, and P. Hosali. 1979. *Indian and British English*. Delhi: Oxford University Press.

Nunan, D. 1989. *Designing Tasks for the Communicative Classroom*. Cambridge: Cambridge University Press.

Parrott, M. 1998. 'A personal response from Martin Parrott'. *The IH Journal 5*.

Pennycook, A. 1994. *The Cultural Politics of English as an International Language*. London: Longman.

Pennycook, A. 2001. *Critical Applied Linguistics: A Critical Introduction*. Mahwah, N.J.: Erlbaum.

Phillipson, R. 1992. *Linguistic Imperialism*. Oxford: Oxford University Press.

Phillipson, R. 1999. 'Voice in global English: unheard chords in Crystal loud and clear'. (Review of Crystal 1997.) *Applied Linguistics* 20/2.

Prabhu, N. S. 1987. *Second Language Pedagogy*. Oxford: Oxford University Press.

Preston, D. 1991. 'Language teaching and learning: folk linguistic perspectives' in J. Alatis (ed.). *Georgetown University Round Table on Languages and Linguistics*. Washington, D.C.: Georgetown University Press.

Preston, D. 1998. 'Why we need to know what real people think about language'. *The Centennial Review* XLII/2.

Prodromou, L. 1996. 'Correspondence'. *ELT Journal* 50/1; 50/4.

Quirk, R. 1985. 'The English language in a global context' in R. Quirk and H. G. Widdowson (eds.). *English in the World*. Cambridge: Cambridge University Press.

Quirk, R., S. Greenbaum, G. Leech, and J. Svartvik. 1985. *A Comprehensive Grammar of the English Language*. London: Longman.

Rampton, B. 1997. 'Retuning in applied linguistics'. *International Journal of Applied Linguistics* 7/1.

Rampton, B. 1998. 'Problems with an orchestral view of applied linguistics: a reply to Widdowson'. *International Journal of Applied Linguistics* 8/1.

Richards, I. A. 1943. *Basic English and its Uses*. London: Kegan Paul. Trench, Trubner.

Richards, J. C. and T. S. Rodgers. 2001. *Approaches and Methods in Language Teaching*. Second edition. Cambridge: Cambridge University Press.

Rosch, E. 1975. 'Cognitive representations of semantic categories'. *Journal of Experimental Psychology* 104.

Said, E. 1994a. *Representations of the Intellectual. The 1993 Reith Lectures*. New York: Pantheon Books.

Said, E. 1994b. *Culture and Imperialism*. London: Vintage.

Schmidt, R. 1990. 'The role of consciousness in second language learning'. *Applied Linguistics* 11/1.

Searle, J. R. 1969. *Speech Acts*. Cambridge: Cambridge University Press.

Seidlhofer, B. 1999. 'Double standards: teacher education in the Expanding Circle'. *World Englishes* 18/2.

Seidlhofer, B. 2001. 'Closing a conceptual gap: the case for a description of English as a lingua franca'. *International Journal of Applied Linguistics* 11/2.

Seidlhofer, B. 2002. 'The shape of things to come? Some basic questions about English as a lingua franca' in K. Knapp and C. Meierkord (eds.). *Lingua Franca Communication*. Frankfurt/Main: Lang.

Seidlhofer, B. 2003. *Controversies in Applied Linguistics*. Oxford: Oxford University Press.

Shohamy, E. 2000. 'The social responsibility of the language testers' in R. L. E. Cooper, E. Shohamy, and J. Walters (eds.). *New Perspectives and Issues in Educational Language Policy*. Amsterdam: John Benjamins.

Sinclair, J. M. 1985. 'Selected issues' in R. Quirk, and H. G. Widdowson (eds.). *English in the World*. Cambridge: Cambridge University Press.

Sinclair, J. M. (Editor-in-chief): 1987/1995. *Collins COBUILD Dictionary*. London: HarperCollins.

Sinclair, J. M. 1991. 'Shared knowledge' in J. Alatis (ed.). *Linguistics and Language Pedagogy: the State of the Art*. Georgetown: Georgetown University Press.

Sinclair, J. M. 1997. 'Corpus evidence in language description' in A. Wichmann, S. Fligelstone, T. McEnery, and G. Knowles (eds.). *Teaching and Language Corpora*. London: Longman.

Sinclair, J. M. 1998. 'Large corpus research and foreign language teaching' in R. Beaugrande, M. Grosman and B. Seidlhofer (eds.). *Language Policy and Language Education in Emerging Nations*. Stamford, Conn.: Ablex.

Skehan, P. 1996. 'Second language acquisition research and task-based instruction' in J. Willis and D. Willis (eds.). *Challenge and Change in Language Teaching*. London: Heinemann.

Skehan, P. 1998a. *A Cognitive Approach to Language Learning*. Oxford: Oxford University Press.

Skehan, P. 1998b. 'Task-based instruction'. *Annual Review of Applied Linguistics* 18.

Skutnabb-Kangas, T. 2000. *Linguistic Genocide in Education—or Worldwide Diversity and Human Rights*. Mahwah, N.J.: Lawrence Erlbaum.

Spolsky, B. 1995. *Measured Words. The Development of Objective Language Testing*. Oxford: Oxford University Press.

Spolsky, B. 1997. 'The ethics of gatekeeping tests: what have we learned in a hundred years?' *Language Testing* 14/3.

Spolsky, B. 1998. *Sociolinguistics*. (In the series *Oxford Introductions to Language Study*.) Oxford: Oxford University Press.

Sridhar, K. K. and S. N. Sridhar. 1986. 'Bridging the paradigm gap: second language acquisition theory and indigenized varieties of English'. *World Englishes* 5/1.

Stern, H. H. 1983. *Fundamental Concepts of Language Teaching*. Oxford: Oxford University Press.

Stubbs, M. W. 1986. *Educational Linguistics*. Oxford: Blackwell.

Stubbs, M. 1996. *Text and Corpus Analysis*. Oxford: Blackwell.

Sullivan, P. 2000. 'Language play and communicative language teaching in a Vietnamese classroom' in J. P. Lantolf (ed.). *Sociocultural Theory and Second Language Learning*. Oxford: Oxford University Press.

Swales, J. 1990. *Genre Analysis*. Cambridge: Cambridge University Press.

Swan, M. and C. Walter. 2001. *The Good Grammar Book*. Oxford: Oxford University Press.

Thornbury, S. 2001. 'Lighten up. A reply to Angeles Clemente'. *ELT Journal* 55/4.

Tribble, C. and G. Jones. 1997. *Concordances in the Classroom*. Houston: Athelstan.

Trudgill, P. 2002. *Sociolinguistic Variation and Change*. Edinburgh: Edinburgh University Press.

Trudgill, P. and J. Hannah. 1994. *International English*. Third edition. London: Edward Arnold.

Weeks, F., P. Strevens, and P. Johnson. 1984. *The SEASPEAK Reference Manual*. Oxford: Pergamon.

Wenden, A. 2002. 'Learner development in language learning'. *Applied Linguistics* 23/1.

West, M. (ed.). 1953. *A General Service List of English Words*. London: Longmans, Green.

West, M. 1960. *Teaching English in Difficult Circumstances*. London: Longmans, Green.

Wichmann, A., S. Fligelstone, and G. Knowles. (eds.). 1997. *Teaching and Language Corpora*. London: Longman.

Widdowson, H. G. 1968. 'The teaching of English through science' in J. Dakin, B.Tiffen, and H.G. Widdowson (eds.). *Language in Education*. London: Oxford University Press.

Widdowson, H. G. 1978. *Teaching Language as Communication*. Oxford: Oxford University Press.

Widdowson, H. G. 1979. *Explorations in Applied Linguistics 1*. Oxford: Oxford University Press.

Widdowson, H. G. 1983. *Learning Purpose and Language Use*. Oxford: Oxford University Press.

Widdowson, H. G. 1984. *Explorations in Applied Linguistics 2*. Oxford: Oxford University Press.

Widdowson, H. G. 1989. 'Knowledge of language and ability for use'. *Applied Linguistics* 10/2.

Widdowson, H. G. 1990. *Aspects of Language Teaching*. Oxford: Oxford University Press.

Widdowson, H. G. 1991 'The description and prescription of language' in J. Alatis (ed.). *Linguistics and Language Pedagogy: the State of the Art*. Georgetown: Georgetown University Press.

Widdowson, H. G. 1992a. 'ELT and EL teachers: matter arising'. *ELT Journal* 46/4.

Widdowson, H. G. 1992b. *Practical Stylistics*. Oxford: Oxford University Press.

Widdowson, H. G. 1993. 'Proper words in proper places'. *ELT Journal* 47/4. Reprinted in T. Hedge and N. Whitney (eds.). 1996. *Power, Pedagogy, and Practice*. Oxford: Oxford University Press.

Widdowson, H. G. 1994. 'The ownership of English'. *TESOL Quarterly* 28/2.

Widdowson, H. G. 1997a. 'Approaches to second language teacher education' in G. R. Tucker and D. Corson (eds.). *Encyclopedia of Language and Education, Volume 4: Second Language Education*. Dordrecht: Kluwer.

Widdowson, H. G. 1997b. 'EIL, ESL, EFL: global issues and local interests'. *World Englishes* 16/1.

Widdowson, H. G. 1998. 'Retuning, calling the tune, and paying the piper: a reaction to Rampton'. *International Journal of Applied Linguistics* 8/1.

Widdowson, H. G. 2000a. 'On the limitations of linguistics applied'. *Applied Linguistics* 21/1.

Widdowson, H. G. 2000b. 'Object language and the language subject: on the mediating role of applied linguistics'. *Annual Review of Applied Linguistics* 20.

Widdowson, H. G. 2000c. 'Essay on literature and language teaching. An epistle to Dr. Edmondson' in C. Riemer (ed.). *Kognitive Aspekte des Lehrens und Lernens von Fremdsprachen*. Tuebingen: Gunter Narr.

Widdowson, H. G. 2001. 'Scoring points by critical analysis: a reaction to Beaugrande'. *Applied Linguistics* 22/2.

Wilkins, D. 1976. *Notional Syllabuses*. Oxford: Oxford University Press.

Wilkins, D. 1979. 'Grammatical, situational and notional syllabuses' in C. Brumfit, and K. Johnson (eds.). *The Communicative Approach to Language Teaching*. Oxford: Oxford University Press.

Willis, D. 1990. *The Lexical Syllabus*. London: Collins.

Willis, D. 1996. 'Accuracy, fluency and conformity' in J. Willis and D. Willis (eds.). *Challenge and Change in Language Teaching*. London: Heinemann.

Willis, J. 1996. *A Framework for Task-based learning*. London: Longman.

Wodak, R. and D. Corson. (eds.). 1997. *Encyclopedia of Language and Education. Volume 1: Language Policy and Political Issues in Education*. Dordrecht: Kluwer.

Woods, D. 1996. *Teacher Cognitions in Language Teaching*. Cambridge: Cambridge University Press.

Index of names

Index